T0311529

How
McGruff and the
Crying Indian
Changed America

How McGruff and the Crying Indian Changed America

A History of Iconic Ad Council Campaigns

WENDY MELILLO

Smithsonian Books
Washington, DC

This book may be purchased for educational, business, or sales promotional use. For information, please write: Special Markets Department, Smithsonian Books, P. O. Box 37012, MRC 513, Washington, DC 20013.

Published by Smithsonian Books
Director: *Carolyn Gleason*
Production Editor: *Christina Wiginton*
Editorial Assistants: *Jane Gardner and Ashley Montague*

Editor: *Duke Johns*
Designer: *Brian Barth*

Library of Congress Cataloging-in-Publication Data

Melillo, Wendy.
    How McGruff and the Crying Indian Changed America : a history of iconic Ad Council campaigns / Wendy Melillo.
        pages. cm.
    Includes bibliographical references and index.
    ISBN 978-1-58834-393-2
1. Advertising, Public service—United States—History.
2. Advertising Council—History.   I. Title.
HF5827.84.M45 2013
659.19′36173—dc23   2013013666

Manufactured in the United States of America
18 17 16 15 14 13   5 4 3 2 1

Contents

Prologue: A Brilliant Public Relations Move   1

1   What Is the Ad Council?   6

2   Advertising's Gift to America   19

3   Smokey Bear: A More Complicated Character
Than His Image Depicts   29

4   The Rosie Legend and Why the Ad Council Claimed Her   49

5   "A Keg of Dynamite and You're Sitting on It": The Manhattan
Project Scientists Launch an Atomic Energy Campaign   69

6   The Struggle for Men's Souls: An Anti-communist
Crusade for Freedom Targets Americans   87

7   The Crying Indian: In America's Debate over Garbage
and Pollution, Does the Campaign Shift Responsibility
from Corporations to Individuals?   103

8   Beyond Integration: Fighting for Historically Black Colleges   128

9   Fighting Back: McGruff Shows Americans
How to Take a Bite Out of Crime   149

10   Public Service Ads and the Public Interest   169

Epilogue: Looking to the Future   186
Acknowledgments   191
Notes   193
Index   215

Prologue

A Brilliant Public Relations Move

Advertising, publishing, and broadcasting played key roles on the American home front during World War II. Their service would prove vital to the war effort, while birthing the organization that would popularize a legendary new media form: public service advertising.

It began in Washington, D.C., on February 5, 1942. With the nation at war, industry leaders met with federal government officials to ask a single question: how could they help their country following the Japanese attack on Pearl Harbor?

Seated in a room at the Social Security Board Building, Donald Nelson, then head of the War Production Board in President Franklin Delano Roosevelt's administration and a former Sears, Roebuck and Co. executive, spelled out exactly how the ad industry could motivate the private sector to aid the war effort. "Just as the manufacturing tools of the nation are going to be converted to the production of war equipment, the tools of mass education should be converted to the dissemination of war information," Nelson told the industry leaders. "Mobilize your organizations and your forces behind the program. Go out and do the job with Yankee ingenuity."[1]

America's communications industry would respond with more than just Yankee ingenuity. By creating the Advertising Council, incorporated February 18, 1942, the industry would use the power of advertising to unify an isolationist American public against a common enemy. To tie the advertising effort more closely to the hostilities with Japan and Germany, industry leaders would change the name to the War Advertising Council on May 28, 1943. This organization, which represented a close partnership forged between business and government, would mobilize the nation's citizens to buy war bonds, plant victory gardens, fight forest fires, and—in the case of women—take tough jobs once held by soldiers.

When it dropped the word "war" from its name after the fighting ended, it would continue to have a profound effect on American society. Its legacy of changing consumer attitudes about seat belts, pollution, education, crime, and drunk driving—to name a few of the many societal issues it has tackled—has proven its patriotism. The Ad Council aims to serve the highest goals of government by protecting the nation's people and resources.

The council's storied public service campaigns created on behalf of clients over its seventy-one-year history are well documented. Efforts for the United Negro College Fund as well as its cultural icons such as Smokey Bear, Womanpower, the Crying Indian, and McGruff the Crime Dog have all changed American perceptions and behavior in memorable ways. Its campaigns have contributed to saving an estimated 14,000 lives each year from vehicular deaths, helped reduce litter by 88 percent, and motivated more than 20 million Americans to join neighborhood watch groups. As Ad Council president and CEO Peggy Conlon sees it, these achievements represent an endowment the advertising industry has awarded to Americans. "The Ad Council is advertising's gift to America," she frequently says.

The way Americans think about social problems and how these problems should be solved has been directly influenced by the messages in Ad Council campaigns. To solve social problems, the campaigns use commercial advertising methods to frame issues with the intention of altering public opinion, changing behavior, and motivating citizen involvement in beneficial causes. Media companies donate more than $1 billion a year in free advertising time and space to Ad Council messages—making it the equivalent of one of the top ten advertisers in the United States. The council receives about thirty inquiries a month from organizations seeking campaigns. About two to five groups file applications each year.

From 1942 to 2012 the Ad Council created 423 separate campaigns, according to the Ad Council Archives at the University of Illinois. The topics covered have included efforts devoted to polio, the Peace Corps, seat belts featuring the Vince and Larry crash dummies, and drunk driving.

What is less well known is that the Ad Council's objective has never been solely to improve society. The council's public service role has also been a remarkably powerful public relations tool that has been wielded by the advertising industry since the council's birth. Its creation was a brilliant public relations move that helped the industry ward off attacks from consumer groups claiming that advertising unfairly lured people into buying goods and services they didn't need, and that fended off unwanted federal regulation. Its access to top government officials through its Washington, D.C., conference, now held once during a presidential term, has given it significant influence in shaping public opinion through campaigns that further the government's domestic and foreign policy goals.

Most Ad Council campaigns have been structured to focus only on the individual actions people can take to solve complex societal problems. This approach raises a broader question about how these campaigns are perceived by the public. If the focus is solely on the individual, does the overall effect create the impression that individuals are exclusively responsible for solving the nation's more difficult issues? This approach seems to ignore the role of other important actors such as corporations and government.

Although he has not studied this particular issue, Todd Gitlin, a professor of journalism and sociology at Columbia University who has written a series of books about the impact of media on American society and culture, thinks it's fair to make the following supposition: "I think it is safe to say, but this is surmise, that these commercials reinforce the propensity that readily exists in our society to reduce social problems to personal challenges."

The campaigns selected in this analysis, while hardly exhaustive, examine the government and corporate interests that influenced the public service advertising viewed by American citizens. The efforts are also worthy of study for what they reveal about the Ad Council itself, what it could have accomplished, and what it did achieve. The cases include both popular efforts and little-known campaigns that have been equally important for the role they have played in American history. While their ultimate goal was to achieve positive social change, most campaigns were more nuanced and affected by more special interests than many Americans—perhaps even the Ad Council itself—realized.

The Ad Council's famous Smokey campaign, explored in chapter 3, is considered a symbol of the U.S. Forest Service's history of conflicting land management policies, making the bear a potent symbol that is widely loved in most parts of America—and fiercely controversial in a few areas. Even if the Ad Council and the U.S. Forest Service only intended the bear to represent the need to protect the nation's forests from uncontrollable wildfires, how American citizens interpret the campaign's message is an important part of the Smokey story.

Until September 2012 the council used the well-known "We Can Do It!" poster (also known as "Rosie the Riveter") symbolizing female empowerment on its website to showcase its noteworthy World War II Womanpower campaign, even though the poster was not created by its ad agency, J. Walter Thompson, or intended for its client, the War Manpower Commission. The council's mistaken interpretation of its own history, examined in chapter 4, created a more favorable public image of the organization because the poster is so liked and well known.

The 1946 atomic energy campaign had the power to establish international control of atomic energy, but it missed its mark because of the fractious Manhattan Project scientists, who requested the effort but then couldn't agree on the best way to achieve their aims. A close examination of this campaign, explored in chapter 5, helps explain why scientists today are not communicating effectively about current concerns such as climate change and intelligent design.

The 1950 Crusade for Freedom campaign discussed in chapter 6, created on behalf of Radio Free Europe and Radio Liberty, trumpeted the Truman and Eisenhower administrations' attempts to rid the world of communism. The public later learned that the Central Intelligence Agency had paid for the campaign, demonstrating just how much the council has helped the U.S. government achieve some of its chief domestic and foreign policy goals.

The 1971 "People Start Pollution; People Can Stop It" campaign featuring the Crying Indian was designed for a client that despite its name—Keep America Beautiful—had a double-edged goal. It wanted to clean up litter, while simultaneously representing the bottled beverage and packaging industries. This campaign, addressed in chapter 7, highlights what can happen when an Ad Council effort represents only one side of a complicated issue such as pollution.

By agreeing to develop a campaign on behalf of the United Negro College Fund in the early 1970s, the council bucked a national trend of support for integration between whites and blacks by arguing that black colleges were critically important too. The resulting "A Mind Is a Terrible Thing to Waste" campaign, analyzed in chapter 8, gave more than 400,000 African Americans the chance to graduate from college.

And who can forget gravel-voiced McGruff, the crime-fighting dog who was patterned in part after actor Peter Falk's detective character in the TV show *Columbo*? The campaign, explained in chapter 9, helped usher in neighborhood watch groups, encouraging citizens to patrol community streets while armed with walkie-talkies to report crimes.

Ad Council campaigns are widely respected, and when the council's logo appears on behalf of a cause, it is the equivalent of the *Good Housekeeping* seal of approval. Corporations, media companies, and ad agencies provide financial support. Industry and government interests are taken into consideration when campaigns are selected, and each effort is backed by the full credibility of the industry's top agencies. The organization has a tremendous responsibility to disparate constituencies: the client, the public, the ad industry, and the media companies that run public service ads free of charge. Balancing the needs and interests of these groups in a way that is equitable to all involved is not always possible. That means that some campaign goals, despite good intentions, may not always be in the public's best interests.

This book offers an overview of the Ad Council's public service campaigns that prompted people to take action to help solve a societal problem, and explores the complexities involved in their creation. Businesses consider the Ad Council their charity. The council believes it is a public service gift. Understanding the Ad Council's formidable history will help illuminate the impact this gift has had on American society.

Chapter 1

What Is the Ad Council?

The enduring success of the Ad Council is a tribute to the organization's special ability to bring individuals and industries together for the public good.

—Marc Pritchard, global brand building officer, Procter & Gamble

On a brisk November day in 2011, the mood in the ninth-floor conference room at Ad Council headquarters in New York City was somber yet hopeful. Public awareness about the Ad Council's infant mortality campaign for its nonprofit client Save the Children were lagging, and visits to the website had peaked at 3 million.[1]

The initial campaign launched in 2009, called "See Where the Good Goes," had focused on the role of health care workers in helping to reduce the number of children under age five from dying of preventable illnesses. Now it was time for Save the Children, the Ad Council, and its New York–based ad agency BBDO (Batten, Barton, Durstine & Osborn), to take the campaign to the next level.

That morning BBDO presented a fully integrated campaign that would include public service ads intended to run on several media platforms, from the Internet to television. These executions—part of the ad development process—would be presented to the Ad Council's Campaign Review Committee, which had the power to kill or change any idea offered. The CRC, as it is called in the industry, is arguably the most powerful and influential of all the council's five committees because it controls the images, messages, and slogans that the public will see.

Presenting work to this committee, a group of some of the top creative minds in the industry, is considered a defining moment for America's leading ad makers. Producing the right public service campaign may help solve some of the world's most vexing problems. This is advertising that can make a difference.

BBDO's challenge that day was to connect Americans with the need to stop children from dying of preventable illnesses such as diarrhea and malnutrition, and to motivate them to act. Using simple messages to prompt individual action is the key to the Ad Council's public service model. If the advertising makes people care about a cause, then people will remember it and act.

"People have a relationship with the Ad Council brand," said Ad Council president and CEO Peggy Conlon. "Most Americans living today remember an anecdotal story about an Ad Council campaign."

Paul Vinod, BBDO's creative director, had been working with a team of art directors and copywriters to create a simple idea that would get Americans to care about dying children in other countries. That idea was the sound of a child's heartbeat. Warming to his theme, Vinod told the committee how sound engineers, using special stethoscopes, would accompany health care workers in Malawi to capture real heartbeats. Back in the United States, the heartbeats would be mixed into a sound track and given to a celebrity musician who would create a song that people could download from the Internet.

The song's proposed price, $1.29, would bring in revenue for Save the Children. "It's not the classical way of 'I do write a check,' 'I do give my credit card,' but another way which is very simple," Vinod said. "We bring the message home by saying 'Keep the heartbeat alive,' and that's how we start a movement."

Vinod and his team presented two sixty-second television spots, each showing a different way to execute the heartbeat idea. The first, called "The Heartbeat Experiment," took a documentary approach. A health care worker in a small village in Malawi listened to a child's heartbeat as engineers captured the sound. The scene morphed to a recording studio in Los Angeles where singer Katy Perry—used as a placeholder to illustrate how a musician could create a song with the heartbeats—started singing over the sound of the heartbeats. (In reality, other musicians would be approached about recording a song to appear in the final campaign.) The words "Keep 9 million heartbeats alive every year" would appear on the screen. A voiceover said, "Help one local health care worker and you can help save hundreds of children from preventable and treatable illnesses." Viewers then would be directed to a website where they could download the song.

The second spot featured the rock band Coldplay, also used as a storyboard placeholder for celebrity involvement, singing another song created with the heartbeats. First the bass guitarist put down his instrument and walked off the stage. The guitarist followed. Then the drummer and keyboardist left. Alone onstage, lead vocalist Chris Martin stopped singing. Only a single heartbeat was now audible. "What you hear isn't just any beat," Martin would say. "It's the heartbeat of a child kept alive by a health care worker."

To the untrained eye and ear, the presentation seemed impressive. But then the committee's advertising experts went to work. Priscilla Natkins, the Ad Council's executive vice president and director of client services, spoke first. Natkins was enthusiastic about the heartbeat idea, but she also wanted to make sure the campaign raised awareness about Save the Children's broader message. "We just can't rely on people downloading songs," she noted. "There's a universe of donors out there who don't download songs."

Nick Law, executive vice president and chief creative officer of the ad agency R/GA (respected for its digital and mobile expertise), was also strongly supportive of the heartbeat idea, but he had a different concern. "A lot of the tactics are great, but they all depend on a brilliant song," Law said. Getting a celebrity musician to agree to make that song could be difficult.

The critique, delivered with rapid-fire precision, kept BBDO's creative team busy for the next thirty minutes. In the end, the committee approved the heartbeat idea, which would later be presented to the client, Save the Children, at a separate meeting.

The final campaign was released to the public in September 2012.

How the Model Works

Conlon, the Ad Council's president since June 1999, is known in the industry as "no drama Conlon." Her cautious management of a nonprofit organization that earned $40.5 million in revenue in 2010 can be seen in the kind of campaigns— about fifty a year—that the council is willing to prepare on behalf of its clients. During the George W. Bush administration, the Administration for Children and Families, part of the U.S. Department of Health and Human Services, wanted a campaign promoting the value of marriage. The Ad Council declined because the subject was too political. "We did not think it was completely objective and nonpartisan," said Conlon, who built a notable career in advertising and publishing before coming to the Ad Council. "Sometimes we have to take into consideration the mood of the country."

That approach may become more difficult to execute in today's highly charged, partisan environment. "The Ad Council always saw itself as nonpartisan, but everything has become a political issue," said George Perlov, the Ad Council's former head of research and evaluation. "They are very careful about choosing campaigns."

Determining what issues will become campaigns is thus a critical task for an organization that generally shuns politics, religion, advocacy, and direct fund-raising campaigns. What becomes a campaign depends on whether the topic aligns with the Ad Council's mission to focus on its core concerns of health, education, families, communities, and safety; whether the applicant can afford the $2.4 to $3 million it costs the Ad Council to produce a campaign that will run a minimum of three years; if other sponsors can be found to back the effort if the applicant can't fund the campaign; and if the topic can be framed in a way that protects the council's own desire to remain nonpartisan and noncontroversial.

Once the Ad Council agrees to undertake a campaign, it signs a contract with the client requesting the effort. Agencies are selected from a roster of fifty to sixty national firms, and the decision about which one to choose is based primarily on the agency's expertise and ability to commit the resources and staff necessary to the effort. Ad agency relationships with their clients also play a role.

The agencies provide their labor, which includes account management, planning, and ad creation teams, for free. The agencies bill the Ad Council for production costs such as contract photographers, TV directors and crews, research, editing of ad copy, web development, and printing. The council reimburses the agency for these out-of-pocket expenses from the client's budget for the campaign. In return, the client receives a series of ads that run in space donated by media companies on network television, cable, radio, newspapers, magazines, online, and on outdoor billboards (the mix depends on the campaign strategy and target audience). The client also receives evaluation reports about the campaign's results.

The Ad Council's donated media model relies on media companies' running public service ads free of charge. Its media team cultivates relationships with national companies and local affiliates by presenting campaigns that will align with their corporate priorities and targeted audiences. The companies decide which campaigns they will support, with some pledging a specific dollar amount while others agree to support individual campaigns. Some companies carve out media inventory dedicated to public service ads, which is shared with the Ad Council and other nonprofit organizations that the company supports.

But media companies will not run public service ads if they are concerned that the ads will offend their commercial advertisers, or if the subject matter is controversial enough that broadcast stations or publications receive complaints. In 1985 the Ad Council worked with the U.S. Department of Transportation to develop a national safety belt education campaign. When Ruth Wooden became the Ad Council's president in 1987, she reported that the council had been criticized for creating a campaign that focused on making individuals responsible for preventing deaths, as opposed to taking the auto companies to task for not building safer cars. "My response was it made no sense to attempt a campaign that would berate the auto industry when the media companies would not donate media time to such a campaign," Wooden recalled. "[The auto companies] are their biggest advertisers."[2]

Wooden does not believe it's the job of public service advertising to criticize corporations. "Public service advertising depends on the donations from the media," she said. "You have to be realistic. The media companies are not going to donate time free of charge to beat up on their advertisers."

This limitation is true for every nonprofit cause seeking donated media time. Broadcast networks have their own standards, and Wooden would argue that they also have the right to decide what ads run in the space they donate to public service. The Ad Council's staff manages the situation by focusing their campaigns on the individual actions a person can take to help address a larger societal problem. As Wooden puts it: "It is two sides of a coin, but the only side we can operate on in a donated media environment is to speak to individuals directly." The limitations of a donated media model affect how every Ad Council campaign is selected.

The Challenge to Avoid Controversy

An August 18, 2011, meeting of the Ad Council's Advisory Committee on Public Issues, which is responsible for helping identify issues that could become campaigns, illustrated the tightrope the organization must walk as it balances public service with avoiding controversial issues. The meeting also offered an important window into understanding how the council's ties to businesses and the federal government influence the choice of campaigns.

The Ad Council sets the agenda about what issues it considers eligible for public service, given the limits established by media companies. At the same time, the council will give any request—even from industry trade associations, which exist to protect the profits of their corporate members—a fair hearing before rejecting it. The purpose of the August 18 meeting was to gather reaction from committee members about potential campaigns. This feedback is shared with a separate Ad Council committee, the Executive Committee, a group of fifteen to twenty board members, which has the final say on what issues can become a campaign. But as the meeting progressed, it became apparent that defining the parameters of public service is not as clear-cut as outsiders might think.

The list of issues on the committee's docket that day was divided into new work (campaigns the council was currently developing) and new issues under review that could become campaigns. Up first for new work was a discussion about the "Caregiving" effort on behalf of the AARP (formerly known as the American Association of Retired Persons). The campaign's objective was to "motivate family caregivers to identify themselves as caregivers and raise awareness that there are resources available to them to ease their care for loved ones." The AARP would contribute some of the money to produce the effort, but it also wanted groups to lend resources and expertise to help extend the campaign's message. The committee recommended companies that offer long-term care insurance.

For support of a campaign sponsored by a group of leading dental organizations to improve children's teeth, committee cochair Risa Lavizzo-Mourey, president and CEO of the Robert Wood Johnson Foundation, recommended MomsRising, a legislative policy group dedicated to increasing family economic security and reducing discrimination against women and mothers. Committee member Donna Klein, CEO of Corporate Voices for Working Families, a non-profit group made up of businesses interested in family-friendly work policies, objected. "They are extremely partisan," Klein said of MomsRising. "Does the Ad Council have a policy on this?" "We are non-partisan," Conlon replied.

The committee turned next to a federal government campaign, requested by the Food and Drug Administration (FDA) and the U.S. Patent Office, to educate Americans about the dangers of using online pharmacies to obtain prescription drugs. The federal government is an important funding source for the Ad Council, but working with the government exposes the council to criticism if campaigns are perceived to further a government policy agenda that some groups disagree with.

The online pharmacy campaign illustrated the dilemma. The campaign's goal would be to increase awareness about the public health risks and dangers posed by illegal online pharmacies, providing consumers with information about how to access safe, legitimate, FDA-approved medicine online. These goals seemed laudable enough, but committee member Francesca Koe, director of special projects for the Natural Resources Defense Council, got right to the perception problem. "Is the rise of the availability [of online medicines] symptomatic of a larger issue of access to health care or affordability?" she asked. "There is another elephant in the room."

As more Americans use the Internet to obtain prescription drugs at cheaper prices, the government is confronted with the problem of controlling access to medicines from other countries—particularly Canada, Europe, Australia, New Zealand, and Japan, where drug costs are much lower because of price controls. U.S. drug manufacturers and the FDA have long opposed allowing Americans to buy cheaper drugs from other countries, citing concerns about counterfeit or contaminated medicines. Critics argue that the drug manufacturers, aided by government policy, are more interested in protecting industry profits. The drug industry's fierce lobbying effort during the 2010 health care overhaul helped defeat a Senate proposal with public and bipartisan support that would have offered a safer way to buy prescription drugs from other countries.

The proposed campaign would have put the Ad Council on one side of a controversial issue, making it harder to remain neutral. The issue was not resolved during the meeting.

Another campaign considered that day was a campaign on climate change sponsored by the Union of Concerned Scientists. Ad Council staff member Kate Emanuel, then senior vice president of non-profit and government affairs, told the committee that the staff "agreed we did not want to get into the science debate about climate change." The campaign was listed on the committee's docket under the "researching" category. This meant that the Ad Council was still trying to determine whether the organization requesting the campaign was the right fit given the sensitivities surrounding the issue. It wanted the committee's help in thinking up ways to change the potential campaign's focus.

"Initially, this organization [the Union of Concerned Scientists] wanted us to brand them that the research is valid, but that is not our model," Conlon said in the meeting. "How can we reframe this? We want [people] to do individual tasks that can affect climate change."

The Natural Resources Defense Council's Koe thought the council had good reason to be cautious about a campaign addressing climate change. "As the person in charge of our public opinion research, even mentioning global warming in the spot will alienate 50 percent of the audience," she said. "I think people pay more attention when [the spot] is driven by self-interest. You see more [effectiveness] in the energy campaigns where people see a way to save money. Weave together [in the strategy] 'Yes, there is a social responsibility, but here is why it is good for you.'"

Priscilla Natkins agreed. "Save money, save the planet," she said. "There is a way for the two to live side by side."

Conlon was doubtful. "How would that language entice the environmentalist?" she asked.

"The key is not only how to make it salient to someone's life, but to promote stewardship," Koe responded.

Conlon remained unconvinced. "It is an issue fraught with labels that are polarizing," she said. Committee member Kevin Donnellan, the AARP's executive vice president and chief communications officer, agreed. "I think you have to be really careful on this one," he said. "Can you look at the legacy issues? People do want to leave the planet a better place."

Cynthia Round, United Way of America's executive vice president of brand leadership, brought the conversation back to what actions individuals could take. "If you finally break through, they [the audience] have to know there is something they can do," she said. "If you can't distill it to a concrete action—that is the problem with all these campaigns."

The committee decided that the Ad Council should continue its research before making a final decision. While it wanted a campaign on climate change, it wasn't sure that the Union of Concerned Scientists was the right group to sponsor the effort. The coalition of citizens and scientists behind the union believe that human activity is the primary reason why the earth is getting warmer. Accepting a campaign from this group would place the council in the middle of this controversial debate.

A possible migraine headache campaign, next on the docket for discussion, raised flags about driving up health care costs, a big concern for businesses. The Migraine Research Foundation, a nonprofit that raises money to promote migraine research, wanted the campaign to encourage migraine sufferers to learn what triggers the headache and make behavioral changes to avoid one.

Natkins said the campaign could have a positive impact on employers, but Lavizzo-Mourey disagreed. "Inappropriate treatment associated with headaches is a big cost driver," she said. "Thirty million Americans have migraines. A headache is scary, and people want an MRI."

Klein of Corporate Voices for Working Families noted the likely objections from the business industry. "From a business perspective, this would be a hard route to go," she said.

The issues discussed in the meeting continued to grow in complexity. The Ad Council had asked committee members for feedback on a potential anti-piracy campaign requested by the Motion Picture Association of America. The trade association, which represents major motion picture studios, wanted the campaign to help it fight rogue websites that feature stolen movies, TV shows, and music. The campaign would raise awareness about the impact of counterfeit and pirated movies, and increase understanding of what happens when consumers purchase stolen goods.

The request raised questions about whether such a campaign would truly be a public service. "What we are torn with is, is this an industry issue for the industry to take on?" the Ad Council's Emanuel asked.

"It is a very contentious issue," said committee member Darren Walker, vice president of education, creativity, and free expression for the Ford Foundation. "People say on top of everything else, do we really have to worry about protecting Sony and Viacom?"

"The latest frame is a safety and counterfeiting issue," Emanuel said. "I am not sure how you teach consumers about this," Conlon said, dismissing the idea.

The next topic was a campaign requested by the Polaris Project, which fights human trafficking and modern-day slavery. They wanted a campaign to educate Americans about the fact that buying and selling people still happens. This wasn't the first time the council had been asked to consider a campaign on this issue.

"Our struggle is, is this a public service issue, or is it more of a crime issue?" asked Danna Kulzer, the Ad Council's director of non-profit and government affairs. "We know it is underreported." "It exists maybe, but is it prevalent?" Klein asked. "We are stepping into an area that concerns me," Conlon said.

"Is there an action message?" Lavizzo-Mourey asked. The committee couldn't come up with one, and the issue was dropped.

Emanuel then introduced the Ad Council's "wish list," a collection of staff-generated issues lacking a sponsoring organization to pay for a campaign. The council wanted an education campaign that would highlight alternatives to a four-year college education. But such an effort raised concerns about different Ad Council campaigns presenting mixed messages. At the time of the meeting, the council had just launched new work for the existing campaign promoting college access ("KnowHow2GO"), which aims to help low-income and first-generation students prepare for college. New advertising for its long-running United Negro College Fund campaign was also being developed. "We have a problem with having a campaign saying 'Go to a four-year university,' and then we push community colleges," Emanuel said.

The possible alternatives to a four-year degree that could be promoted grew murkier. The Ford Foundation's Walker brought up the report by the 2010 Government Accountability Office, Congress's investigative arm, detailing the unethical—and at times illegal—recruiting practices of some for-profit colleges. Online universities created other problems. "Academia writ large is not in favor of online universities," Klein observed. The subject was eventually dropped.

"The Industry's Charity"

A discussion of how much the Ad Council can do on its own with so many campaigns on its docket—an average of fifty a year—prompted Herbert Pardes, president and CEO of New York–Presbyterian Hospital, to suggest in the meeting that the council might narrow its focus by concentrating on "one or two topics to really have the biggest possible impact."

His comment underscored an aspect of the Ad Council's model that the organization has been criticized for. Although the majority of council campaigns run beyond three years, a campaign could potentially end after three years if other sources of funding can't be found. And three years is not always enough time to achieve the awareness and change clients may desire.

"We ask for a three-year commitment because, in a donated media model, it takes time to build that awareness," Conlon said in response to Pardes's comment.

Unlike many nonprofits, which raise money from individual donors and grants, the council derives its funds from the $2.4 to $3 million average cost nonprofit organizations and the federal government pay to underwrite a three year campaign, and from direct contributions from corporations. In these respects the Ad Council's revenue structure appears more like that of an industry trade association than a nonprofit, except for the growing role played by the government. The actual fees charged to clients vary, depending on the size of the campaign. For example, the anti-childhood obesity effort undertaken with the U.S. Department of Health and Human Services and the U.S. Department of Agriculture, can cost more than $3 million because the campaign delivered different messages reaching both adults and kids, and multiple target audiences.

Based on an analysis of the Ad Council's Form 990 tax returns, its total revenue—including campaign income and corporate contributions—has grown from $20.3 million in 2001 to $40.5 million in 2010. The council raised more than $31.3 million from its public service campaigns in 2010, according to the tax forms, and about $20.8 million of that was spent on the cost of producing the advertising and distributing the campaigns. Nearly one-third, or about $10 million of the $31 million income, was used to cover the council's campaign-related operating expenses: $6 million for salaries and wages; $995,000 for compensation of current officers, directors, trustees, and key employees; $958,000 for other employee benefits and payroll taxes; $942,000 for occupancy; $150,000 for information technology; and $50,000 for office expenses, among other items.

These statistics raise a different question: If the bulk of the Ad Council's revenue comes from taxpayer money as opposed to private sources, is the organization truly independent of the federal government?

"I think that is a valid question that people have to ask," Wooden said. "It is true for any nonprofit that does work with the federal government. It doesn't mean it is wrong, but it means you are a different organization. You are a government service contractor."

Conlon believes that placing too much emphasis on the income derived from the federal government is the wrong way to analyze the revenue. She said corporate contributions nearly match what the government pays for campaigns. What's more, the Ad Council provides a "unique value" to its government and nonprofit clients alike. "Our combined obesity prevention work [for the government] got over $100 million in donated media in one year, and that's just one example," Conlon said. She also points out that nonprofit clients benefit from the Ad Council's practice of leveraging dollars. "If we passed along every single [cost], we would price ourselves out of the market for them," she said.

Critics argue that Ad Council campaigns are expensive. The council counters that its partnerships with advertising, business, foundation, and media organizations enable it to provide something unique to its clients through donated media. In its pamphlet "When There Is a Need, We Are There," the council reports that since 1998 it has received more than $1 billion a year in donated advertising time and space on behalf of its campaigns.

"That's why the industry puts cash into the Ad Council, because they believe it is the industry's charity," Conlon said.

Chapter 2

Advertising's Gift to America

The Ad Council is advertising's gift to America.

—Peggy Conlon, Ad Council president and CEO

Today the U.S. ad industry employs more than 462,000 people and has annual revenues of $100 billion. At midcentury, however, this sunny future was in peril.

James Webb Young, a senior consultant to the J. Walter Thompson agency, delivered bitter news to industry executives gathered in Hot Springs, Virginia, on November 14, 1941. Young recalled how he had recommended several "outstanding advertising men to a former president of a 'great' university for a promotional campaign," and the educator had exploded. "Surely you recognize that advertising is a déclassé profession!" he cried. "To put such men in charge of a cultural relations program would kill it at the start." Young then told his audience a second example of an ad industry smackdown. He'd just read a book about the nervous system, written by a prominent scientist. "Perhaps it will surprise you to know your last book was very helpful to an advertising man," he told the author. Staring at Young over his glasses, the scientist responded, "I am not only surprised; I am shocked. So far as I can see, there is no connection between brains and advertising."[1]

Nevertheless, advertising had its champions, especially in Washington.

Business Interests Trump Consumer Protection

The political and economic climate that gave birth to the Ad Council was rooted in the history leading up to the Wheeler–Lea Act of 1938, which strengthened the Federal Trade Commission's authority to regulate advertising.

The legislation, passed during the New Deal and approved by the Roosevelt administration, represented the one time in American history when Congress "formally considered exactly what the role of advertising should be in our society and how it should be regulated."[2]

Between 1900 and 1930, the U.S. population had increased by 65 percent, and the volume of goods produced by manufacturers had risen by 151 percent.[3] Because products were similar in both quality and price, companies needed a new way to help their goods stand out in a crowded market. Advertising increasingly focused on establishing brand loyalty to attract new consumers. Instead of appealing to a consumer's reason by emphasizing product attributes and price in the advertising copy (the standard practice up to around 1900), companies shifted to using emotional appeals based on image enhancement.

"The most obvious source of distortion in advertising's mirror was the presumption by advertisers that the public preferred an image of 'life as it ought to be' . . . to an image of literal reality," Roland Marchand wrote in *Advertising the American Dream: Making Way for Modernity, 1920–1940*. Thus, "ad creators tried to reflect public aspirations rather than contemporary circumstances, to mirror popular fantasies rather than social realities."[4]

In their quest for a competitive advantage, advertisers also shaded the truth, misled, and lied to consumers to increase product sales, as Inger Stole, a University of Illinois advertising professor, observed in a 2000 article. "It did not take long before such marketing strategies caught the attention of a feisty and burgeoning consumer movement."[5]

Signs of the growing consumer backlash that Young referred to in his speech can be found in the dozens of books published in the late 1930s and early 1940s that criticized advertising. Some—such as *100,000,000 Guinea Pigs* (the first in a series), *American Chamber of Horrors*, and *Poisons, Potions and Profits*—assailed the advertising of food and drugs in particular. Others such as *Partners in Plunder*, *Our Economic Society and Its Problems*, and *The Industrial Discipline and the Governmental Arts* attacked advertising and business in general. Scores of articles in newspapers and magazines echoed these concerns. And some representatives of the consumer movement found positions in the administration and Congress, where they could use the power of regulation and legislation to fight for consumer protections.

In the food category alone, consumers had no way to judge the ingredients in malted milk or jarred chicken. The fat content in ice cream remained a mystery, and deceptive packaging often led consumers to believe they were getting more of a product than they actually were. The use of different bottle shapes and sizes added to the confusion.

Not all of the discourse was negative. Some voices in the consumer movement recognized the potential of advertising to improve society. Stuart Chase and F. J. Schlink wrote in their 1927 book, *Your Money's Worth,* "It's a magnificent technique. Sanely applied it could remake the world. Think of what might be done with applied psychology in a great publicity drive for public health, for better housing, for cleaning up the slums, for honest and timely information about goods, for genuine education in a hundred fields!"[6]

Advertisers had not ignored the need to correct abuses in their industry. In 1911 the publishers of the advertising trade magazine *Printers' Ink* developed a model statute to regulate untruthful advertising. This would eventually become law in twenty-six states, and seventeen other states adopted similar legislation. The Better Business Bureaus established policies to review unfair or unscrupulous advertising practices. Newspapers and magazines developed advertising standards. The International Advertising Association adopted a "Code of Business Ethics" in 1929, and the Advertising Federation of America, another industry trade association, followed with its own code in 1932.[7]

But consumer groups complained that self-regulation was failing because the industry did not enforce it. In June 1933, the year of President Roosevelt's inauguration, Senator Royal S. Copeland, a Democrat from New York, introduced a bill to revise and amend the existing Food and Drug Act. It was known as the Tugwell bill, named after Rexford G. Tugwell, then assistant secretary of agriculture, who strongly endorsed it. It called for new labeling laws and mandatory grading of goods, and it would give the Food and Drug Administration (FDA)—established with the passage of the 1906 Pure Food and Drugs Act—the power to prohibit false advertising of any food, drug, or cosmetic. Of particular concern to the industry was a provision that would define an ad as false if it created a misleading impression by the use of ambiguity or inference.[8] This represented an effort to eliminate advertising puffery by making it "close to impossible for manufacturers to infer ambiguous rewards such as popularity, marital happiness, and social acceptance in exchange for product loyalty." [9] (Such later ads as those that promoted Folgers coffee as "the best part of wakin' up," or the skies of United Airlines as always "friendly" would have been in jeopardy under this proposed law.)

Then, as now, lobbying could alter political outcomes. The advertising industry mounted a vigorous lobbying and public relations effort against the bill. Advertising had already suffered a big hit during the Great Depression, dropping more than 50 percent from a 1929 level of $2 billion. In letters to newspapers, magazines, and radio stations, advertisers warned that the industry would suffer an even greater loss of profits if the Tugwell bill passed. The media industry, largely supported by advertising revenues, did its part by not reporting on the proposed legislation. Drug manufacturers formed the Joint Committee for Sound Democratic Consumer Legislation to oppose the bill.[10]

The bill's supporters, with far fewer resources, could not compete. A more extreme faction of the consumer movement even opposed the bill, believing it did not provide enough protections. By late 1933 it was clear the bill would not pass. Revisions to the bill over the next two years would make it far more palatable to advertisers. The use of ambiguity or inference would be permitted. There would be no mandatory grading of goods. And the FDA would not be given the authority to regulate advertising.[11]

In the end, the passage of the Wheeler–Lea Act of 1938 gave the Federal Trade Commission (FTC) jurisdiction over false and misleading advertising, and the ability to regulate the advertising of food, drugs, cosmetics, and therapeutic devices. An ad would be considered false when "it misrepresented the character, quality, or therapeutic effect of an advertised commodity." The FTC could issue cease-and-desist orders to companies for false ads, and injunctions against companies for ads that "were injurious to consumers' health."

Stole concludes that consumer protections were sacrificed to the more powerful business interests of the advertising industry. "Unlike the Tugwell bill, which had intended to place the burden of proof with advertisers, the Wheeler–Lea bill placed the task of proving false and misleading advertising claims with the FTC. Although the bill proposed fines for dissemination of false advertising, it did not propose prison terms for such offenses."[12] At best, the FTC "was left to prosecute false and misleading advertising after consumers already had been hurt."[13]

The Attacks Continue

With the threat of war looming in the early 1940s, the federal government needed money to pay for national defense. The advertising industry faced a serious threat when a bill was introduced in Congress that would restrict the amount of advertising costs businesses were allowed to deduct from their income taxes. At that time, businesses could deduct up to 80 percent of their advertising costs as tax-deductible expenses. Proponents of the bill believed that the stricter tax burden would increase needed government revenues and curb excessive advertising, which could lead to price inflation. As Inger Stole writes, "If business wanted to advertise, they argued, they should pay for it out of their own pockets and not charge it to the government as a tax-deductible business expense."[14]

Industry concerns mounted further when Assistant Attorney General Thurman Arnold claimed that advertising was conducted in some cases as a monopoly practice, which violated the Sherman Antitrust Act. He alleged that manufacturers would use large advertising campaigns to increase demand for their products. They would then force merchants to accept their less popular brands to prevent competitors from building up a large stock of competing products in a store, not unlike some Walmart practices today. Arnold called this practice "full-line forcing" and considered it illegal. In mid-1941 the Justice Department sent questionnaires to twenty-two major oil companies asking for information on their advertising costs, media placements, advertising copy, names of their advertising agencies, and the amount spent in each media category.[15] An article in *Printers' Ink* said of the survey: "At the basis is the belief that advertising itself is uneconomic as well as anti-social."[16]

Clearly the industry was in trouble and needed a powerful public relations campaign. One idea proposed in *Printers' Ink* called for a $5 million campaign to educate the public about advertising.[17] Another urged the advertising community to create a "united front" against the attacks. In a 1941 memo, Paul B. West, president of the Association of National Advertisers, asked the American Association of Advertising Agencies (widely known as "the 4 A's") for a joint meeting in Hot Springs, Virginia, where a plan for "a forceful, dramatic presentation" of the facts about advertising could be developed. "Let us take advantage of this opportunity to show what advertising has to offer the national economy," West urged.[18]

The November 14, 1941, meeting addressed three key areas: the regulatory threats, advertising's benefit to the economy, and a plan of action. Young delivered the plan of action in his speech. He was already well-known in advertising circles, having worked his way up within ten years from an office boy at the age of thirteen for a religious book publisher to "magazine mailer, shipping clerk, stenographer . . . book salesman and advertising manager."[19] Later he joined the J. Walter Thompson company as a copywriter, becoming a vice president in 1917. He had then retired from advertising in 1928 at the age of forty-two. His "retirement" included a five-year stint as an advertising professor at the University of Chicago, then serving as a consultant to the secretary of the interior, director of the Bureau of Foreign and Domestic Commerce, and director of communications for the coordinator of inter-American affairs. He rejoined J. Walter Thompson as a senior consultant and director shortly before the joint meeting in 1941.[20]

In the Hot Springs speech, Young rallied his troops to "ask ourselves whether we, as an industry, do not have a great contribution to make in this effort to regain for business the leadership of our economy." He called on his audience to use the power of advertising to combat the threats to the industry. "We have within our hands the greatest aggregate means of mass education and persuasion the world has ever seen—namely, the channels of advertising communication. We have the masters of these techniques of using these channels. We have power. Why do we not use it?"[21]

Young's remarks were followed by a luncheon, where William L. Batt, director of the materials division of the Roosevelt administration's Office of Production Management, warned that the looming signs of war meant the ad industry could no longer conduct business as usual. "I suggest that you find out what your clients ought to be doing to help save paper, or to save cardboard, or to save anything of which we are short for defense purposes," he said.[22] "We have not formally declared war, but how any man or woman can conclude that we are not in the war, in effect, I don't see."[23]

Between sessions, Batt asked West if the advertising industry had a Washington office, and was surprised to learn there was none. He urged West to spend a week in Washington to meet with administration officials. West boarded a train with his wife on Sunday, December, 7, 1941, the day Japanese planes bombed Pearl Harbor.[24]

Suddenly, in a time of war, the advertising industry could showcase its value by serving the nation.

The Birth of an Advertising Council

After the Hot Springs meeting, Chester LaRoche, then chairman of the board for the ad agency Young & Rubicam (Y&R), sparked the plan of action that would create the Ad Council. People tended to notice LaRoche, a graduate of Phillips Exeter Academy and Yale University. While LaRoche was serving as the southern advertising manager for *Collier's Weekly*, John Orr Young, Y&R's cofounder, had jotted his name down in a little black book he kept that listed people Young wanted to work for him. He noted, "Chet LaRoche: Aggressive, Irish, football type, Colliers."[25]

LaRoche joined Paul West in Washington for a meeting on December 15, 1941, with Donald Nelson, the former Sears, Roebuck and Co. executive who had become director of priorities for the U.S. Office of Production Management. Nelson had written to West on December 9 to ask for a meeting between advertising representatives and government officials. "One of the pressing requirements of the Government is to have the help of the established organizations representing the creative ability of advertising and the channels of communication reaching the public," Nelson wrote. "There are, and will be many campaigns having to do with public education, morale, problems of conservation, use of alternative materials in place of those now urgently needed for war purposes; in short, we must have the means of quickly and effectively disseminating facts to the American people in all ways that are necessary and proper to bring about a united effort of all the people of the country."[26]

Harold B. Thomas, president of the Centaur Company, then the maker of the patented laxative Fletcher's Castoria, recalled the tense meeting in his book about the history of the Ad Council: "Those in attendance at this small meeting December 15 remember well the . . . gravity of the situation—the seriousness, down-to-earth attitude of Nelson as he said in effect—we must produce as we have never produced before—we must fight for our lives—we must be ready for anything and everything."[27]

Nelson wanted the ad industry's help with "conservation, health and welfare, civilian defense, [speedy] production and others."[28] But such a partnership between the ad industry and government would not be easy, as one meeting attendee later recalled in his December 19 memo based on conversations with Washington insiders. The memo detailed the bureaucracy and indifference ad agency personnel faced in Washington, concluding:

> They feel that the only solution is for the Office of Civilian Defense to have either an existing advertising agency, or a specially created advertising agency of their own, staffed by people who can sell this package—Protection—to the American people, and headed by an individual or individuals independent enough to go to the primary powers that be and see that stuff is pushed through fast and that it appears. They point out that Americans are not going to be guarded by piles of material stacked on somebody's desk in Washington for months. They feel that somebody with vision enough to see what is actually needed and with courage enough to fight for it, has got to head things up— somebody whose opinions will be respected enough so that even the "brass hat" element will acknowledge their worth. They say it is no job for a fumbler, no matter how earnest or sincere he is.[29]

As a result of this meeting, the focus soon shifted from creating a council to combat government attacks to create a council to facilitate the ad industry coming to the aid of a government fighting a war. Two needs could be met by a single solution that would be a win–win for both sides. The government would harness the power of the industry to help win the war, and the industry would improve its image with the government.

When representatives of the ad industry and media companies met again on January 5, 1942, a plan was put in place to develop a council that would meet the advertising needs of the federal government through projects such as "conservation and proper use of civilian goods and materials, the promotion of public health, nutritional use of food, consumption of gasoline, sale of war bonds, etc." Chester LaRoche was named chairman of the council, with Paul West as secretary.[30]

When the opportunity presented itself, the industry seized the moment. In a memo outlining the council's purpose, Nelson wrote, "This nation must be converted from peace-time habits and customs (luxuries, spendthrift attitude, wastefulness, expectations that anything can be replaced with something just-as-good or better) to an all-out war basis (conserve, scrimp, save and do without)." The memo recognized that "advertising is essential in getting this job done and the government has asked our cooperation toward that end."[31]

In this memo, the seeds were planted for the Ad Council's future "Washington conferences," during which the council would meet once a year (today the Washington conference is held once every presidential term) with the executive branch.[32]

LaRoche and West saw two key purposes for the council: providing a point of contact between the government and the advertising industry, and helping coordinate ad campaigns needed by the government. During the war, representatives from what would become the War Advertising Council would attend meetings with senior-level government officials, and would advise and consult on questions of policy and procedures as they related to the overall public relations mission.

The donated media model's roots can be found in the minutes from the Ad Council's January 14, 1942, meeting at the Cloud Club on Lexington Avenue in New York. During a discussion of how the council should function, LaRoche suggested concentrating first on government needs such as conservation and hoarding. "One way to expedite the job," LaRoche said, "would be to get several agencies to volunteer a certain amount of their services and the Council would then assign an agency to the specific job for which it was best qualified."[33]

By the time the council met again in Washington on February 5, 1942, prior to a second meeting with Nelson, the 4 A's had already pledged $25,000 for operational expenses until a fund-raising plan could be developed. Advertising, publishing, and broadcasting executives would then meet with Nelson that same day for an off-the-record conversation in a room at the Social Security Board Building. LaRoche and Leo Burnett, president of the Chicago-based Leo Burnett Company, represented the ad agency world at the meeting. Thomas of the Centaur Company represented advertisers. Harry Butcher, vice president of the Columbia Broadcasting Company, filled in for company president Paul Kesten when his plane was grounded in New York. Nelson told the attendees that the War Production Board would develop the plans for the public information program, and it would be up to industry and labor to execute them.

Government officials listed seven messages that they wanted the council to convey to the American people through advertising: "the necessity of fighting to keep from losing our shirts"; pointing "out the way that the enemy operates" and "how we would have to live under their kind of system"; creating "an understanding of who and what our allies are and the importance of pooling our resources"; "the need to work more, to produce more"; "the need to sacrifice, to give up a lot of things we have been accustomed to"; "to maintain a fight-to-win morale, especially among men going into service"; and "later on, when we are winning, not to let down, not to be satisfied with any compromise and to keep alive the ultimate goals for which we are fighting."[34]

Nelson and Grover understood that the nation's business and communications companies would be crucial to involving citizens in a production program to help the country fight the Axis powers. President Roosevelt had warned the nation of the hardships ahead in his January 6, 1942, State of the Union address. "Our war program for the coming fiscal year will cost $56 billion or, in other words, more than one-half of the estimated annual national income," he said. "That means taxes and bonds, and bonds and taxes. It means cutting luxuries and other nonessentials. In a word, it means an 'all-out' war by individual effort and family effort in a united country."[35]

When the Ad Council was incorporated on February 18, 1942, its members included the owners and executives of magazines, newspapers, radio, and outdoor advertising, printing, and direct-mail firms. Leading ad agencies, as well as major companies that advertised their goods and services, participated in this unprecedented effort. Its mission: "To provide a means for marshalling the forces of advertising so that they may be of maximum aid in the successful prosecution of the war and in the preservation of American democracy."[36]

The name would later be changed to the War Advertising Council at the May 28, 1943, meeting.[37] "Advertising's gift to America" would become the industry's greatest public relations tool. As long as the war lasted, advertising would no longer be a nasty business in the public's mind.

Chapter 3

Smokey Bear

A More Complicated Character Than His Image Depicts

*Smokey Bear ranks alongside Santa Claus and Mickey Mouse
as one of the most recognizable icons of our time. . . . Kids love him.*

—*Ad Council,* Public Service Advertising That Changed a Nation

*In this region, Smokey dolls have been hanged and nailed to posts,
posters bearing his image have been riddled with bullet holes, and
he has commonly been characterized as a vicious and despotic land
thief.*

—*Jake Kosek,* Understories: The Political Life of Forests in Northern New
Mexico

On a sunny Friday in August 2007, Scott Murray stood before the Ad
Council's Campaign Review Committee. At ad agency Draftfcb, the
thirty-five-year-old creative director had promoted Taco Bell, State Farm Insurance and Doubletree Hotels (he is now a creative director at R&R Partners
in Los Angeles). But none of that work matched the opportunity now before
him. The U.S. Forest Service's Cooperative Forest Fire Prevention (CFFP) program wanted a new Smokey Bear campaign. Murray would have the chance to
help create the advertising for this important image.

As the longest-running public service advertising campaign in U.S. history, Smokey is embedded in America's cultural zeitgeist. He has his own zip
code, postage stamp, website, Facebook page, and school lesson plan. His mail
once exceeded more than a thousand letters a day, and he counts more than
ninety-three thousand friends on Facebook. His image is protected by an act of

Congress, and he remains one of the most popular characters ever produced by the ad industry.

Three out of four adults recognize him, and he was once second only to Santa Claus among the nation's favorite characters. Smokey has been promoted by Alvin and the Chipmunks, the Grateful Dead, Aretha Franklin, and Sammy Davis Jr. Actors such as Gregory Peck, John Wayne, and Rodney Dangerfield have sung his praises. Since Smokey debuted in 1944, the amount of land burned because of wildfires dropped from an average of 22 million acres to less than 8 million per year.[1] Many consider Smokey one of the Ad Council's most successful creations.

Smokey is also a symbol of conflict. Critics argue that his message promotes contradictory land use policies: it urges citizens both to protect forests from human-caused fires so everyone can enjoy the wonders of nature, and to save trees so that the wood can be harvested to benefit America's economy. Smokey is simultaneously a beloved icon of many children and their parents, a loathed symbol of colonialism to some American Indians and Chicanos who believe the government took their land (according to Jake Kosek's research), and a character who communicates the wrong message, according to a growing audience of amateurs and experts who believe controlled fires are actually good for forests.

The U.S. Forest Service, the National Association of State Foresters, and the Ad Council—the three members who make up the CFFP coordinating committee—are aware of the criticisms, but they maintain that Smokey does not represent official Forest Service policies. While some audiences consider Smokey a symbol of how the federal government addresses land use, the CFFP argues that Smokey's message focuses solely on wildfire prevention education. The Forest Service believes Smokey also protects watersheds, wildlife habitats, and homes threatened by fires, and it insists that Smokey has never said that all fires are bad for forests, just dangerously out-of-control ones.

The number of people in the Ad Council's conference room the day Murray presented his work, typically about ten for such a meeting, had swelled to forty, reflecting the excitement associated with the new Smokey advertising campaign. Nina DiSesa, then chairman of the McCann Erickson ad agency, headed the committee. An advertising legend herself, DiSesa had become the first female executive creative director of McCann's flagship New York office in 1994. She later presided over the well-known MasterCard "Priceless" campaign.

For "creatives" such as Murray, appearing before this Ad Council committee represented a rare chance to meet and work with giants such as DiSesa.

Murray opened with a pitch for a new Smokey print ad, and his audience was hooked. The goal of the campaign was to reintroduce Smokey to Americans as a hip bear who understood the modern world and still had a relevant message to share. What better way to do that than give him a profile—done in *Vanity Fair* style—to accompany the TV spot? Copying the questions that appeared in the monthly profile at the back of the magazine, readers would learn that Smokey's idea of perfect happiness was "a day fishing in the wilderness, followed by a nap under a shady, towering oak tree, hat over my eyes, no wildfires to worry about." When asked on what occasion he might lie, Smokey answered, "The only lying I do involves hibernation."

Relieved at the committee's welcoming response, Murray turned to the thirty-second TV spot. The concept: Smokey is always watching you. On the three screens in the room, a carved Smokey statue—the one present at many national parks and based on the work of artist Rudy Wendelin—appeared behind people about to commit a careless act that could cause a wildfire. To Murray, it seemed like only ten seconds into his description of the spot when DiSesa interrupted. "I hate it," Murray recalled her saying, unable to tolerate an ad in which Smokey did not move or express emotion. "What else do you have?"

Murray, reeling from the committee's sudden change, could only talk about his other idea since no other presentation was ready: in this scenario, people would step into Smokey's shoes as they admonished others for potentially starting a fire. Fortunately, the alternative was enough. With orders from the committee to develop it, the result would be the 2008 campaign called "Get Your Smokey On."

Preserving Nature's "Great Solemn Cathedral"

To understand Smokey's complicated history, it's necessary to start with a pivotal May 1903 Yosemite mountain camping trip that President Theodore Roosevelt took with naturalist and Sierra Club founder John Muir.

While lying prone on a pile of pine needles and surrounded by giant sequoia trees, Roosevelt learned why preserving forests needed to be a part of future land management policies. Staring at the trees, he felt like he was "lying in a great solemn cathedral, far vaster and more beautiful than any built by the hands of man."[2]

Over the four-day hike, Muir, with unlimited access to Roosevelt, explained the importance of preserving America's parks and forests in their pure state. This position would be combined with "the greatest good for the greatest number" approach favored by Roosevelt's good friend and chief of the Division of Forestry, Gifford Pinchot, to create the Forest Service's mix of preservation and management in its land policies.[3] It was likely the staggering beauty of his surroundings, even more than Muir's eloquence, that worked its magic on the president. Roosevelt delighted in the wild land he encountered, including the four inches of snow he found himself buried under after awakening one morning at Glacier Point. If Roosevelt considered the land "bully," as Edmund Morris described in his book *Theodore Rex*, the unexpected snow was "bullier."[4]

Muir did not emerge from the trip empty-handed. Roosevelt issued an immediate presidential order ceding the already well-developed Yosemite Valley back to the national park system and granting an extension of the California forest. The word "preservation" also appeared in Roosevelt's May 19, 1903, speech that he delivered in Sacramento immediately after the Yosemite trip. He said:

> Lying out at night under those giant Sequoias was lying in a temple built by no hand of man, a temple grander than any human architect could by any possibility build, and I hope for the preservation of the groves of giant trees simply because it would be a shame to our civilization to let them disappear. They are monuments in themselves. I ask for the preservation of the other forests on grounds of wise and far-sighted economic policy. I do not ask that lumbering be stopped at all. On the contrary, I ask that the forests be kept for use in lumbering, only that they be so used that not only shall we here, this generation, get the benefit for the next few years, but that our children and our children's children shall get the benefit. I ask that your marvelous natural resources be handed on unimpaired to your posterity. We are not building this country of ours for a day. It is to last through the ages.[5]

Roosevelt's words characterized the fundamental conflict that would permeate federal land use policy for generations to come. The land should be used to benefit the country's economic interests, yet also be preserved for the future enjoyment of all citizens. It was a conflict that would pit rancher against tourist, and tree cutter against tree-hugging environmentalist.

To further understand how one cartoon bear's advertising messages would generate such disparate reactions, it's necessary to first explore the land management policies practiced by the federal Forest Service, part of the U.S. Department of Agriculture. The Multiple-Use Sustained-Yield Act of 1960 gave the Forest Service authority to combine both preservation and management in its approach to the nation's land.[6] Pete Dunne, in his book *Prairie Spring*, defines the terms as follows: "Multiple use means hiking, hunting, bird watching, camping, gas and oil drilling, timber harvesting, and cattle grazing. Sustained yield means you can do what you want to do as long as the ecological integrity of the habitat is not diminished or destroyed."[7]

In the mid-nineteenth century, land dominated American thought in the form of manifest destiny—the idea that the United States had a God-given right to expand its territory. The phrase first appeared in the July/August 1845 edition of the *United States Magazine and Democratic Review*, where author John L. O'Sullivan, writing about the annexation of Texas, declared "the fulfillment of our manifest destiny to overspread the continent allotted by Providence for the free development of our multiplying millions."[8] How to manage the land became a chief concern even before shots rang out at noon in Oklahoma on September 16, 1893, and the final acres were claimed in the last of America's great land rushes.

Manifest destiny brought unwelcome consequences. Concern about depletion of lumber and the need to preserve the forests gained greater attention in 1872, when Franklin B. Hough, a physician and statistician, was appointed to a New York state commission to study the necessity of a public forest park. His paper, "On the Duty of Governments in the Preservation of Forests," which called for stopping the destruction of trees and promoting reforestation, became the basis of a August 15, 1876, bill authorizing $2,000 for a forestry study.[9] Previous attempts at passing a version of the bill through the Public Lands Committee had failed. So a motion was made to transfer the bill as a rider to the Department of Agriculture's general appropriations bill. This move was significant because it foreshadowed the future 1905 shift of forestry matters from the Department of the Interior to Agriculture, where the Forest Service remains housed today.[10]

The Forest Reserve Act of 1891 authorized the government to designate public land as forest reserves.[11] To protect water supplies, President Benjamin Harrison set aside fifteen federal land reserves with more than 13 million acres, including the Yellowstone Forest Reserve. President Grover Cleveland created an additional thirteen reserves of 21 million acres. A bill signed by President William McKinley on June 4, 1897, authorized the U.S. Geological Survey to examine the forest reserves. No reservation could be established "except to improve and protect the forest within the reservation, or for the purpose of securing favorable conditions of water flows, and to furnish a continuous supply of timber for the use and necessities of the citizens of the United States."[12] The secretary of the interior was directed to develop rules to protect the reserves, and the bill permitted the sale of mature or dead lumber.

Gifford Pinchot used his friendship with Teddy Roosevelt to broaden the government's management of public lands. The two had successfully kept control of the forests from "men they castigated as robber barons and plunderers of the public domain."[13] Preserving the land was considered radical in the eyes of those such as William A. Clark, the Montana copper baron and U.S. senator who brought the railroad to southern Nevada; J. P. Morgan, who controlled the Northern Pacific Railroad; and E. H. Harriman, head of the Union Pacific Railroad. Like many of their powerful colleagues, all three were eager to gain riches from the final fruits of manifest destiny. Clark's attitude that he was above the law and bore no responsibility toward average citizens particularly irked Mark Twain. In a 1907 essay entitled "Senator Clark of Montana," Twain posited him as the essence of Gilded Age corruption: "He is as rotten a human being as can be found anywhere under the flag; he is a shame to the American nation, and no one has helped to send him to the Senate who did not know that his proper place was the penitentiary, with a ball and chain on his legs. To my mind he is the most disgusting creature that the republic has produced since [William 'Boss'] Tweed's time."[14]

When Pinchot met with Roosevelt in 1899, while the former Rough Rider was governor of New York, they agreed that "Americans had become much too shortsighted with the continent they now straddled. . . . In an eye blink, the great bounty had been exhausted; more than a billion acres had been given away to corporations, states, or private landowners to do with as they pleased."[15]

An assassin's bullet on September 6, 1901, took the life of President William McKinley and made Roosevelt, at forty-two, the nation's youngest president.

Although Roosevelt said publicly that little would change in his administration, his goal was to move the Republican Party away from big business to become what he saw as "a fairly radical progressive party."[16] In his first message to Congress, Roosevelt said, "The forest reserves should be set apart forever for the use and benefit of our people as a whole and not sacrificed to the short-sighted greed of a few."[17] To achieve this, he asked Pinchot to stay on as the country's forester and presidential advisor.

Through the use of executive decrees, Roosevelt got to work. Pelican Island in Florida became America's first wildlife refuge. When Roosevelt won the 1904 election, Congress passed the Transfer Act of 1905, which moved responsibility for the forests to the Department of Agriculture, changed the Bureau of Forestry to the U.S. Forest Service, and renamed the reserves national forests. Pinchot, as the Forest Service's first chief, now had control of 60 million acres. Together, Roosevelt and Pinchot would push an agenda of conservation.

In 1907 Roosevelt further expanded federally protected lands, despite an attempt by a rebellious Congress to eliminate the president's power to create more national forests in seven western states. When Congress added an amendment to a spending bill that would eliminate the president's authority to create new national forests without congressional approval, Roosevelt felt stymied.[18] He had one week to sign the bill, which was necessary to keep the government operating. Pinchot, however, felt emboldened. Why not spend the week protecting as much land as possible by creating more national forests that Roosevelt would add to the bill before signing it?

Pouring over maps of the seven states in question, Roosevelt was elated by his friend's plan. "Oh, this is bully," he exclaimed. "Have you put in the North Fork of the Flathead? Up there once I saw the biggest herd of black-tailed deer."[19] By week's end, 16 million acres of additional land had been declared national forests by executive decree. In just two years, Roosevelt, with the help of Pinchot, had tripled the amount of land in the national forest system to 180 million acres. Backed by Pinchot's army of forest rangers, conservation became the new buzzword.

Dismantling Roosevelt's Legacy

These successes, however, were fleeting. The Forest Service would barely survive the William Howard Taft presidency, which started in 1909. In the early days of Taft's administration, Roosevelt's foes in Congress pledged death to the Forest Service by a thousand little cuts. The budget was slashed, causing mayhem among Pinchot's forest rangers: "As policemen, game wardens, rescuers and peacemakers, rangers were expected to organize and lead fire-fighting crews, build roads, negotiate grazing fees and timber sales contracts, direct reforestation and disease control projects and run surveys."[20] The pay cuts were crippling, and there were insufficient funds for roads, telephones, trails, or the hiring of fire patrols in advance of the coming wildfire season.

Worse, Pinchot, held over from the Roosevelt administration, now found himself at odds with his mentor John Muir. Muir thought conservation should mean preserving the land in its pure state, but Pinchot disagreed. His policy for how the Forest Service should operate rested on the core principle that "use was not contrary to conservation. Decisions on use would consider the needs of the local industries first."[21] Any conflicts would be resolved from the standpoint of "the greatest good of the greatest number in the long run."[22]

Roosevelt may have handpicked Taft to carry on his legacy, but Taft, once in office, believed Roosevelt's conservation movement had gone too far. He fired Pinchot on January 7, 1910.[23] Roosevelt's enemies in Congress made plans to abolish the Forest Service. Their sharpened knives slashed the service's ability to publicize itself, making it nearly impossible to recruit new forest rangers. Senator Weldon Heyburn of Idaho, long a Roosevelt foe, said no further federal money should be spent on forests. Meanwhile, Taft quickly returned some of the land Roosevelt had protected to private interests.

Then nature intervened. In July of that year, a series of wildfires, started by electrical storms, erupted in the dry forests of Washington, Idaho, and Montana. Other fires, started for work-related reasons at logging, ranching, and railroad sites, were also spread by fierce winds over a three-day period. Up until then, fire protection chiefly had fallen to the forest rangers, since the states enacted few laws and allocated insufficient resources to address the issue. But the decimated Forest Service could do little to stop the wildfires from turning into a raging inferno in August. As eloquently told in Timothy Egan's book, *The Big Burn: Teddy Roosevelt and the Fire That Saved America*, the fire consumed 3 million acres in two days, destroying a good part of towns such as Wallace, Idaho, and taking the lives of at least eighty-five, many of them firefighters.[24]

Pinchot used the fire as an opportunity to attack the enemies of conservation. He called people like Senator Heyburn part of a group of "ironbound reactionaries" with blood on their hands.[25] "The men in Congress like Heyburn who have made light of the efforts of the Forest Service to prepare itself to prevent such a calamity as this, have in effect been fighting on the side of the fires against the general welfare," Pinchot said. "If even a small fraction of the loss from the present fires had been expended in additional patrol and preventive equipment some or perhaps all of the loss could have been avoided."[26]

Although it was doubtful that anything could have stopped the fire, Pinchot used it to rouse support for the Forest Service and to lambaste Congress for the budget cuts. Roosevelt joined in, calling for an expanded Forest Service, a new crop of rangers to protect America's forests, and more land to be set aside for the enjoyment of future generations.

With public sentiment now favoring conservation, Pinchot was able to spearhead a movement that culminated in Congress passing the Weeks Act in early 1911, placing 20 million acres of eastern lands within the public land system. Forests in the Appalachians, the Great Smoky Mountains, New England, and southern Ohio would be added. The bill also allowed the federal government to purchase land to protect the headwaters of rivers and watersheds in the East, and called for federal, state, and private authorities to cooperate in preventing forest fires.[27] The Clarke-McNary Act in 1924, which provided money for controlling forest fires, further extended the authority of the Forest Service to buy timber-producing land.[28]

Nevertheless, Forest Service officials believed that more needed to be done to prevent forest fires. Addressing Americans directly, the Forest Service created a radio program, *Uncle Sam's Forest Rangers*, which debuted in 1932 on the NBC radio network as part of the "National Farm and Home Hour."[29] The program introduced listening audiences to two characters: an experienced ranger named Jim Robbins and his young protégé Jerry Quick, who had recently graduated from forestry school. When young Jerry forgot to break his match in two after lighting up a cigarette, he quickly learned the dangers of carelessness in the forest. Each weekly episode of the program, which lasted into the 1940s, showcased a different part of the forest ranger's job. The program also highlighted different Forest Service goals advocated by President Franklin Delano Roosevelt. After FDR launched a Civilian Conservation Corps that would put a quarter of a million men to work in the forests ten days after his March 4, 1933, inauguration, an episode featuring the program appeared on the show that

September. The corps played an important role in combating forest fires, and program funds were used to buy more acres for national forests, build campgrounds, and establish trails.[30]

Even before Smokey Bear was created, the Forest Service would speak to the nation with forest fire prevention advertising messages that pushed the theme of protecting America's forests from the Axis powers. It was the threat to national economic and security interests that galvanized the War Advertising Council to create a forest fire prevention campaign. Preserving the forests for future generations was not the chief concern.

Another Enemy to Conquer

When a Japanese submarine surfaced off the coast of California during World War II on February 23, 1942, near Ellwood Beach, seven miles north of Santa Barbara concern about protecting the nation's forests intensified. As William Clifford Lawter Jr. writes in *Smokey Bear 20252: A Biography*, the ship was under orders to attack a coastal target and thus divert American warships northward. "Five nervous sailors scrambled on deck and fired a quick volley of almost two dozen five-inch shells," Lawter observes.[31] Nobody was injured, and damages, which included the loss of a shed owned by the Barnsdall-Rio Grande Oil Company, barely reached $500.[32]

But the psychological impact was enormous. This was the first wartime attack on the U.S. mainland. Threats to America's national security and critical lumber supply were now uppermost in the minds of government officials and business leaders alike. Ellen Earnhardt Morrison, writing in *Guardian of the Forest: A History of the Smokey Bear Program*, explains why lumber was considered so critical to the war effort:

> It is estimated that during World War II, our military forces used enough lumber to construct 9,500,000 average size houses (about one-fourth the number of family homes in the United States at that time). . . . The building of a "Liberty" ship required about 350,000 board feet of lumber. Any ship of 10,000-ton capacity needed 250,000 board feet of lumber and timber just to brace every load it transported. About 28,000 board feet went into building a PT boat, and a sub-chaser required 200,000 board feet for its foredecks, bulkheads,

and other parts. High quality wood was used to make gunstocks, and every year of the war saw 50,000,000 board feet consumed for this purpose. When a soldier was shipped overseas, he was outfitted with supplies and equipment sent in packing crates. These crates used many more board feet of lumber.[33]

Human carelessness in forests was a grave concern even before the Japanese submarine attack. In 1941, the year America entered the war, 208,000 forest fires consumed 30 million acres of land. The Forest Service claimed that nine out of ten of these fires were caused by people and could have been prevented.[34] Preventing accidental fires became a top priority for William V. Mendenhall, the supervisor of Angeles National Forest in Southern California, who was ap-pointed the forest defense coordinator for the area. To educate the public about how carelessness causes fires, Mendenhall and his fire prevention officer, Arnold B. Larson—a former newspaperman—asked advertising agencies to include fire prevention messages in their ad copy or to donate posters to the cause.[35]

Mendenhall addressed his April 28, 1942, letter to ad agencies around the country. The copy sent to Sigurd Larmon, president of Young & Rubicam, read, "We need your help in arousing the public to join us, as never before, in pro-tecting America's 160 national forests. It's a big part of the job of defeating the Axis."[36] Mendenhall urged Larmon to use his agency to "hammer home, in newspaper, periodical and radio advertising, this year's extraordinary need for vigilant care with fire, matches and cigarettes in forest country."[37] In his tele-graph response, Larmon referred Mendenhall to the newly formed Ad Council: "It is our considered judgment that your cause can be served more promptly and completely through this organization than through individual agencies."[38] In turn, the Ad Council recommended Don Belding, then head of the Los Angeles office of Lord & Thomas (which would later become Foote, Cone & Belding, and then Draftfcb) to help create the campaign.

Belding was ideally suited to take on a national fire prevention campaign. Within his office, which was a part of the Lord & Thomas Chicago-based firm run by advertising giant Albert Lasker, Belding handled the prestigious Sunkist (California Fruit Growers Exchange) account.[39] In his acceptance speech for president of the Pacific Coast Advertising Clubs, Belding told his audience: "It is advertising which makes free enterprise possible in the United States and

Canada. It is advertising which makes a solvent press possible and without a solvent press we cannot have a free press."[40]

Forest Fires: "Allies of the Axis"

Belding presented the first forest fire prevention campaign at a May 12, 1942, meeting of the Los Angeles County Conservation Association. The slogan was: "Careless Matches Aid the Axis—Prevent Forest Fires."[41] These words appeared below the "head of [a] Jap soldier (against forest fire background) holding [a] burning match to his face," according to a memo listing highlights of the campaign.[42] Fire prevention officer Larson of the Angeles National Forest described the poster of the Japanese soldier, featuring a menacing grin, to his superiors in Washington, D.C., as having "a power of evil magnetism that draws and binds attention."[43] Smokey would not appear in the campaign until 1944.

The Ad Council showed the campaign to Secretary of Agriculture Claude Wickard on May 18. The Forest Service would pay for the production of the posters, radio transcripts, movie trailers, and billboards at an estimated cost of $43,000.[44] But additional support was needed from industry to place newspaper and magazine ads nationwide. Belding had first proposed Kiwanis International as the sponsor of the program, but the Forest Service rejected the idea: "Kiwanis usually puts on a good opening show, but does not follow through on a long campaign such as this will have to be, since it is not believed they are equipped to do so."[45]

The Forest Service also believed that a national campaign was necessary to attract the support of big business: "If the Advertising Council program is not put on as a nation-wide campaign, we had better not have any campaign at all. Big companies all over the country, represented by the Advertising Council, will not come in on any sporadic local campaigns."[46]

Wickard liked the campaign.[47] The Forest Service assigned Richard Hammatt to direct the campaign and began preparations for a national announcement of the effort.[48] Hammatt, who had graduated from Harvard University's first forestry class in 1906, had served the Forest Service in California and Oregon. After leaving to become the executive officer of the California Redwood Association, he had returned to the service in 1933 to help organize President Roosevelt's Civilian Conservation Corps.[49]

When Secretary Wickard launched the campaign on CBS's radio network on July 24, 1942, he told listeners that "destruction in our forests today by carelessness with fire is equivalent to sabotaging the nation's war program."[50] The announcement followed a July 16 letter to all the Forest Service's regional offices describing the role each office and ranger would have in the "greatest mass attack on the carelessly caused forest fire in the history of conservation."[51]

By September, problems with the campaign began surfacing. The Ad Council had created a new rule requiring all campaigns to have advertising coordinators, which forced Belding to find a corporate sponsor to fill the role he played on the campaign. When he suggested an executive from the Los Angeles Fruit Growers Exchange, Hammatt initially balked. In his September 12 reply to Belding, he wrote: "There are many owners of stumpage and manufacturers of lumber who are very suspicious that the Forest Service will use this Wartime Forest Fire Prevention campaign as a vehicle through which to preach public control of cutting practices on privately owned forest land, and there are members of the Forest Service who believe some of those owners and manufacturers might be glad to throw a spoke or two in the wheel of the . . . campaign undertaken in any large way by the Forest Service."[52]

Others questioned the campaign's theme. As in other early Ad Council campaigns, the ads pushed a patriotic theme. But the patriotic fervor embedded in the campaign's slogan, combined with the evil grin on the face of the Japanese soldier in the poster, resonated more with Americans living in the West, while Hitler seemed a greater threat to those in the eastern states.

In response to a questionnaire Hammatt circulated to regional foresters about the 1942 campaign, the California region office reported: "The criticism of this year's design was that the Jap head was more applicable to the West than nationwide, and that the slogan 'Careless Matches Aid the Axis' was too impersonal and did not bring home the fire problem to the individual citizen."[53] Foresters in the South agreed: "While the Jap face was an excellent symbol, it must be remembered that the Japs are somewhat far away to the people in the South while the Nazis are much closer. Pictures and mats possibly using a combination of the Nazi and Jap would be more effective."[54]

As a result, the faces of Hitler and Japanese prime minister Hideki Tōjō appeared on the 1943 poster, with a forest fire raging in the background. The slogan, "Our Carelessness, Their Secret Weapon," had won out against the Ad Council's proposed "Carelessness Is Treason." Some Forest Service officials objected to the word "treason" as being too forceful and possibly even dangerous.[55]

By 1944, with the war nearing an end, the Forest Service wanted the campaign to extend beyond a ceasefire, continuing to educate Americans about the need to prevent fires. The use of war-related scare tactics no longer applied, and Hammatt was eager for new material. Walt Disney's *Bambi*, a popular hit film after its 1942 release, inspired the idea of making a Disney poster for the fire prevention effort. Responding to the familiar fawn in the 1944 campaign, children and schoolteachers no longer found the campaign intimidating. In the poster, Bambi looked out at the audience with a cartoon rabbit and squirrel seated by his side. The slogan, which promoted a personal responsibility theme, said, "Please Mister, Don't Be Careless. Prevent Forest Fires."

Though well received, Bambi was not a permanent solution. Hammatt considered the Disney art "fine, but the information I get from all sources back here is that there always are too many strings to it to make it practicable for us as a basic design," he wrote in a letter to Foote, Cone & Belding on August 17, 1944.[56] He wanted a "good basic design 'a la Disney,'" and a squirrel emerged as one possibility. But a bear was considered more suitable. An earlier memo described a collective vision of what the bear should look like. Hammatt wrote: "Characterization (Disney manner?) of a (cub?) bear in a green (unburned) setting. Nose short (Panda type), color black or brown; expression appealing, knowledgeable, quizzical; perhaps wearing a campaign (or Boy Scout) hat that typifies the outdoors and the woods. A bear that walks on his hind legs; that can be shown putting out a warming fire with a bucket of water; dropping by parachute to a fire; reporting a fire by phone from a lookout; plowing a fire-line around a new-made clearing; building a campfire in the right place and way; carrying a rifle like G.I. Joes, etc."[57]

Hammatt also knew what he didn't want: "Do not simulate bears drawn by Cliff Berryman of the *Washington Star* (Teddy bears); used in Boy Scout publications; used by Piper Cub (airplane); the bear that symbolizes Russia; the bears on attached Forest Service bookmark."[58]

The assignment for drawing the bear was given to New York artist Albert Staehle. The Munich-born Staehle, who had emigrated to the United States at the age of fourteen, was a popular animal artist. He drew the "flop-eared cocker spaniel Butch on *Saturday Evening Post* covers."[59] His poster of a cow had inspired the Borden Company's Elsie the Cow.[60]

Staehle's interpretation of Hammatt's description resulted in a tender-looking bear pouring a bucket of water over a campfire. Published reports credit Hammatt for naming the bear Smokey, based perhaps on "Smokey Joe" Martin, the deceased assistant chief of the New York City fire department, who had been fearless in fighting fires.[61] Hammatt and his team added jeans and a hat to Staehle's naked bear, and the icon was born.

Within weeks of the poster's 1944 release, Hammatt knew he had a hit when large requests for Smokey Bear materials came rolling in.

The Forest Service and Madison Avenue

In 2007 Fire Prevention Program Manager Helene Cleveland, a group of state foresters, and other Forest Service officials listened intently as Draftfcb's Scott Murray presented his ideas for a new Smokey public service ad (PSA), including the same Smokey statue spot that would later draw such a negative response from Nina DiSesa. Murray was new to the Smokey account, as was Cleveland. He worked in Irvine, California, she in Washington D.C. But more than distance separated the two.

Cleveland, in the tradition established by Gifford Pinchot, had entered the Forest Service in 1981 as a forester working in Vermont's Green Mountain National Forest. She became an expert in both forestry and fire management, battling blazes in forests, grasslands, swamps, and peat bogs. She understood the smoldering threat of a dry peat moss bog, but she knew nothing about how advertising was created. Murray, on the other hand, knew how to weave elements of popular culture into successful ads, but he had only limited knowledge of the forests. That became quickly evident to Cleveland when he constantly referred to Smokey as a grizzly bear. He later recalled that, after he had ended his pitch, Cleveland said, "We have a lot of issues here, but the first one is Smokey is not a grizzly bear. He's a black bear."

Everyone cared about creating the right Smokey message, but Cleveland and Murray brought different experiences to the table. In Cleveland's world, having Smokey communicate the right message was critical. To Murray, what mattered was whether the PSA moved the audience or not.

After his statue idea bombed in New York, Murray headed back to Irvine. With less than a month to come up with another Smokey spot, he was back to square one. The research showed that people started nine out of ten wildfires, with campfires being one of the top three causes of the problem, according to Cleveland. Cigarettes, parking heated cars too close to dry brush, starting terrain vehicles in the wilderness where a spark could ignite, and burning trash in the backyard also played roles.

How could Smokey best communicate the complicated issues involved given the time limits imposed by a TV commercial? There were other special considerations as well. The Smokey Bear Act of 1952 had given control of Smokey and any revenue generated through the marketing of his image to the Department of Agriculture's Forest Service. The revenue goes into a fire prevention fund, which can only be used for that purpose. What Smokey can say is carefully controlled. His well-known slogan had changed from "Only You Can Prevent Forest Fires" to "Only You Can Prevent Wildfires" in 2001.

Murray asked his creative partner Dan Neri: "What would happen if people turned into Smokey?" Advertising concepts always reflect a core idea. The best in the business know that the simplest concepts usually work most effectively. The idea here would be: step into Smokey's shoes. The "Get Your Smokey On" campaign would show people morphing into Smokey as they instructed people to pick up their cigarette butts, not to leave a smoldering camp or bonfire, and to watch how they burn debris in their backyard. "We [were] asking people to become advocates, and the second you take on that role, you become Smokey," Murray explains.

Murray knew from his Campaign Review Committee experience that a single idea wasn't enough. So another—"Let's Put Smokey Back on the A-list"—featured the bear hanging out with George Clooney and Brad Pitt at a diner, or trying on jeans with Cameron Diaz. The slogan was, "Times have changed, but his message hasn't."

Back at the Ad Council in New York that September, Murray opened with the "Get Your Smokey On" pitch. Thirty seconds in, DiSesa said, "I love this." Ditto for the celebrity idea. The review committee argued about which campaign should move forward. Both got a green light, but "Get Your Smokey On" later won out when it became too difficult to secure the celebrities needed to put Smokey back on the A-list. Meanwhile, Cleveland and her team also liked Murray's revised ideas. "We always figured Smokey was on the A-list," she later said in a statement.

An updated, more muscular Smokey in the 2008 "Get Your Smokey On" campaign appeals to a younger generation. (Smokey Bear image used with the permission of the USDA Forest Service.)

The bear himself also got a new look. Thanks to computer-generated animation, a more muscular, less cartoonish Smokey emerged with lifelike fur, human teeth and fingers, and updated jeans. Although Smokey is targeted at people eighteen to thirty-four, children are likely to see his commercials. "He had to look more like a black bear but not terrify children," says Hilary Hamer, Draftfcb's senior vice president, who has managed the account since 2004. "He's authoritative, yet approachable."

The Controversial Side of Smokey's Message

Everybody loves Smokey, or so Jake Kosek thought. When the associate professor of geography at the University of California at Berkeley interviewed New Mexican residents for his 2006 book, *Understories: The Political Life of Forests in Northern New Mexico*, a frightening picture of the bear emerged. Posters of his image were found in the forest full of bullet holes. In his book Kosek quotes one district ranger of the Carson National Forest who said that "posters of Smokey have more bullet holes in them than any sign we post around here."

In the forests of northern New Mexico, American Indians and Chicanos retained bitter feelings over contested land claims that dated back five centuries. To them, Smokey was a bitter symbol of a U.S. government only too willing to give away land to robber barons such as William A. Clark (the "Copper King") and J. P. Morgan, but to take it from Indians and Latinos with more legitimate claims. Kosek's chief argument was that "racialized nationalist histories underlying the Smokey Bear campaign have infused the bear and the forest with exclusionary formations of U.S. nationalism and, together with the acquisition and misuse of forest lands by the Forest Service in northern New Mexico, have made Smokey more of a symbol of conquest than a benevolent protector of public forests."[62]

To people whose livelihood and existence depended on the forests, a fire prevention message was a threat. In northern New Mexico it was a common practice to burn areas of the forest so that sheep might graze, but Smokey's message urged the prevention of all forest fires. As Kosek recounts, one Forest Service supervisor wrote to his superior, "I am reducing the distribution of the war posters due to negative reaction to them on the part of the local people." The supervisor went on to say, "The fire prevention posters have made people feel like they are being accused of aiding the enemy." He recommended that "we do a more intensive education campaign before actively enforcing fire prevention in the area."[63]

By enforcing fire prevention, the government would take control of the region's natural resources away from the inhabitants. The greater national good would be imposed on local residents, prompting conflict between Smokey as a government representative and the people living in or near the forests who disagreed with his message. Tensions were inevitable.

Of even greater significance to the people living near New Mexico's forests was the notion that Smokey protected the forests to further the economic interests of others. Saving lumber to fight a war was one thing. But protecting the forests for America's timber manufacturers was a different matter. Smokey's message protected the manufacturers, who were allowed to cut trees in the forests, but excluded the grazers, hunters, and farmers who had a long history of using fire to further their own interests. The needs of local residents were pitted against larger manufacturing interests deemed vital to strengthening America's economy.

Smokey's message also imposed blame. As Kosek argues in his book, the Smokey campaign reflected the belief, deeply rooted in the history of the Forest Service, that people who set fires in forests were deviants and evildoers. The 1942 Japanese submarine attack only intensified this notion. When the Ad Council started its campaign with the Forest Service, it was the first national effort to protect the nation's forests. The strategy behind the campaign linked protecting lumber with national patriotism. So anyone who ignored the campaign's message was guilty of treason, the word some ad men had wanted to use in the 1943 poster featuring Hitler and Tōjō.[64]

Early messages from the fire prevention campaigns preceding Smokey urged citizens to "Volunteer Now as Forest Fire Watchers" and "Keep a Watchful Eye for Enemy Saboteurs."[65] Such messages only encouraged Americans to distrust people who were different—including the Asians behind the submarine attack, or the Indians and Chicanos who burned areas of forest so their animals might graze. "The boundaries of that patriotism," Kosek writes, "as was made painfully clear throughout the nation at the time through expression in the Japanese American concentration camps, the zoot suit riots, and the Tuskegee Project testing syphilis on African Americans, among many other exclusionary nationalist practices, became manifest in forest fire prevention. The campaign made those 'elements' that had traditionally used forest fires more suspect to their neighbors and unpatriotic collaborators with the enemy."[66]

The ad makers depicted fire as the enemy and linked it with images of the menacing Japanese soldier in the 1942 poster and the scary faces of Hitler and Tōjō in the 1943 poster. As time went on, the embodiment of evil in the message shifted from foreign enemies to any American citizen who was careless with matches.

Smokey's influence on how Americans view their forests remains prevalent today. Although the campaign exacerbated long-standing disagreements about land claims and land usage in specific regions, to the majority of the public Smokey remains a positive iconic image. He has been rebranded and refashioned for the twenty-first century, but his message of taking personal responsibility for the well-being of public parks, forests, and wetlands endures. In recent years, when wildfires have ravaged California and Arizona, Smokey's message, whatever its conflicting or controversial aspects, has served Americans well.

Chapter 4

The Rosie Legend and Why the Ad Council Claimed Her

The most successful advertising recruitment campaign in American history, this powerful symbol recruited two million women into the workforce to support the war economy. Those ads made a tremendous change in the relationship between women and the workplace.

—Ad Council website, June 2012

Some accounts claim that Norman Rockwell drew the "We Can Do It!" poster, while the Ad Council recently claimed her as their own. But . . . "We Can Do It!" was not a government poster. It did not appear everywhere during the war. [It] was far from the feminist icon it has retroactively become. The poster has come to represent a past that never was.

—James J. Kimble and Lester C. Olson,
"Visual Rhetoric Representing Rosie the Riveter"

Peggy Conlon's face peered out of the famous World War II poster of Rosie the Riveter—the one where a tough yet feminine Rosie sports a polka-dot red bandana as she rolls up her sleeve to reveal a shapely muscle. The words "We Can Do It!" appear above the compelling image.

To mark its seventieth birthday in February 2012, the Ad Council created a new Facebook application called "Rosify Yourself." Fans could insert their own picture into the memorable 1942 poster and become, as the Ad Council's press release called it, "riveters of social change." Conlon's Rosie appeared at the end of her February 13, 2012, *Huffington Post* article where she asked readers,

Pittsburgh freelance artist J. Howard Miller created this 1943 poster for the Westing-house Electric and Manufacturing Company to spur worker productivity. (National Archives)

"You know about Rosie the Riveter, but did you know that she helped recruit over two million women to join the workforce during the war?"

Because there are no copyright restrictions, the Rosie poster is as ubiquitous in American visual culture as images of Marilyn Monroe, appearing on memorabilia from napkins and mugs to aprons and T-shirts. Two known copies of the original poster still exist and were purchased by the National Archives and the Smithsonian's National Museum of American History. A third may survive in a private collection. The National Archives first displayed the poster in its 1994–95 exhibition, "Powers of Persuasion: Poster Art from World War II." This exhibition has been credited for making the poster more widely known to the public.

"[The National Archives] produced a reproduction for their shops, and the image took off after that," says Harry Rubenstein, chair and curator of the National Museum of American History's Division of Political History. "It's amazing to me that what has become one of the most famous World War II posters is largely famous because of a postwar exhibit."

Since 2002 the Ad Council has used the "We Can Do It!" poster in its publicity and advertising materials as a symbol of its well-regarded World War II Womanpower campaign, even though the poster was not part of that campaign (which was created by the council's ad agency, J. Walter Thompson, for its 1942 client, the War Manpower Commission). This was not a deliberate intention to mislead the public, but rather a mistaken interpretation of its own history. The mistake is revealing, because the words and images that any organization chooses to shape its public image demonstrate how the organization thinks about itself and its role in society.

The Rosie poster and the myth she represents—that of dramatically changing the perceptions of the role women played in American society—have been intricately woven into the council's publicity materials to bolster the image it wanted the world to see. The Ad Council's Womanpower campaign did have a significant and positive impact on spurring worker productivity to help America win the war, but at the time it did not drastically alter prevailing attitudes about the nurturing and domestic role of women in American life, or eliminate resistance to women entering the workforce. By selecting a popular image to depict this campaign retroactively, the council linked its important effort to all the misconceptions that surround the "We Can Do It!" poster.

Until 2012, the "We Can Do It!" poster appeared under "The Classics" section of the Ad Council's website featuring its work. The site credited the campaign and the poster with making employment outside of the home "socially acceptable and even desirable" for women. The poster also graced the cover of the Ad Council's September 2004 report, "Public Service Advertising That Changed a Nation." In another Ad Council publication, "Matters of Choice: Advertising in the Public Interest," the blurb next to the Rosie poster reads, "Ads like this made an abiding change in the relationship between women and the workplace."

The U.S. government viewed the Ad Council's Womanpower campaign as temporary: The goal was to get women into the workplace to aid the war effort. There was no drive to keep them there, once the war was over. However, even if the government viewed its Womanpower campaign as finite, American women in the 1940s may not have known that. The Ad Council helped plant a potent seed. When women were forced back into homes postwar, the stage was set. Women already knew that they could do many men's jobs; in the ensuing decades, this came to mean that they could do all men's jobs.

Examining the story behind the poster and the campaign will shed light on the historical role the Ad Council did play in mobilizing women to enter the workforce for a critical period until soldiers returned from World War II. The motives were bottom-line: this was not a push to gain public acceptance for working women, but rather to help the government secure the necessary labor needed during a specific period to win a war. The push was patriotic and practical rather than overtly feminist, and it appealed to the nurturing side of women to gain their help.

When the hostilities ended, American soldiers returned to the jobs they held before the war, and massive industrial layoffs left women with lower-paying clerical or domestic positions—when they could find work at all. When they couldn't, they returned to their homes. (It would be decades before women again entered the U.S. workforce in record numbers.)

The Not-So-Rosy Lives of American Women in the Early 1940s

On the eve of the bombing of Pearl Harbor, unemployment rates following the Great Depression remained stubbornly high. Women's lives were consumed by the domestic tasks that had dominated the days of their mother's generation.

Images of tough-talking career women portrayed by actresses such as Joan Crawford, Barbara Stanwyck, and Katharine Hepburn appeared on Hollywood's picture screens, but not in America's offices. As Sherna Berger Gluck argues in *Rosie the Riveter Revisited: Women, the War, and Social Change*, "The Depression reinforced women's role as the mainstay of family life, and their household chores often harked back to a past when women provided food and clothing for the family with their own hands. Bread had to be baked, fruit and vegetables canned, clothing sewn. Working-class women often performed these tasks without the benefits of modern household technology."[1]

In 1941 one-third of American households still cooked with coal or wood, Gluck observes. Water was often brought in from an outside source. Of the 11.5 million women employed in 1940, the majority did so in order to survive. But because unemployment rates for men remained high, there was active hostility toward women in the workforce. "Despite the militancy of some of the unemployed, people by and large did not blame their problems on capitalism," Gluck writes. "They tended, instead, to internalize them or, through the medium of cultural forms like the popular gangster films of the 1930s, to attribute social problems to personal evil."[2]

Women had an unprecedented opportunity to enter a workforce with plentiful jobs because the country had to mobilize quickly after the Japanese attack on Pearl Harbor. The government's goal was to unify the American public against the nation's enemies and to find the workers needed to produce enough airplanes, ships, and firearms to ensure victory. This scenario provided only a temporary place for women in the workforce.

But the government's need for temporary workers did not match the long-term aspirations of the students, wives, and widows who needed work and were seeking permanent places in the labor market. Maureen Honey, in *Creating Rosie the Riveter: Class, Gender, and Propaganda during World War II*, examined surveys among women conducted in 1944. "The economic advantages to women of wartime hiring patterns, when viewed against a history of systematic exclusion from better-paying jobs, are one indication that the war meant more to women workers than an opportunity to defend the country," she reports. "Another is that surveys taken in 1944 revealed that 75 to 80 percent of women in war production areas planned to remain in the labor force after victory was won, and they wanted to keep the jobs they were then performing."[3]

Honey's analysis of Census Bureau reports reveal the underlying government assumptions behind the Ad Council's Womanpower recruitment campaign. One Census Bureau report concluded that the best group of female workers to recruit would be married women whose children were fourteen or older. A second report by the War Production Board's Labor Division showed that government officials anticipated that women's participation in the labor force would be finite: "There is little doubt that women will be required to leave their jobs at the end of the war to permit the return of men to their jobs as they are released from the armed forces."[4]

Thus, the Womanpower campaign was geared toward using women to fill temporary work positions. Government officials assumed that women would return to their familiar roles of homemaking and child rearing when the war ended. The fact that the government geared the campaign toward woman without young children underscored its reluctance to hire young mothers. This was also reflected in the lack of adequate day care for children throughout the war.[5]

The government may have wanted temporary women workers, but it had no mechanism for forcing reluctant companies to hire them. President Roosevelt's War Manpower Commission and the War Department encountered strong industry resistance to hiring women and minorities. As Eleanor Straub noted in her analysis of government labor policy during the war years, "Prejudices against women, blacks, aliens, and Jews in the labor force were often frequently deep-seated and employer specifications were often not modified until [migration from other cities] had strained community facilities to the breaking point."[6]

Straub's analysis was supported by a May 1942 U.S. Employment Service survey of attitudes about the use of women in the labor force, which found:

> Over four-fifths of the skilled, professional and managerial openings and well over half of the semiskilled and unskilled jobs will continue to be barred to women. Even among clerical and sales occupations, almost half the job openings are with employers who will not consider women for such jobs.
>
> In spite of the increasing shortage of male labor, employers indicate some relaxation of discrimination against women in but [sic] 12 percent of the reported openings.[7]

Knowing how critical it was to keep American production operating at full force, FDR did his part to overcome the prejudices toward women and minorities in the workplace. In his 1942 Columbus Day speech, the president said, "In some communities, employers dislike to hire women. In others, they are reluctant to hire Negroes. We can no longer afford to indulge such prejudice."[8]

Some bias against women in the workforce was even held by women themselves. A January 1943 public opinion survey by the University of Denver's National Opinion Research Center found that 81 percent of women with children who were not currently in the labor force thought they could contribute the most to the war effort by not working and continuing to care for their children.[9]

Labor shortages created a difficult challenge for the government. Among many options the government considered to deal with the worker shortage was a law that would require people to work. But if Congress were to pass such an unpopular law, it would have difficulty enforcing it. If no law were enacted, the government would have to exert powers of persuasion to get people into the labor force. A 1942 government strategy document outlining the War Manpower Commission's objectives for its recruitment campaigns noted the dilemma:

> If there is no Manpower law, millions of job shifts must be brought about by persuasion. We are not asking people to do something they can take in their stride—like saving sugar or conserving tires. We're asking many to change their lives radically.
>
> If there is a Manpower law, persuasion is just as necessary. An unpopular law cannot be enforced. (Witness the Prohibition Law.) Without a law, refusal to do what the government asks would pass—is passing—unnoticed. With a law, wholesale violations would be a national scandal—an advertisement to the whole world of our disunity.[10]

Government officials saw several advantages in creating what Honey calls a "propaganda" recruitment campaign. First, publicity about recruitment would help overcome industry resistance to hiring women and minorities. Second, a campaign promising jobs could divert attention from the ugly domestic realities of a country at war, where food rationing, gasoline shortages, and overcrowded public transportation services were common problems. Third, the propaganda campaigns launched by the Ad Council could provide a type of "ideological framework" for the war to help Americans overcome their isolationist mentality and better understand what their nation was fighting for.[11]

But the campaign would never achieve the "tremendous change in the relationship between women and the workplace" that the Ad Council's website claimed in 2012. Under the Servicemen's Readjustment Act of 1944—popularly known as the G. I. Bill—returning soldiers received federal aid to buy homes, start businesses, and further their education. After the war, most women went back to their homes—and the 1950s only reinforced the domesticity that had become the hallmark of their lives. In *The Greater Generation: In Defense of the Baby Boom Legacy*, Leonard Steinhorn writes: "The ... norm of domesticity was so powerful that it not only shrank women's expectations but made those lowered expectations seem normal, the way things ought to be, so much so that both men and women internalized them and created patterns of behavior to accommodate them. So of the women who attended college in the Fifties, two-thirds failed to receive their bachelor's degrees, and of all the BA degrees granted in 1950, only 23.9 percent went to women. Even at elite women's schools, college was seen as a stepping-stone not to a career but to a good and respectable marriage, what many called the Mrs. degree."[12]

Women's experiences in the 1950s would also later prompt Betty Friedan to explore why "the proportion of women attending college in comparison with men dropped from 47 percent in 1920 to 35 percent in 1958" in her groundbreaking book *The Feminine Mystique*.[13]

"A Past That Never Was"

The revisionist work of Gluck, Honey, and other researchers such as Karen Anderson and Susan M. Hartmann have contributed significantly to debunking the Rosie myth of feminine empowerment in the wartime workforce. Yet the myth endures. That's due, in part, to the numerous media reports that echo the Ad Council's promotion of the famed poster as a widely circulated image during the war that helped mobilize millions of women to replace men in the workforce.

In an article examining the origins of the Rosie poster, James J. Kimble and Lester C. Olson have established that the poster came neither from the Ad

Council nor the government, and that it did not appear broadly during the war—as numerous media accounts have subsequently claimed. The authors also debunk another common myth attributing the poster's creation to well-known artist Norman Rockwell, who drew his own Rosie illustration on the May 29, 1943, cover of the *Saturday Evening Post*. Rockwell's painting emphasized— perhaps even more strongly than the "We Can Do It" poster—a woman's capability to do factory work. His image was attired in denim clothing, and she held a sandwich. A riveting gun rested in her lap. Across the front of her lunch-box, the name "Rosie" appeared.

It was Pittsburgh freelance artist J. Howard Miller, working for the West-inghouse Electric and Manufacturing Company, who created the "We Can Do It!" poster. It appeared only in Westinghouse factories for two weeks in late February 1943, according to Kimble and Olson. The only people who saw it were Westinghouse workers, which included women.

The "shop poster," Kimble and Olson explain, was made for the "War Pro-duction Coordinating Committee," the name of which appears on the bottom of the poster. Even though the name sounds similar to the government's War Pro-duction Board, which existed during the war to spur industry manufacturing, Kimble and Olson establish that this was really the wartime labor–management organization within Westinghouse. The authors quote an issue of *Westinghouse Magazine*, which describes the aim of this group as follows: "Propose methods for increasing output of war material, receive suggestions for greater production from both employes [*sic*] and management, and study such subjects as taking care of tools, preventing breakdowns, reducing accidents, adapting old ma-chines to new uses, cutting wastage, breaking production bottlenecks and using every machine to the fullest extent."[14]

At the time, the government's War Production Board encouraged defense plants to organize labor committees to avert any problems that could slow down production lines. Kimble and Olson report that one of the Westinghouse com-mittee's principal functions was to provide an ongoing supply of these posters as labor incentives throughout the plants. They conclude: "Seen in this light, 'We Can Do It!' was clearly one company's response to a government initiative, not an official government product. Indeed, it is unlikely that the government would have allowed the Westinghouse logo, which was widely known, to appear on a government poster. Yet the familiar *W* logo was imprinted prominently on

Miller's poster to feature Westinghouse along the bottom edge, just in front of Rosie's waist. The Westinghouse name recurred on Rosie's badge, located on her collar. Therefore, the idea that Miller's poster was an official government publication is a misconception."[15]

Kimble and Olson note the many Rosie inaccuracies that have appeared in respected publications over the years. A June 2, 1997, *New York Times* article called the poster "a worldwide symbol of women in the defense industry in World War II." A 1999 CNN web-based special report on the twentieth century said, "Spurred on by higher wages and a propaganda poster featuring a muscle-bound 'Rosie the Riveter' exclaiming 'We Can Do It!' millions of American women helped assemble bombs, build tanks, weld hulls and grease locomotives." A *San Diego Union-Tribune* September 8, 2001, article said the image "was used in propaganda posters to encourage women to work during the war." On November 11, 2003, *USA Today* told its readers that wartime women in the workforce "were known as 'Rosies,' after the muscle-flexing 'Rosie the Riveter' in the iconic 'We Can Do It!' poster." The article said the poster was "part of a government campaign to bring women into the workforce to replace the men who had left to fight the war." A *San Francisco Chronicle* story on March 29, 2004, noted that "Rosie the Riveter was a popular icon, whose slogan, 'We Can Do It!' helped mobilize millions of American women to replace the men who left to fight in battle." A *Houston Chronicle* report on May 21, 2004, claimed that "the original Rosie the Riveter, Rosie Will Monroe, worked on the assembly line at Ford building B-29 and B-24 military planes. She caught the eye of Hollywood producers who were casting a 'riveter' for a promotional film. Her exposure in the film resulted in the 'We Can Do It!' poster. She came to symbolize the generation of women who entered the workplace during the war."[16]

Scholars have made similar mistakes. Emily Yellin, writing in *Our Mothers' War: American Women at Home and at the Front during World War II*, refers to Miller's poster as "government commissioned," which further reinforces the myth's credibility.[17]

Kimble and Olson argue that these representations of the Rosie myth demonstrate the power of the media to reinforce cultural symbols. Once embedded in the cultural psyche, images such as Miller's poster become what Michael Osborn calls "fiction, which often passes for history."[18] Kimble and Olson also believe that the poster achieved legitimacy as a "representative character," defined by Robert N. Bellah et al. in *Habits of the Heart: Individualism and Commitment in American Life*, as "a kind of symbol. It is the way by which we can bring together in one concentrated image the way people in a given social environment organize and give meaning and direction to their lives. In fact, a representative character is more than a collection of individual traits and personalities. It is rather a public image that helps define, for a given group of people, just what kinds of personality traits it is good and legitimate to develop."[19]

Writing in *American Monroe: The Making of a Body Politic*, S. Paige Baty elaborates on the role representative characters play in American society: "The representative character embodies and expresses achievement, success, failure, genius, struggle, triumph, and other human possibilities: one representative character's story may be written as a cautionary tale, while another's may be erected as a monument to human achievement."[20] Images such as the Rosie poster, therefore, are given new values and histories that can change over time, depending on how people remember the poster in relation to female workers during World War II. The immediate rationale for the poster fades; what's left is the image. The strong, upbeat sense of 1940s female empowerment is arresting. What's missing is the context: The empowerment was actually limited and finite: a means to a wartime end. By claiming Miller's poster as its own and linking it to its Womanpower campaign, the Ad Council gave more credit to the role the campaign played in history. At the time, the campaign did not make an abiding change in the relationship between women and the U.S. workforce.

The Womanpower Campaign

In 1942 the Ad Council began working with the Office of War Information (OWI) and the War Manpower Commission to produce a campaign encouraging women to take war-related civilian and military jobs. FDR had established the OWI in June 1942 to function chiefly as a propaganda arm to promote "understanding of the status and progress of the war effort and of war policies, activities, and aims of the U.S. government."[21] In addition to coordinating advertising, the OWI would work with radio shows interested in integrating "government material into their regular efforts." It would also contact radio programs directly to interest individual producers "in giving treatment to Manpower themes occasionally."[22]

To help give these activities legitimacy, Roosevelt appointed Elmer Davis, a respected journalist who opposed government control of the press, to head the agency. The Womanpower campaign fell under the OWI's Bureau of Campaigns, which coordinated all of the government propaganda efforts during the war. Ken Dyke, a former NBC marketing official and advertising director for Colgate-Palmolive, became chief of the bureau and later the War Advertising Council's chief contact with the government. Requests for campaigns from federal agencies would be sent to Dyke's office, which then contacted the Ad Council. Much as it does today, the council would find an ad agency to prepare the copy for print ads, pamphlets, and posters and to work with firms to place the advertising.[23]

The War Manpower Commission, responsible for mobilizing civilians for the war effort, requested the Womanpower campaign. The Ad Council selected the J. Walter Thompson Company agency in August 1942 to prepare the effort. At the time, government officials were discussing the idea of requiring women to register with their local employment bureaus. The Thompson Company made it clear to the government that it "would have no interest whatsoever in working on any women's campaigns which involved registration or enrollment." The commission assured the agency that "a well rounded, professionally planned educational program, stressing recruitment was the only way a general labor draft might be avoided."[24]

Given the size and importance of the effort, the Thompson Company assigned more than forty people to work on the campaign. It considered the Womanpower campaign to be its major contribution to the war effort. One internal project report noted that "attention was particularly centered on surveys on what women and their husbands and friends felt about war work, and eliminating causes of difficulty. This involved problems of transportation, child care, factory conditions, and many others."[25]

Although the government needed women to work, Leila J. Rupp, writing in *Mobilizing Women for War: German and American Propaganda, 1939–1945,* points out that the War Manpower Commission made it clear in its early directives that it believed a woman's first duty was to her children: "The WMC directed that no women with dependent children be encouraged or compelled to seek employment until all other sources had been exhausted, and if such women had to be employed, that adequate care be provided for the children."[26]

Paul McNutt, head of the War Manpower Commission, explained the policy this way: "Even in a national emergency as critical as this, the welfare of our children must be of paramount importance, since it is for them that our civilization is to be preserved and by them that it will be maintained and bettered."[27]

A summer 1943 pamphlet titled "How Industry Can Help the Government's Information Program on Womanpower," prepared by the War Advertising Council, the OWI, and the War Manpower Commission, spelled out the policy to advertisers preparing ad copy: "Women with young children should not be urged to apply for full-time work unless provisions can be made for their care."[28]

The campaign itself had three main objectives: the government wanted "to create an understanding of manpower needs," "persuade as many people as possible to take such action as is called for in their own localities," and "to build public sentiment which can work as a force behind the orderly execution of the manpower program."[29] The campaign's theme was boiled down to a simple slogan: "the right workers in the right war jobs." The emphasis on "right war jobs" suggests how government officials thought the campaign should be positioned in the minds of the target audience: "It takes men to fight our planes, guns, and ships. And it takes men and women to make them. Manpower—Womanpower—that's what will win or lose this war! It takes the right worker in the right war job!"[30]

The effort was rolled out in three phases. The first phase focused on making citizens aware that there were labor shortages, and that the problem needed to be solved locally. The second phase targeted skilled workers not engaged in war work. The third emphasized the importance of labor in winning the war.[31]

A specific recruitment campaign targeting women was carried out in the third phase of the overall national effort. One strategy document described how women could help speed the war to victory day, "when that fighting man comes home to you!" Ad copywriters were directed to tie the skills needed in war work to the same skills used in housework: "Millions of women find war work pleasant and as easy as running a sewing machine, or using a vacuum cleaner." The writers were also encouraged to appeal to a woman's desire to shop: "And you'll have fun buying extra things with your war pay."[32]

The copy platform for the campaign, which outlined what content the ads should include, emphasized the need to pitch the copy "on a highly emotional patriotic appeal." The ads were to make clear that, by taking a war job, a woman was "protecting her own loved ones from death on the battlefield—that she is a total war soldier just as surely as if she were with her husband, brother or father in the front lines." Of particular note was the direction to copywriters that the ads "should dramatize her acceptance of a war job as another symbol of woman's rise to her rightful place in society—with status equal to men's."[33] The implication was that, by taking a war job, a woman would be considered equal to a man. This foreshadowed one of the campaign's unintended consequences. Future generations of women would expect that they belonged in the workforce as much as men did.

The Womanpower campaign geared up in late 1942 and launched in April 1943. Pamphlets produced for the effort reinforced the notion that women were a temporary part of the labor force. "This soldier may die unless you man this idle machine," read the headline on one 1943 pamphlet, prepared by J. Walter Thompson staff to answer questions women had about war work. The pamphlet, with the slogan "America at War Needs Women at Work," encouraged women to apply for traditional female labor positions such as teachers, telephone operators, child care workers, and waitresses.[34]

Even the logo J. Walter Thompson designed for the campaign linked all female employment to the war and patriotism. Inspired by the Statue of Liberty, the crown on a woman's head formed three initials standing for "Women War Workers." A letter from Thompson account executive William Berchtold to the War Manpower Commission stated, "You will note the spokes of the crown have been so designed that they form 3 'W's'—standing for 'Women War Worker.' Quite obviously, the design has been inspired by the head of Liberty, the symbol of freedom for which the world fights."[35]

An early 1943 J. Walter Thompson newspaper ad targeted influential groups in women's lives. The ad underscored the themes of patriotism, while attempting to break down some of the obstacles women faced when seeking a war job. Directed at husbands, the ad implied that the war was the only reason the traditional division of labor between men and women should be changed. Under the headline "Should Your Wife Get a War Job?" the copy read:

Maybe you know how badly she is needed and are helping her get her right war job. Chances are you've put off discussing the subject frankly—have secretly hoped she wouldn't be needed because you're making enough money to take care of your family.

Well, it's only fair that you both know the facts.

By the end of 1943 one-third of all the workers in the United States must be women, if we are to maintain our war production and essential civilian activities on a level to insure victory.

If your wife is physically fit, and has no children under 14, she should get a war job immediately. If you have children under 14, and can make good provision for their care, she should consider a war job.

Naturally, with both of you working, your family income will be increased. You can get the things you've always wanted—and put away enough in War Bonds to insure your children's education . . . get the new things you'll want when victory comes.[36]

When industries in New Britain, Connecticut, needed women war workers, a November 7, 1942, newspaper ad featured an illustration of Uncle Sam appearing over the shoulder of a woman washing dishes in her home. The copy said, "Mothers, wives and daughters now have a chance right here at home to help win the war by producing vital materials in New Britain plants. Count yourself in on this patriotic opportunity." Testimonials from women war workers also appeared in the ad. "My two boys in the service know I am helping them to win the war," said one Anna Miastkowski.[37]

J. Walter Thompson's copywriters took a different approach to their ads than the galvanizing message depicted in the J. Howard Miller poster. Take the 1944 "Last night I listened to the clock" newspaper ad as an example. In this evocative ad, a woman muses about what her life has been like since her husband Jack left to fight in the war. The appeal was subtler than the forceful approach of the "We Can Do It!" poster, and certainly more emotional. Carefully placed between images of a small grandfather clock and pipe on the left and the face of a woman looking at the clock on the right, the copy read:

Have you a clock that talks? Ours does—has ever since I married Jack. "*Hap-py* . . . *Hap-py* . . . *Hap-py!*"—that's what it always said to me until the time he left to fight. Then we—the clock and I—were left

Created by the J. Walter Thompson ad agency, this 1944 newspaper ad encouraged women to take a war job. (Hartman Center for Sales, Advertising and Marketing History, David M. Rubenstein Rare Book and Manuscript Library, Duke University)

alone.... Since then it haunted me. *"How-long?... How-long?... How-long?"* ... it kept on ticking. How could a woman answer that?... There *is* a way. Not one that will set the day, month and year when all our enemies will finally be beaten—but a way to help make certain that the date of victory shall not be extended one single, needless day!... *Work!* Work in war industries ... in the armed services ... in any one of the hundreds of essential jobs that are begging to be filled. The jobs that must be filled. The jobs that can't be filled unless we women do it![38]

J. Walter Thompson was one of the first agencies to base its advertising approaches on psychology. It had hired behaviorist John B. Watson in 1920, and it helped pioneer the use of the testimonial.[39] Tugging at heartstrings became a typical approach in the Womanpower campaign, and this differed dramatically from the "roll up your sleeves and let's get to work" message of the J. Howard Miller poster, which was intended for a different purpose.

A magazine ad "Put it there, Sister!"—published in the June 1944 issue of *Good Housekeeping*—demonstrated the approach. A soldier in uniform extended his left hand in greeting to compensate for his missing right arm. The carefully pinned-up sleeve of his right arm told readers the tragic story. The copy read:

Put it there, Sister! And thanks for pretending not to notice it's my left. But, then I might have known that you'd understand. You've understood a lot of things.

Nobody had to shout about the things our Country's up against ... or tell you twice how desperately our women's help is needed. Not to you!

You took a job. You went to work. You knew this was a full-time war ... that there's a crying need in war plants, other necessary jobs and in the Armed Services, for women who'll pitch in and fill the gap.

It's girls like you who make a feller proud. You're not afraid to get in there and work at whatever you can do.

The doctors say that I'll be good as new—well, almost. Soon I'll be working, too.[40]

In the remainder of the ad, the soldier urges other women to find war jobs. The patriotic appeal is carefully woven in: "Remember, any job you take which releases a man to fight becomes a major contribution to a speedy victory."[41]

The evocative language in these J. Walter Thompson ads appealed to women precisely because the words recognized the position women found themselves in during the war. Some were left alone while their husbands fought. Others felt compelled to act when a fictional wounded soldier appealed to their sense of patriotic duty. Ads like "Last night I listened to the clock" and "Put it there, Sister!" helped the War Manpower Commission reach "an all time peak" of 15.2 million women in the workforce by March 1943, 1.9 million more than the previous year.[42]

In addition to the ad campaign, the OWI helped boost publicity for the War Manpower Commission by blanketing as many publications as possible in a concentrated period with feature stories about women holding jobs in the war effort. A plethora of magazine covers in September 1943 carried images of women workers. The *National Republic*'s cover showed women fixing cars, changing tires, and operating machines. *House & Garden* carried the image of a woman dressed in farmer's clothing over one half of her body, and wearing an apron on the other half. Even *Best Crossword Puzzles* depicted a woman dressed in a worker's uniform, a plane behind her as she ate a sandwich and worked on a puzzle.[43]

The campaign's radio spots reinforced the theme of doing one's part to win the war. In a one-minute spot, a woman worker said, "Learning a War Job was easy! It's fun, learning to check materials used in a War Plant. And it's exciting, too. Because you—well, you get the feeling that you're actually helping to win the War. I mean—you feel you're really doing something important."[44]

Other radio ads continued the theme of connecting a woman's war work at home with her fighting soldier abroad: "One thing Dave said to me before he went to Bataan—he said, 'Honey . . . take care of things at home!' Well, I learned a War Job as a lathe-operator, and started work in a tank factory. I think I'm 'taking care of things' the way Dave wanted me to."[45]

Some even suggested to women in shrill tones that no other work, including housework or child care, was more important than war work. "What are you doing to make unconditional surrender come as soon as possible?" asked one radio spot. "Are you doing all you can?"[46] Another queried, "Is the work you're doing helping to win this war? If you can't answer 'yes' then you should do something about it."[47] Such radio spots appeared on news programs like *Raymond Gram Swing*, daily soap operas like *Joyce Jordan, M.D.*, and entertainment programs like *Gracie Fields*.

Speeches made by government officials about the campaign further reinforced the expectation that work for women would be temporary. "War is not the time to satisfy career ambitions," Margaret A. Hickey, chairman of the women's committee formed to advise the campaign, told a group of War Manpower Commission officials. "The practical experience gained through wartime jobs will make American women better citizens and homemakers."[48]

But Hickey also suggested that this campaign would change how women viewed themselves. When Hickey discussed the nation's postwar needs, she envisioned women having opportunities to balance work with their home responsibilities: "There will be voices, there always are, pleading that women's place is in the home. The answer is that most certainly her place is in the home, but not within the isolated four walls with the vines of prejudice and intolerance closing the view to community and nation and the world."[49]

The "We Can Do It!" poster took on new meaning over time, which is apparently what eventually led Ad Council officials to believe that the poster was a part of the Womanpower campaign. For the Ad Council, which must balance its public service commitment with its deep and at times conflicting ties to industry, claiming Rosie's public image emphasized the kind of organizational traits it wants to show the world. Rosie's legend helped perpetuate the public narrative that the Ad Council is the advertising industry's beneficent gift to American society.

To support its later claim to the "We Can Do It!" poster, the Ad Council cited a 1952 history of its organization, *The Background and Beginning of the Advertising Council*, by Harold B. Thomas, a founding member. The council said that Thomas "connects the phrase 'Rosie the Riveter' with the Womanpower campaign." Thomas's forty-seven-page document covers the period from 1920 to March 1942. No mention is made of Rosie the Riveter in the original document, but an appendix added about 1990 likely caused the confusion by referring to the "recruitment of war workers campaign" as "Rosie, the Riveter," according to the Ad Council Archives at the University of Illinois.

The connection between the poster and the Ad Council was also likely reinforced by a statement made by former Ad Council president Robert P. Keim, who served from 1966 to 1987. In his 2002 memoir, Keim wrote that the War Advertising Council "had breathed life into the image of Rosie the Riveter as the ideal for women to get into war work."[50]

The Ad Council's use of the J. Howard Miller poster was not a deliberately manufactured event planned with the intention to deceive. Instead, Ad Council staff believed the poster belonged to its Womanpower campaign based on its own historical documents, and selected the powerful image precisely because of what it depicted: a strong working woman who helped America win its battle against fascism.

But it didn't need to. The superior, evocative Womanpower ads prepared by the J. Walter Thompson agency tell the story far more eloquently. These images did more to lure women out of their homes and into war jobs than the "We Can Do It!" poster ever could. Only Westinghouse factory workers saw the "We Can Do It!" poster, and for only two weeks, according to Kimble and Olson's definitive study. The Rosie poster was not influential in getting women into war jobs, simply because that was not the intent behind its creation. It was made to spur worker production within Westinghouse factories.

The "We Can Do It!" poster went on to become an iconic symbol of female empowerment in the workplace, while the J. Walter Thompson ads faded into history because the Ad Council didn't showcase that part of its past.

The Ad Council has defended the legacy of its Womanpower campaign, as it should, pointing out in a written response: "It is important to note that it is not disputed that the Ad Council did create an iconic campaign that changed the way women viewed the workforce and contributed to the recruitment and empowerment of over 2 million women to fill needed positions during a time of instability. More importantly, it produced lasting generations of women who came to believe that working outside of the home was a possibility, this being what Rosie the Riveter also exemplifies."[51]

What the Ad Council did with its Womanpower campaign was even greater than that. Not only did American women realize that working outside the home was a possibility, they learned that they were capable of doing any job a man could do. And that message resonated with generations of women to come.

Chapter 5

"A Keg of Dynamite and You're Sitting on It"

The Manhattan Project Scientists Launch an Atomic Energy Campaign

Long before the atom bomb, civilization had created the machinery for its own destruction, and was learning to use it with all the moronic delight of a gangster trying out his first machine gun.

—Raymond Chandler

In one brief moment on October 25, 1945, what didn't happen would cost the United States a sane nuclear policy.

World War II was finally over. The normally eloquent nuclear physicist J. Robert Oppenheimer was overcome by emotion as he faced President Harry Truman in the Oval Office. Truman had just told the former Manhattan Project director that he thought the Soviets would never develop their own atomic bomb.

Oppenheimer's incredulity at such a ridiculous statement robbed him of the persuasive voice he needed to accomplish his critical mission—convincing President Truman about the need to control atomic weapons to avoid an arms race and possible war with the Russians. Instead of summoning his usual articulateness, Oppenheimer made an overtly emotional response: "Mr. President, I feel I have blood on my hands."

As Kai Bird and Martin J. Sherwin describe the conversation in *American Prometheus: The Triumph and Tragedy of J. Robert Oppenheimer*, the physicist's distress may have been a contributing factor in his failure to gain Truman's support for control of atomic weapons.

Afterwards, the President was heard to mutter, "Blood on his hands, dammit, he hasn't half as much blood on his hands as I have. You just don't go around bellyaching about it." He later told [Undersecretary of State] Dean Acheson, "I don't want to see that son-of-a-bitch in this office ever again."

Even in May 1946, the encounter still vivid in his mind, he wrote Acheson and described Oppenheimer as a "cry-baby scientist" who had come to "my office some five or six months ago and spent most of his time wringing his hands and telling me they had blood on them because of the discovery of atomic energy."[1]

Oppenheimer's failure to persuade Truman led scientists to make a dramatic decision: a direct appeal to the public. To reach a mass audience, William Higinbotham, chairman of the newly formed Federation of American Scientists (FAS), turned to the ad industry for help. His February 14, 1946, letter to Theodore Repplier, executive director of the War Advertising Council, proposed a bold move: an atomic energy campaign. He and his fellow scientists were fearful of the destructive capabilities of atomic weapons after the bombings of Hiroshima and Nagasaki. As other nations developed such weapons, the threat of nuclear warfare would grow—unless something was done to stop it. Convinced that international control was the only answer, the scientists wanted the War Advertising Council to trumpet this vital message.

"The advertising business can render a great public service at this time and in the near future by undertaking to present to the American public the basic facts which lead to the decision that some form of world control of atomic energy is necessary," Higinbotham wrote. "The Federation of American Scientists has as its primary objective the establishment of international controls of atomic armaments, so that the great peaceful potentialities of nuclear energies can be realized in science, medicine and industry, and the world may enjoy an epoch of unhampered cultural, scientific and commercial interchange between nations."[2]

When he met with War Advertising Council officials a few weeks later, Oppenheimer would add his own appeal to Higinbotham's. Like many of the postwar Manhattan Project scientists, Oppenheimer worried that the device he had helped create, with a capacity to kill more than 100,000 people, could be used against the United States. His January 1946 comments, published in the *Proceedings of the American Philosophical Society*, emphasized the urgency of international control. "It will not help to avert such a war if we try to rub the edges off this new terror that we have helped to bring to the world," he wrote. "As a vast threat and a new one, to all the peoples of the earth, by its novelty, its terror, its strangely Promethean quality, it has become . . . an opportunity unique and challenging."[3]

Controlling atomic energy was a cause that Albert Einstein, the most famous physicist of the twentieth century, embraced. In 1946 he lent his name to a $1 million fund-raising drive. "We scientists recognize our inescapable responsibility to carry to our fellow citizens an understanding of the simple facts of atomic energy and its implications," he wrote in a letter for the campaign on December 11, 1946. He believed that the only effective way to defend against atomic warheads was to take the facts about such weapons to the citizens of America. Only if all nations exercised control and pursued the peaceful development of atomic energy would the world be safe.[4]

This chapter will argue that the scientists' belief in rational thinking led them to naively assume that if they gave people enough information about the dangers of atomic weapons, the public would act on their message. But giving people knowledge is not always enough to change behavior. Disagreements among the scientists contributed to the campaign's lack of a strong public message that would have explained what Americans could do individually to help establish international control. What's more, the scientists' inability to raise enough money prevented the effort from expanding beyond radio to print advertising, where more information about the need to control atomic energy could have been provided.[5]

The scientists' collective failure to recognize the need for the atomic energy campaign to include an action message represents a missed opportunity at a pivotal moment in the postwar era to establish an international authority to control the proliferation of atomic weapons. After Oppenheimer stood in President Truman's office and did not effectively articulate why international control was so critical, the scientists had few options left when negotiations between the United States and the Soviet Union broke down a year later. The atomic energy campaign was the scientists' best hope to use public opinion to persuade President Truman to negotiate further with the Soviets. Their failure to fully support it partly opened the door to an arms race that did not end with the breakup of the Soviet Union. Nearly seventy years after President Truman used the force of atomic energy on Hiroshima and Nagasaki to stop a war, America's leaders still struggle to contain the threat of nuclear warfare from other countries.

To understand the atomic energy campaign's failure, it's necessary to explore the sense of fear that gripped the nation once the atomic bomb was unleashed on Japan, how the scientists sought to harness the bomb's destructive power through international control, and why the internal disagreements and disorganization among the scientists proved so fatal to the campaign.

Atomic Gloom

The atomic energy campaign grew out of a climate of anxiety that engulfed postwar American society once V-J Day elation quickly turned to confusion and fear as the devastation of Hiroshima and Nagasaki sank in. In a radio address the day the first bomb was dropped, President Truman told the nation, "The force from which the sun draws its power has been loosed against those who brought war to the Far East."[6]

Cold War historian Paul Boyer captured the mood of Americans at the time in *By the Bomb's Early Light: American Thought and Culture at the Dawn of the Atomic Age*. "Just below the surface, powerful currents of anxiety and apprehension surged through the culture," Boyer wrote. "Contemporary social observers agreed that the news of the atomic bomb had had a devastating effect."[7]

The First One Hundred Days of the Atomic Age, published by the Woodrow Wilson Foundation in 1945, charts "the ever-widening concern and alarm" echoed in the comments of world leaders, newspaper editorials, and scientists made immediately after the bombs were dropped. Winston Churchill hoped "that these awful agencies . . . instead of wrecking measureless havoc upon the entire globe . . . may become a perennial fountain of world prosperity." The *New York Times* editorial page called for "a revolution in mankind's political thinking. The mentality and the national and world political institutions necessary to make certain that mankind gets only immense benefits, and not the unthinkable destruction that this great discovery can bring, must be created without delay." Einstein argued that the release of atomic energy did not create a new problem: "It has merely made more urgent the necessity of solving an existing one. . . . As long as there are sovereign nations possessing great power, war is inevitable."[8]

Norman Cousins, the editor of the *Saturday Review of Literature*, opened his 1945 book *Modern Man Is Obsolete* with a discussion of fear. "The beginning of the Atomic Age has brought less hope than fear," Cousins wrote. "It is a primitive fear, the fear of the unknown, the fear of forces man can neither channel nor comprehend. This fear is not new; in its classical form it is the fear of irrational death."[9]

Perhaps the gloom was most keenly felt by a group of scientists who had helped make the bomb but believed that President Truman should not have used it on Japan. These scientists had wanted the president to demonstrate the bomb's destructive power on an uninhabited island and then let the United Nations decide whether to use it if Japan did not immediately surrender. Supporters of this approach included Hungarian-born physicist Leo Szilard, who is credited with writing the famous 1939 letter, signed by Einstein to President Roosevelt, that stimulated the launch of the Manhattan Project. In July 1945 Szilard circulated and submitted his own petition to Truman, urging him not to use the bomb unless the terms imposed on Japan were made public.[10]

Another concerned scientist, Eugene Rabinowitch, was the Manhattan Project chemist at the University of Chicago; he later became the founder and editor of the *Bulletin of the Atomic Scientists*. He recalled his immediate reaction to the news of Hiroshima in the article "Five Years After," published in the *Bulletin* in January 1951. "In the summer of 1945," Rabinowitch wrote, "some of us walked the streets of Chicago vividly imagining the sky suddenly lit by a giant fireball, the steel skeletons of skyscrapers bending into grotesque shapes and their masonry raining into the streets below, until a great cloud of dust rose and settled over the crumbling city."[11]

Fear became a galvanizing force for action. The small groups of scientists that formed around the Manhattan Project centers at Chicago, New York, Los Alamos, New Mexico, and Oak Ridge, Tennessee, became the Federation of Atomic (later American) Scientists in November 1945. Among its goals: "To create a realization of the dangers that this nation and all civilization will face if the tremendous destructive potential of nuclear energy is misused," and "to help establish an atmosphere of world security in which the beneficial possibilities of nuclear energy may be developed."[12]

International Control

Higinbotham's 1946 letter to the Ad Council was stark. There was no defense against atomic weapons, and the United States could not keep the scientific knowledge necessary to build a bomb secret for long. Therefore, the scientists rationally concluded, some form of international control must be established. Susan Caudill, in a paper on Albert Einstein's publicity campaign for world government published in *Journalism Quarterly*, notes that international control "usually was interpreted to mean either international control through an expanded United Nations, or through a supra-national structure with the power to control atomic energy development and to keep the peace. The latter plan required that nations would have to disarm and surrender military control to a world government."[13]

The scientists had the support of a number of opinion leaders who believed that either international control or the more controversial idea of a world government was the only solution to avoiding future atomic wars. Cousins, whose *Modern Man Is Obsolete* first appeared as an editorial in the *Saturday Review* four days after Japan surrendered on August 12, 1945, argued for world government. "Can it be that we do not realize that in an age of atomic energy and rocket planes the foundations of the old sovereignties have been shattered?" he wrote. "The need for world government was clear long before August 6, 1945, but Hiroshima and Nagasaki raised that need to such dimensions that it can no longer be ignored."[14]

Following the bombings, Raymond Gram Swing, the American Broadcasting Company newscaster, would devote each Friday's radio broadcast to the influence of atomic energy. In his book, *In the Name of Sanity*, Swing adopted the slogan "One world or no world," a phrase he credited to Louis Adamic, the editor of the magazine *Common Ground*: "There must be one world, or the many worlds into which we still are divided by our archaic concepts of sovereignty will wipe each other out."[15] Boyer, in *The Bomb's Early Light*, considers Swing to have been an "extremely influential opinion-molder in the early postwar period."[16]

Another important voice favoring world government came from University of Chicago president Robert Hutchins, whose speeches, magazine articles, and weekly radio program, the *Chicago Roundtable*, reached a broad audience. In his radio program on August 12, 1945, Hutchins called for "the necessity of a world organization." He established the Committee to Frame a World Constitution, promoting the idea through his speeches and radio appearances. Boyer notes the irony of this position, given the University of Chicago's prominent role in making the bomb, and cites modern historians who suggest that Hutchins was engaged in a public relations campaign of his own to replace the university's image as a "bomb factory" with the more positive movement for a world government.[17]

University of Chicago Nobel Prize–winning chemist Harold Urey called on the need for an informed public in a democracy to understand the options available for addressing the atomic threat. In an influential November 1945 article in the magazine *Science*, he considered and then rejected options ranging from establishing security by building more atomic weapons to ceding control of the bombs to the United Nations, before concluding that a world government was the only choice. "We are inevitably led to the conclusion that a superior world government of some kind possessing adequate power to maintain the peace and with the various divisions of the world relatively disarmed, is the only way out," he wrote. "What will be needed is a most efficient inspection service which will detect and report promptly any attempt to produce atomic bombs . . . and a sufficient force to prevent such activities."[18]

A Public Education Campaign

The scientists had three reasons why they wanted an Ad Council campaign. The first can be traced to an American Institute of Public Opinion poll taken in October 1945, two months after the bombings, which found that only 17 percent of Americans believed that "making atomic bombs should be put under control of the new United Nations Security Council." While many nuclear scientists and a number of the nation's opinion leaders considered some form of international or world control necessary to the survival of civilization, the American public was hardly convinced. In the same poll, 85 percent of the Americans sampled approved of Truman's use of the bomb. It would take a national ad campaign to sway public opinion.[19]

The second reason was articulated in Urey's comments in the *Science* article about the need in a democracy "to have an informed people if proper decisions are to be made and executed." The scientists believed that garnering public support for their cause was the best way to influence American leaders.

As chairman of the Emergency Committee of Atomic Scientists (ECAS), the group that would raise money for the scientists' educational efforts, Einstein argued that any national policy on atomic energy must stem from an informed public. "America's decision will not be made over a table in the United Nations," Einstein wrote in a June 23, 1946, article, "Only Then Shall We Find Courage," published in the *New York Times Magazine*. "Our representatives in New York, in Paris, or in Moscow depend ultimately on decisions made in the village square. To the village square we must carry the facts of atomic energy. From there must come America's voice." This quote would be used in the ECAS statement of purpose, and the need for informed citizens become a central theme in the atomic energy campaign's radio messages.[20]

The third reason was the scientists' bedrock belief in rational thinking. If they could convince Americans of how destructive the bomb would be if placed in the wrong hands, citizens would naturally favor a way to control it to prevent future wars. This reasoning prompted the scientists to use fear messages in the campaign's radio copy—an approach that would backfire when they were unable to raise enough money to prepare an information pamphlet to accompany the radio messages.

The War Advertising Council's newly formed public advisory committee approved the atomic energy campaign on June 5, 1946. Its nineteen members included Vassar College president Sarah Blanding; Harvard University president James Conant; General Foods Corporation chairman Clarence Francis; American Institute of Public Opinion director George Gallup; Studebaker Corporation president Paul Hoffman; and Allen Gregg, director of medical science at the Rockefeller Foundation. At this first meeting, the committee determined it would create campaigns on controversial topics only when "a public question shall be considered to have passed from the stage of controversy to the stage where action or understanding is desirable by the whole people or important segments of them." If committee members decided an "action" or "understanding" was needed beyond what could be expected from newspaper and broadcast editorials, then the "Council will . . . attempt to add the power of advertising to the securing of this action or understanding." When the committee approved the atomic energy campaign that day, it did so with one provision: "that primary emphasis be given to the need for international control, with support for a specific form of international control whenever a proposal shall become national policy."[21]

No clear national policy on regulating atomic energy had yet emerged. Earlier that year, forty-five members of the War Advertising Council had met with White House and congressional leaders in what would become a yearly Washington conference, where Ad Council members would discuss campaign subjects with government officials. At lunch with council members, Connecticut Senator Brien McMahon, chairman of the Senate's Special Committee on Atomic Energy, said it would likely be three years, not ten, before another nation developed the bomb (indeed, the Soviet Union tested its first atomic bomb on September 24, 1949).

McMahon advocated an "effective scientific system of international inspection, with emphasis on the constructive side of atomic energy." Although other government officials doubted that the Soviets would agree to such a proposal, McMahon remained optimistic. He opposed military control of atomic energy and argued that the United States should not manufacture more weapons. He believed that civilian scientists (not the military) should evaluate the results of the upcoming Bikini Island tests planned for that July. And he encouraged the peacetime use of atomic energy, predicting that such energy plants would exist "in our time."[22]

The War Advertising Council assigned G. Edward Pendray, president of the American Rocket Society, to coordinate the campaign, and enlisted the Young & Rubicam (now Y&R) ad agency to prepare the advertising, which would be delivered to the public through radio spots until the scientists could raise enough money to broaden the campaign to newspaper ads. With input from the State Department and the U.S. delegation to the United Nations Atomic Energy Commission (UNAEC), Y&R prepared a radio fact sheet that would serve as the campaign focus. They recognized the limitations of radio to deliver lengthy explanations on such a complicated topic, but it considered the medium a good first step.

"Obviously, the problems raised for Americans by the release of atomic energy and its use in weapons of war cannot be dealt with completely in a single radio message," the fact sheet said. "All we can hope now is to make a beginning by bringing to the public rudimentary facts about the devastating power of atomic bombs and the efforts being made to secure the United States and the world against their use. As events develop and clarify themselves, it will become possible to present new information—until, when our government is ready to approve or disapprove international control plans, or otherwise take national action, the public will be sufficiently informed to assume a position on the issues." Y&R believed the fact sheet and radio messages could stimulate "listeners to inform themselves about the subject, to start discussing its problems, and thus to form opinions based on sound information."[23]

The campaign was based on a national proposal favored by the scientists and put forth by Bernard Baruch, U.S. representative to the UNAEC, recommending that an international authority such as the UN have control over atomic energy. Before distrust of the Soviet Union mushroomed into the Cold War, some nations were receptive to the idea of international control of atomic weapons. In the "Declaration of November 15, 1945," the United States, United Kingdom and Canada had agreed that "the responsibility for devising means to insure that the new discoveries shall be used for the benefit of mankind, instead of as a means of destruction, rests not on our nations alone, but upon the whole civilized world."[24]

To develop the atomic energy campaign messages, Y&R followed a set of objectives outlined in a January 1947 Ad Council report to its Public Advisory Committee: "Tell the facts about atomic energy and the atomic bomb without indulging in scare copy; state that our government has initiated efforts to establish international control of atomic energy; state the principal points in the so-called Baruch Plan; and emphasize the need for international control." The ad agency proposed a two-part strategy: first to promote awareness of the issue and highlight the arguments for international control favored by the scientists, and then to change behavior by swaying public opinion in favor of the need for international control.[25]

The radio ads, read by program announcers or the hosts of specific shows, began in late summer 1946 and aired on such programs as *Quiz Kids, This Is Your FBI, Famous Jury Trials, Martin Agronsky, Arthur Godfrey, Bob Hope,* and *Amos 'n' Andy.* News broadcasters such as Walter Winchell and Elmer Davis discussed the issues outlined in the radio fact sheets. A September 13, 1946, spot on NBC's *Echoes from the Tropics* said, "The problem of atomic energy is your immediate problem.... As a citizen of a democratic society, it is your duty to keep yourself informed of all proposals to share, limit or control the development of atomic energy. Read the newspapers. Form discussion groups. Remember—your vote may someday help determine whether atomic energy will be used for war or peace."[26]

Another spot, on November 22, 1946, on Nelson Olmsted's program, announced: "The discovery of atomic weapons of warfare . . . with their terrific destructive power . . . has raised one of the most vital problems ever to face you and the rest of the world. But you must know about atomic energy itself before you can have any idea what to do about it. Learn all you can about what leading scientists have to say about the atom. Be informed. Remember . . . ignorance may be bliss . . . but in this case it's a keg of dynamite . . . and you're sitting on it."[27]

The radio spots ran for at least one week each month between August 1946 and February 1947. By February the Ad Council reported that the radio campaign had garnered more than 658 million listener impressions.[28] (The council defined a "listener impression" as one message heard by one listener.) Council members, knowing that the radio spots would not be enough to persuade people to take action, wanted a pamphlet that "would be a well-illustrated primer on atomic energy and the essentials of the Baruch Plan, which would be offered without charge over the air in connection with our radio allocations."[29] Thus, the radio ads would encourage listeners to write for a pamphlet with more information—a strategy that would work well in future Ad Council campaigns such as McGruff the Crime Dog. In this case, however, the council would spend several months unsuccessfully pushing the scientists to raise enough money to broaden the campaign's scope.

Disagreements, Disorganization, and Few Dollars

A number of scientist advocacy groups needed money, but the scientific community seemed unable or unwilling to prioritize the various needs. The ECAS originally had launched a $1 million fund-raising effort under Einstein's leadership in the fall of 1946 to help the National Committee of Atomic Information (NCAI), a group dedicated to improving communication between scientists and the public. But the ECAS soon began fielding requests for funds from other FAS member associations, the newly formed *Bulletin of the Atomic Scientists*, and the Ad Council. After meeting with Ad Council officials in October 1946, an NCAI consultant recommended that $50,000 be raised to prepare the atomic energy information pamphlet.

"I think that either the National Committee or the Emergency Committee [ECAS] should quickly produce such a pamphlet that could be tied in as a mailing piece with what the Advertising Council is already doing over the radio, otherwise there is no way that we could capitalize on what they are doing," the consultant reported. "At present their help chiefly amounts to shooting a lot of stuff into the air, since there is no follow-up."[30] The council also talked of starting its own fund-raising effort to support a pamphlet and newspaper ads, an idea that alarmed the consultant, since he thought this would compete with the $1 million ECAS drive. "I have tried to get them to put the brakes on this," the consultant told the scientists. In retrospect, this was counterproductive advice. Had the Ad Council been able to raise funds itself from business sources, the atomic energy campaign would not have ended when it did.[31]

After dropping its separate fund-raising plans, the council turned to the ECAS for money. Theodore Repplier wrote Joseph Schaffner, the executive director of the ECAS, on October 10, 1946, asking for $100,000 to prepare an information booklet about atomic energy in "simple non-technical layman's language." The money also would be used to prepare newspaper ads and possibly car cards for streetcars and buses. Repplier recommended forming a committee with representatives from the State Department, Baruch's advisers, and the NCAI to review the ad copy.[32]

By November, however, it was clear that the number of scientist groups involved was making fund-raising and coordination of the atomic energy campaign more difficult. "I am worrying now about [the] means of properly coordinating the various activities and the most sensible arrangement for determining the distribution of educational funds," the FAS's Higinbotham wrote to the ECAS's Schaffner.[33] In response to a query from Schaffner in January 1947 about what could be done to promote the campaign for less than $100,000, the Ad Council stated it would need a minimum of $50,000 to prepare the pamphlet or $10,000 to produce six newspaper ads.[34] The council also sent a second letter to Einstein January 14, saying that the atomic energy campaign had been "handicapped by the total lack of funds."[35]

Meanwhile, the FAS also pressured Einstein. Higinbotham sent his own appeal January 17, calling the atomic energy campaign "the most powerful single weapon in the propaganda and education field." He told Einstein that the FAS had asked the Ad Council not to raise money in competition with the ECAS. "I feel that the scientists should either contribute directly to the support of this campaign or else help them to raise money for it."[36]

Disagreements among the scientists further hindered the campaign. Some questioned the need for it, while others refused to donate funds for other activities without it. Szilard, a particularly powerful and colorful figure, opposed the use of mass media at a November 1946 FAS meeting. Yet a San Francisco group of scientists planning to raise $75,000 for the ECAS wanted reassurance that "the scientists would have professional advice on how to educate the public and would be prepared to use proven mass media."[37]

Scientists were also split on what form of international control to support. While the majority favored a UN type of structure, key members of the ECAS —specifically Einstein, Urey, Szilard, and physicist Hans Bethe—wanted a full-fledged world government.[38] The more controversial world government idea appeared in the ECAS fund-raising appeals, alienating those who preferred a less ambitious strategy. Einstein's December 11, 1946, appeal letter launching a $1 million fund-raising drive emphasized the need for a world government. "Through the release of atomic energy, our generation has brought into the world the most revolutionary force since prehistoric man's discovery of fire," he wrote. "This basic power of the universe cannot be fitted into the outmoded concept of narrow nationalisms."[39] Attached to the letter was Einstein's "Only Then Shall We Find Courage" article, where he called for a need to be "actively eager to submit ourselves to binding authority necessary for world security."[40]

The ECAS's tepid agreement to raise $50,000 for the atomic energy campaign at its meeting in early February 1947 angered Ad Council officials, who believed that the scientists wanted to raise money for their other projects first. Einstein's group offered to pay in monthly installments of $5,000 or $10,000 starting in April, several months away. The council's response was hardly enthusiastic. Commercial radio programs were already resisting carrying the atomic energy messages, "primarily because there is no action message," as Allan Wilson, the council's assistant to the president, wrote to Pendray, the campaign's coordinator. "I have tried several times to impress Schaffner with these facts, but . . . he doesn't yet understand what we need if we are to do a real job, and

I am afraid that he still thinks that it is more important to finance group meetings than it is to implement our mechanisms for reaching the public."[41]

Wilson soon delivered an ultimatum to Schaffner. "The effective use of our advertising facilities in this particular campaign depends, not on the possibility of getting a few thousand dollars each month, but on having definite assurance of a sum of not less than $30,000 available in a lump sum reasonably soon," he wrote February 27.[42]

Petty bickering and bureaucracy had imperiled the scientists' hopes for mobilizing public opinion. But before they could sort out their fund-raising conflicts, world events unfolded that would seal the fate of the atomic energy campaign.

Politics Intervenes

In the months following Hiroshima, the scientists first believed that President Truman truly supported international control of atomic energy. Only later would they learn that Truman's definition of international control did not include sharing U.S. scientific knowledge or giving up plans to build more atomic weapons. The president's words in his October 3, 1945, address to Congress were encouraging. "The hope of civilization lies in international arrangements looking . . . to the renunciation of the use and development of the atomic bomb," Truman said then. "The alternative . . . may be a desperate armament race, which might well end in disaster."[43]

The first sign of trouble for the scientists came the next day, when legislation introduced by Senator Edwin C. Johnson of Colorado proposed giving a nine-member commission appointed by the president complete power over U.S. atomic energy policy. Known as the May-Johnson bill, it would have allowed military officers to sit on the commission and endorsed punishing any scientist with up to ten years in prison for any security violations. After newspaper headlines captured their intense lobbying effort against it, the scientists prevailed, and the bill was defeated.[44]

Senator McMahon of Connecticut then introduced a bill that would turn control of atomic energy over to a civilian Atomic Energy Commission, which many scientists supported. By the end of January 1946, the United States, the Soviet Union, and several other nations reached an agreement to establish the UNAEC (United Nations Atomic Energy Commission). President Truman appointed a special committee headed by Dean Acheson to prepare a proposal for international nuclear control, for the UNAEC's first meeting in June 1946. To write the proposal, the committee named a board of consultants that included Oppenheimer and was chaired by David Lilienthal, the Chicago lawyer previously appointed by President Roosevelt to head the Tennessee Valley Authority.

The "Report on the International Control of Atomic Energy," known as the Acheson-Lilienthal report, issued March 28, 1946 (and mostly written by Oppenheimer), recommended that an international authority such as the UN should have control over atomic energy. Participating nations would share information, divide research facilities, and allow inspections by the UN.[45]

Even before the Acheson-Lilienthal plan was presented at the UN, historian Boyer notes, there were warning signs of Truman's concerns. Truman not only disapproved of sharing atomic knowledge, he had also grown increasingly suspicious of the Soviet Union, as more countries disappeared behind what Winston Churchill called the Iron Curtain. These concerns were reflected in a cover letter to the Acheson-Lilienthal report, which declared that the United States would continue testing and building atomic bombs until an international control plan became fully operational. "Even then . . . the United States could reject it and carry on with its atomic weapons program. The United States thus preserved a de facto veto over the entire plan: not until Washington agreed that the raw-materials survey was complete and the inspection system satisfactorily in place would the international-control arrangement begin." The Soviets hardly welcomed this news, since they would have to submit to inspections while the United States continued making bombs.[46]

In a speech to the UNAEC on June 19, 1946, Soviet delegate Andrei Gromyko announced that the Soviet Union would not give up the right to veto decisions made by an international control authority, and he called for the destruction of existing stocks of atomic weapons.[47] His second speech almost a year later on March 5, 1947, in which he again attacked the American plan and called it "an attempt to impose American capitalistic domination on the economic life of the Soviet Union," showed how far the two sides were from coming to an agreement, less than a year after the atomic energy campaign had begun.[48]

Gromyko's second speech in 1947 prompted the Ad Council to discuss scaling back the campaign. "It is generally agreed that there is no point in running a full-scale campaign of mass education on atomic dangers, until we are fairly close—say a year, or six months—to the time when we can reasonably expect some kind of atomic treaty which American voters can support, or not support, through the Senate," Repplier wrote in a memo to the scientists March 7. "Gromyko's speech is quite important to [the campaign], for now there is very little immediate possibility of the average man having any decisions whatever to make upon atomic problems."[49]

On March 12, 1947, Truman delivered a speech to Congress where he announced a U.S. commitment to help noncommunist countries resist Soviet expansion. The policy, which became known as the Truman Doctrine, would "help free peoples to maintain their free institutions and their national integrity against aggressive movements that seek to impose upon them totalitarian regimes," he said. The Truman Doctrine further solidified the growing reality of the Cold War.[50]

By now it was clear that the United States and the Soviet Union would not come to any agreement on establishing an international authority to control atomic energy. The Ad Council's board of directors called for the campaign to be dropped. On hearing this news, the ECAS did not offer to increase the $50,000 it had agreed to allocate, and left it up to the Ad Council "to decide what its responsibilities to the American people are in this matter."[51] Still hoping to move the campaign forward, the council's Public Advisory Committee met in early April and agreed to continue it, provided that more funding could be obtained from the scientists.[52]

It was precisely at this critical moment that the scientists' support of the atomic energy campaign would have had the greatest impact. But instead of tackling the money problem with the same vigor the group had used to defeat the May-Johnson bill, some leaders, including physicist Hans Bethe, called for a cutback in ECAS fund-raising efforts. In his April 29, 1947, letter to the ECAS's Schaffner, Bethe wrote, "The repetition of our statements about the horrors of atomic war will in the present situation only increase the hysteria of the public. It will make rational thinking less possible, it will increase our intransigent attitude against Russia, and . . . it will give new force to the witch hunt . . . proceeding in this country."[53]

Had the scientists pushed ahead with their fund-raising efforts and given the Ad Council enough money to produce the pamphlet, or let the Ad Council raise the money on its own as it wanted to do, the campaign could have urged the public to pressure government officials for further negotiations with the Soviets. But with only $42,290.34 in the bank as of April 30, 1947, the scientists were broke, and the ECAS was in danger of shutting down. As the scientists scrambled to address the problem of dwindling contributions, the Ad Council stopped running the radio spots.[54]

For want of $50,000, the course of history may have been changed.

Why the Campaign Failed

Fear appeals are tricky. While they can be highly effective in political races, they can also alienate. People can avoid or deny dire warnings they think they can do little or nothing about. The atomic energy campaign's lack of an action message hindered its effectiveness. An examination of the copy from nine public service ads reveals the vague language used in the first phase of the campaign. An August 13, 1946, spot on CBS's *The Light of the World* told listeners that "every American who makes any pretense of good citizenship should inform himself of the proposals made by our government to the United Nations Atomic Energy Commission." A November 23, 1946, message on ABC's *The American Farmer* continued the educational theme: "Inform yourself and discuss the current trends [that] thinking scientists and statesmen are proposing in international . . . meetings."[55]

Such amorphous messages left listeners uncertain about how international control was defined in the Baruch Plan, which favored UN control of atomic bombs. Listeners were also unclear about what they should do, since the messages did not urge them to request a pamphlet, or to write Congress to show their support for the Baruch Plan.[56]

Without developing a clear message asking the public to support a specific form of international control, the radio spots simply communicated a generalized fear of atomic energy, which the scientists had articulated since the bombs were first dropped on Hiroshima and Nagasaki. One ad aired on ABC's *The American Farmer* on November 23, 1946, told listeners that "the discovery of atomic energy creates the most serious problem ever to face this nation and the world. Scientists and experts agree there is no effective defense against it and none can be expected." A second, on ABC's *At Your Request*, focused on the weapons' destructiveness: "Never forget, enough atom bombs could kill one American out of three without warning in a single day." A third, on NBC's *Car-*

nation Contented Hour, told listeners they could not protect themselves: "If we can't control it, no country is safe—no city—no man, woman, or child."[57]

Ironically, promotion of such fear-filled messages achieved the opposite result: fostering a reliance on nuclear weapons. The main effect of the campaign was to induce fear, denial, and a sense of despair that the average person could do nothing to prevent another attack. Manhattan Project chemist Rabinowitch argued as much in his *Bulletin of the Atomic Scientists* article in 1951: "While trying to frighten men into rationality, scientists have frightened many into abject fear or blind hatred." He concluded that the scientists' influence on public affairs had produced some undesirable results: "It has made, in some instances, for more and not less passion and confusion, and has made some rational solutions more and not less difficult."

As U.S. negotiations with the Soviets broke down, there was little outcry from an informed public to stop the inevitable march toward an arms race. Indeed, nuclear brinksmanship would weigh heavily on U.S. foreign policy for several decades, injecting fear of the atomic bomb into American children, who would practice "duck and cover" drills in public schools.

The atomic energy campaign had aired at a time when it could best capitalize on the post-Hiroshima concerns about nuclear weapons. Polls taken in early 1946 showed that American support for a world government had risen since the bombs were first dropped. The ABC newscaster Raymond Gram Swing published an Ohio survey in early 1946 that "showed overwhelming support for world government" when the poll question linked the idea of a world government with abolishing future wars. An August 1946 Gallup poll found that 54 percent of Americans favored transforming the UN into a structure that could control the armies of all nations, including the United States.[58]

Disorganization among the scientists and their inability to raise a minimum of $30,000 to create an information pamphlet hurt the atomic energy campaign. The Ad Council, under pressure from networks refusing to air the spots without an action message, ultimately stopped the campaign in May 1947. This decision ended any hope of placing atomic energy under the control of the UN or a world government. The cost of that lost opportunity—in political, social, and financial terms—was incalculable.

Chapter 6

The Struggle for Men's Souls
An Anti-communist Crusade for Freedom Targets Americans

*Radio Free Europe, like the Berlin Airlift, was one of our most successful
Cold War ventures that helped result in cracking open the Iron Curtain.*

—Robert Keim, Ad Council President

*Why not, in fact, turn the enormous persuasive power of American
advertising in advertising's own defense—or at least in defense of
those values and institutions of which advertising was an integral
part? Advertising was the keeper of the American Way, and the
American Way, in its turn, was the keeper of advertising.*

—*Frank Fox,* Madison Avenue Goes to War

Early in 1967, Ad Council president Robert Keim returned to New York
from a visit to Radio Free Europe's headquarters in Munich. Browsing
through the newspapers, he noticed an ad for an upcoming *60 Minutes* report
called "In the Pay of the CIA: An American Dilemma." The March 13, 1967,
report would accuse the Ad Council of being paid by the CIA to run its Crusade for Freedom campaign to raise money for Radio Free Europe and Radio
Liberty (known collectively as "the Radios"). Keim immediately called CBS,
requesting that Mike Wallace interview him or another Ad Council official on
the air, but it was "no dice," as he wrote in his memoir. Keim said the Ad Council knew nothing about a relationship with the CIA. Writing in 2002, Keim
said, "I feel then and I feel today that Radio Free Europe, like the Berlin Airlift,

was one of our most successful Cold War ventures that helped result in cracking open the Iron Curtain."[1]

The CIA established the nonprofit National Committee for a Free Europe (later the Free Europe Committee) on May 11, 1949, as a front organization to sponsor the Ad Council's Crusade for Freedom campaign. Working through this committee, the CIA made an initial grant of $180,000 to start the campaign and contributed an additional $5 million over the next five years. This arrangement enabled the U.S. State Department to claim that American citizens supported the Radios, when the Soviet Union complained that the broadcasts were a government-sponsored American propaganda tool. The Radios were part of a broad effort by the CIA to promote American values and ideology without the use of military force. This overall cultural initiative involved an array of U.S. institutions and professionals, from corporations and foundations to journalists and advertisers.[2]

Much has been written about the Radios, the CIA's clandestine funding of the broadcasts, and the part journalists played in maintaining the "open secret" about CIA involvement.[3] But little is known about the Ad Council's role, under the guise of public service, in the Crusade for Freedom campaign's efforts to destabilize the Soviet Union's control of Eastern Europe. The Ad Council's campaign used public service advertising messages to further a Cold War liberation strategy promoted by Eisenhower protégé and political warfare specialist Charles Douglas (C. D.) Jackson, a Princeton graduate who had joined Henry Luce's Time-Life empire as an advertising and public relations executive.

The campaign also directly targeted Americans with messages aimed at supporting capitalism and democracy while vilifying the evils of communism. During the Cold War, the Ad Council was governed by men and women whose desire to promote the democratic way of life at home and abroad continued well beyond World War II, when the conflict's urgency helped justify the advertising industry's use of propaganda to aid the federal government. Like Jackson, Ad Council officials embraced the idea, outlined in Henry Luce's 1941 editorial "The American Century," that it was the United States' manifest destiny to promote the global spread of freedom, capitalism, and democracy.

To understand the Crusade campaign, it's necessary to explore how the effort was rooted in Cold War beliefs and strategies. One analysis of the Cold War has described this period as a psychological contest, in which the combatants used "peaceful" methods to undermine each other.[4] The establishment of the CIA, the birth of the Radios, and the creation of the Crusade for Freedom campaign to support the Radios would all play their part in using nonmilitary techniques to fight communism.

American Culture and the Cold War

In 1947 most of Europe was going broke. On June 5, 1947, General George Catlett Marshall, the former U.S. Army's wartime chief of staff and current secretary of state in the Truman administration, delivered a plan at the 296th Harvard commencement to address the crisis in Europe. Marshall, along with Manhattan Project physicist J. Robert Oppenheimer, D-Day commander Omar Bradley and poet T. S. Eliot, would receive honorary degrees that day. He called on the United States to intervene with cash and material assistance to stop European economies and governments from collapsing. "Aside from the demoralizing effect on the world at large and the possibilities of disturbances arising as a result of the desperation of the people concerned, the consequences to the economy of the United States should be apparent to all," Marshall told his audience.[5]

The Marshall Plan was designed in part to carry out the Truman Doctrine, which had been delivered a few months earlier in the president's March 1947 address to Congress. Truman called for American support in Greece and Turkey, where Communist takeovers threatened. "I believe that it must be the policy of the United States to support free peoples who are resisting attempted subjugation by armed minorities or by outside pressures," Truman said.[6] It was America's responsibility, he argued, to save Western Europe.

The Truman Doctrine and Marshall Plan would be bolstered in nonmilitary ways to support and encourage democracy and capitalism abroad and at home. The promotion of American ideas and culture abroad became a key foreign policy strategy in the aftermath of the war. In October 1947 General Lucius Clay—U.S. military governor of Germany from 1945 to 1949—initiated Operation Backtalk. This plan promoted American ideas in Germany to counteract the negative images coming from Soviet sources, and its success encouraged the adoption of the Marshall Plan in the postwar reconstruction of Europe.[7]

In this climate, Melvin J. Lasky, a journalist with the *New Leader* and *Partisan Review* who had remained in Germany after the war, proposed the creation of a literary review that would "support the general objectives of U.S. foreign policy in Germany and Europe by illustrating the intellectual, spiritual, and literary achievements from which American democracy takes its inspiration."[8] The resulting *Der Monat* (The Month) first appeared in October 1948 during the Berlin blockade. Initially printed in Munich and airlifted to Berlin, it quickly established itself as an anti-communist literary journal, attracting contributions from George Orwell, Thomas Mann, Saul Bellow, and T. S. Eliot, among others. Frances Stonor Saunders, in *The Cultural Cold War: The CIA and the World of Arts and Letters*, describes how *Der Monat* was financed through "confidential funds" of the Marshall Plan, then later the CIA, then the Ford Foundation, and finally the CIA again.[9]

Other cultural initiatives would follow. The Congress for Cultural Freedom, established in West Berlin in 1950, sought to solidify anti-communist opinions among the Western European intelligentsia through the promotion of a viewpoint "more accommodating to the American way of life," and its CIA connections have been well documented.[10] The congress was backed by an impressive array of noted thinkers at the time, including Austrian writer Franz Borkenau, American philosopher James Burnham, British philosopher Bertrand Russell, and American historian Arthur Schlesinger Jr. In May 1952 it held its first major event, a "Masterpieces of the Twentieth Century" festival in Paris. The monthlong series of ballets, literary events, concerts, and theater was intended as a demonstration of the cultural vitality of the West versus the cultural sterility of the East, and of the Soviet Union in particular.[11]

The CIA strategists who advocated the use of psychological warfare to promote American ideals were veterans of the CIA's predecessor, the Office of Strategic Services (OSS).[12] President Roosevelt had established the OSS in 1941 to coordinate national intelligence functions after Wall Street lawyer and friend William "Wild Bill" Donovan convinced him of the need for an intelligence agency. After the war, when Truman disbanded the OSS, about one third of the OSS staff would go to work for the newly created CIA.

The CIA and the Birth of Radio Free Europe

The National Security Act of July 26, 1947, established the CIA, formed the National Security Council (NSC) to advise the president on political and military strategy at home and abroad, and reorganized the armed services. One of the first questions the CIA had to address was whether Congress, in authorizing the act, had granted the agency constitutional authority to conduct clandestine, psychological warfare. To authorize the use of clandestine psychological warfare, the NSC took two actions on December 9, 1947. The first, known as NSC 4, granted the assistant secretary of state for public affairs responsibility to lead "the immediate strengthening and coordination of all foreign information measures of the U.S. government to counteract the effects of anti-U.S. propaganda."[13] The second, NSC 4A, directed that the newly approved overt propaganda programs "must be supplemented by covert psychological operations."[14] These two directives became the first formal authorizations for public propaganda and clandestine operations in the postwar period.

Diplomat George F. Kennan, a chief architect of the Marshall Plan and director of the State Department's policy and planning staff, embraced the necessity of covert activities to advance America's objectives abroad.[15] He would later defend the CIA's role during the Cold War to critics of the covert operations: "This country has no Ministry of Culture, and [the] CIA was obliged to do what it could to try to fill the gap. It should be praised for having done so."[16]

NSC directive 10/2 in June 1948 created the Office of Policy Coordination (OPC), a division of the CIA, which was funded through the State Department. This arrangement enabled the State and Defense Departments to avoid defending appropriations for covert activities before Congress. The OPC charter defined its tasks as "propaganda, economic warfare, preventative direct action, sabotage, assassinations, and kidnappings."[17] The NSC directive said such activities must be "so planned and executed that any U.S. government responsibility for them is not evident to unauthorized persons, and that if uncovered the U.S. government can plausibly disclaim any responsibility for them."[18] The OPC would oversee the operation of the Radios.

Liberation was one of two foreign policy objectives that dominated the early Cold War period. Containment, promoted by Kennan, aimed to reduce Soviet power by loosening its grip on Eastern Europe and resisting its further expansion. Kennan selected Frank Wisner, another Princeton graduate, who had spent the war working in Romania and the Balkans for the OSS, to head the OPC. But Wisner, like C. D. Jackson, favored a more aggressive liberation strategy that would free Eastern Europe without open warfare. He agreed with a State Department analysis which argued that refugees could be used for intelligence purposes, and he believed people in Eastern Europe could be encouraged to revolt openly against Soviet rule. To destabilize Soviet control, Wisner would use "writers, speakers, propagandists, printing presses, and radio transmitters to carry the message back into Eastern Europe."[19]

The National Committee for a Free Europe's membership included Henry Ford II, the president of General Motors, Time-Life executive John C. Hughes, Arthur Schlesinger, Cecil B. DeMille, Dwight D. Eisenhower, and a host of businessmen, lawyers, diplomats, media officials, advertising executives, and journalists.[20] A budget of $10 million was set aside for the creation of Radio Free Europe (RFE), established in Berlin in 1950. As far as the public knew, it was operated and funded by the private, nonprofit Free Europe committee. Within two years, RFE would broadcast from twenty-nine stations in sixteen different languages. It would use informers behind the Iron Curtain, monitor communist news reports, and sponsor anti-communist lectures. Radio Liberty, which targeted listeners in the Soviet Union, was established in 1951. Creation of the Radios addressed two important goals for American intelligence officials: slowing Soviet expansion westward and creating a communications outlet for the refugees fleeing communist regimes. As early as 1947, the Soviets had already established allied governments in Bulgaria, Hungry, and Poland, and were seeking to solidify their position in East Germany.[21]

In the minutes of a Free Europe committee board meeting on July 29, 1949, mention is made that "a finance committee is being organized to give attention to fundraising." The resulting Crusade for Freedom became a nationwide fundraising drive to support the Free Europe committee and the Radios in particular.[22]

But the campaign would never raise a significant amount of money for the Radios. Its real propaganda purpose would be to aim pro-democracy messages at Americans, to gain popular domestic support for the liberation objective of freeing Eastern Europe and rolling back communism. As Christopher Simpson has observed, "in reality, one of the most important reasons for the [campaign] was to bring to America the analysis of foreign affairs that had been developed by the [Free Europe committee]." That meant "a more aggressive, hard-hitting version [of foreign affairs] that would soon come to be known as Liberation."[23]

Abbott Washburn, a public relations executive from General Mills, and Nate Crabtree, an account executive at the ad agency Batten, Barton, Durstine & Osborn (now BBDO), created the campaign's strategy. The Freedom Bell, based on the Liberty Bell in Philadelphia, would be the symbol. Once cast in Croydon, England, by the noted manufacturer Gillett & Johnston, the bell traveled across America and generated rallies where people could sign "Freedom Scrolls" and pledge "Truth Dollars." General Lucius Clay, the man credited with the success of the Berlin Airlift, was named the head of the Crusade for Freedom's board of directors.[24]

C. D. Jackson and Liberation Strategy

C. D. Jackson, a Time Inc. vice president in charge of public relations and publisher of *Fortune* magazine, is considered the chief architect of America's psychological warfare efforts during the early Cold War. During World War II, Jackson had served as deputy chief for the Office of War Information for North Africa and the Middle East. He was also deputy chief of the Psychological Warfare Division under Dwight D. Eisenhower's command of the Allied Expeditionary Force. During his presidential administration, Eisenhower appointed Jackson as a special adviser to the president for psychological warfare. Jackson would also run the CIA's Psychological Strategy Board, established April 4, 1951, with direct control of the Radios, the National Committee for a Free Europe, and the Crusade for Freedom campaign.

When Jackson graduated from Princeton in 1924, his plan for an academic career teaching French had been interrupted by his father's sudden death. Saddled with losses in the family business, Jackson ended up selling it and then applied to his friend Henry Luce of Time-Life for a job. He was hired as an assistant to the president of Time Inc. and then became general manager of *Life* after Luce created the publication in 1937. In 1949 he became publisher of *Fortune*. Although Jackson would often take extended leaves to work in the government, he regularly returned to Luce's media empire during a career that lasted thirty-three years.[25]

In 1941 Jackson founded the Council for Democracy, an anti-communist group. He also worked in the Office of War Information in North Africa in 1942. He traveled with Eisenhower to Sicily and England, where he became deputy chief of the Psychological Warfare Division. In this position he wrote propaganda for D-Day before being given the task to "appraise the reactions and ideas of liberated and conquered peoples toward the Allies in general and the U.S. in particular."[26]

Jackson fully embraced the ideas Henry Luce had set forth in a February 1941 *Life* editorial titled "The American Century." Luce urged citizens to "accept wholeheartedly our duty and our opportunity as the most powerful and vital nation in the world and in consequence to exert upon the world the full impact of our influence, for such purposes as we see fit and by such means as we see fit."[27] He referred to the twentieth century as "ours . . . because it is America's first century as a dominant power in the world." As historian Blanch Wiesen Cook has argued, "not only did Henry Luce, the creator and owner of Time-Life-Fortune and ancillary publications and broadcast media, envision the Americanization of the world, he believed that his vision was shared by most men living."[28]

In the early postwar years, Jackson headed up a number of organizations that would help promote American influence abroad. His work with Nelson Rockefeller and the World Trade Foundation, which sought to expand U.S. international business interests, reflected his concept of "Enterprise America"—a notion of partnership between business and government that would seek to expand America's economic interests worldwide. He encouraged "businessmen to end their enmity toward government and to lend their services to the state for the purpose of taking over the operation of foreign economic policy."[29]

Jackson was also a strong proponent of a Cold War liberation strategy based on the June 1948 NSC directive 10/2, which called for "subversion against hostile states, including assistance to underground resistance movements, guerrillas and refugee liberation groups, and support [for] indigenous anti-Communist elements in threatened countries of the free world."[30] Another NSC directive in September 1949, NSC 58/1, was a draft policy about the European satellite states prepared by Kennan's Policy Planning Staff at the State Department and widely circulated in the Truman administration. The paper encouraged using several different methods, including "overt, covert, informational, diplomatic, and economic," with the purpose of undermining Soviet power over their satellite states. Following this approach, "the Truman administration orchestrated a vast and provocative anti-communist psychological warfare program to break up the Soviet bloc by encouraging revolution behind the Iron Curtain."[31]

The compromise between the containment and liberation strategies that emerged in the 1952 Republican platform was called "peaceful liberation," with "peaceful" being defined as "psychological" or "political" warfare to encourage revolution within the Soviet-controlled countries. After Eisenhower's election, Jackson took on the task of making peaceful liberation a reality, through his position as psychological warfare adviser in Eisenhower's administration, his role in writing speeches for Eisenhower, and his involvement with organizations such as the National Committee for a Free Europe and the Ad Council.[32]

The Postwar Ad Council

The Ad Council was created and managed by business leaders who espoused the same beliefs about America's destiny as Luce had articulated in his "American Century" editorial. These executives would use advertising to carry out Jackson's advocacy of psychological warfare to achieve "peaceful liberation." James Webb Young, the J. Walter Thompson consultant and a founding member of the Ad Council, believed that the organization he had helped create was part of an important propaganda tool in fighting communism at home and abroad. "If we win the battle for the minds, the hearts, and the loyalties of the peoples of the world, many of the other problems on the military, economic, and political fronts will disappear," Young said in a January 15, 1951, speech titled "Socially Conscious Capitalism," delivered to the Advertising Council of Rochester.[33]

Young feared that the United States was losing the propaganda war in Europe to more effective Soviet techniques because the American approach lacked a doctrine as comprehensive as communism's. He characterized the communist doctrine as "a well-developed, thorough study that was projected as a scientific study of society and its inevitable development," and argued that the United States needed an effective message to communicate the benefits of a free society. He believed the "lack of doctrine" prevented the Western powers from countering Soviet claims.[34]

Young proposed a "free world doctrine," promoted through the use of advertising, to combat the influence of communism in Europe. This doctrine would address four elements: religion, political freedom, capitalism, and social welfare. Young argued that there were few religious and political differences between the United States and Europe but believed capitalism was little understood outside American borders. In his view, American capitalism differed from how Europeans conducted business because it included widespread competition, diffusion of ownership, high productivity, engineered marketing, and free trade. He believed that U.S. capitalism was also significantly different because it combined the pursuit of wealth by private individuals and corporations with the acknowledged need for businesses to be socially responsible.

"And now we have advanced from this sense of responsibility on the part of the individual businessman to a sense of corporate responsibility," Young said. "We have done it on the national scale in the Advertising Council." Young coupled the elements of capitalism with social responsibility to propose a new doctrine that he called "socially conscious capitalism." Highlighting this new doctrine, Young told his audience that "we must get behind it, we must sell it . . . or we must preach it with the same kind of fanaticism, and the same kind of intensity and power and skill that the Russians put behind their doctrine."

Young's concept of socially conscious capitalism had strong parallels with Jackson's Enterprise America. In effect, the Ad Council became the embodiment of Jackson's desire to forge a partnership between business and government that would protect American business interests at home while expanding American economic interests across the globe. As Blanche Wiesen Cook has observed, Jackson's "vision of Enterprise America would transform private domestic business into government's most devoted working partner."[35]

The Ad Council's Washington conference, established in the mid-1940s, gave the council's staff close access to government officials, who would provide off-the-record reports about the state of domestic and international affairs. Two conferences took place during the war, and then yearly after.

Leo Burnett, then president of the Chicago-based ad agency that bore his name, wrote a report summarizing the events of the February 1950 Washington conference. After listening to briefings by Secretary of State Dean Acheson and Paul Hoffman, administrator of the Economic Cooperation Administration, Burnett wrote, "A new 'package' is clearly needed to sell the democratic way of life under a capitalistic system not only to freedom-loving people who are special targets of the slick salesmanship of the Soviet Union, but generally to the American people."

Thus American citizens were identified as crucial targets for a message promoting capitalism. Burnett based his assessment on Acheson's "total diplomacy" strategy and Hoffman's emphasis on the disastrous political consequences if the Marshall Plan failed. By using total diplomacy, Acheson told the advertising executives, the United States would "help great areas of the world where the desire for liberty is strong to gain social, economic and political strength." Hoffman framed the situation in Europe as "the most titanic struggle the world has ever seen. It is a struggle for men's souls. The weapons of the enemy are chaos and confusion. The propaganda never lets up."[36]

When the advertising executives left Washington, they were primed to take on the Free Europe committee's request for a fund-raising campaign to support the Radios. The 1950 Crusade for Freedom campaign launched on September 4, 1950, with a radio address by General Eisenhower and ended with the dedication of the World Freedom Bell in Berlin on United Nations Day, October 24, 1950. During this period, 16 million Americans contributed $1.3 million "Truth" dollars to the effort. America's destiny of bringing freedom to the world was outlined in the 1951 Crusade for Freedom fact sheet summing up the 1950 effort: "These millions of Americans gave their support to the Crusade because they believed—as does Radio Free Europe—that the world cannot exist half slave half free; that unless Communism is aggressively countered, it will inevitably destroy freedom everywhere, even in America." The Crusade campaign delivered a powerful political warning to Americans: fight communism, or be overwhelmed by it.[37]

The Crusade campaign messages reinforced Jackson's "peaceful liberation" strategy by promising people living behind the Iron Curtain that they would one day be free of communist rule. Consider the 1950 Crusade campaign, which targeted both domestic and international audiences. Eisenhower, Eleanor Roosevelt, and Cardinal Francis Joseph Spellman appeared in the newspaper ads. Roosevelt's message called on Americans to support freedom by urging them to sign the Freedom Scroll, while Spellman encouraged American prayers "to save mankind from this cancerous growth of Communism." Eisenhower expressed the liberation message. "Your contribution to the Crusade for Freedom will help Radio Free Europe pierce the Iron Curtain . . . give hope and courage to the . . . people now living in Eastern Europe, who keep alive in their hearts the hope of freedom and self-government," he said in one ad.[38]

Lucius Clay, national chairman of the Crusade campaign, pushed for the 1951 campaign messages to be even stronger. "It is imperative that we quickly build up our strength on the psychological warfare front," he wrote in a February 21, 1951, letter to Charles P. Taft, a Cincinnati lawyer and son of William

Howard Taft in charge of raising money for the Ohio region. "The world struggle will ultimately be resolved more through the force of ideas than through
the force of arms."[39]

"Peaceful liberation" gave the United States broad latitude to pursue an
aggressive Cold War strategy with psychological warfare efforts. In these messages, truth and freedom belonged to America. Lies were manufactured by the
Kremlin to depict the United States as an imperialist nation whose main am-
bition was materialistic pursuits. The headline from a January 1951 Crusade
campaign print ad screamed, "The Commissar lies . . . I heard the Truth from
Radio Free Europe!" The accompanying picture featured a man and woman in
a country behind the Iron Curtain, listening to a radio. "Your dollars have built
two vital radio transmitters on the very doorstep of Red dominated Europe,"
the text read. "These broadcasts, delivered by escaped patriots from the satellite
nations, are countering Communist fictions with facts and helping to win the
Cold War for us all."[40]

Using the concept of escape as a metaphor for hope and liberation was a
central theme in the ads. But liberation also meant that the countries behind the
Iron Curtain would have to move toward a system that was in America's best
interests. World conditions had to be changed in a way that suited the United
States. Thus, Mr. Jankowski's son "escaped" to Cleveland. "Mr. Jankowski . . . your
son escaped . . . he is safe in Cleveland," read the headline of a September 1951
newspaper ad. The picture showed a smiling man and woman holding telephone receivers to their ears. The copy read, "By helping to fight Communism
with truth—the truth over Radio Free Europe—you are delivering the most
telling setbacks the Kremlin has ever felt—defeats that can win the cold war
and prevent a global hot war. It's work that can insure the peace of the world."[41]

The Ad Council encouraged newspapers to directly sponsor the ads so that
it would appear that America's press was supporting the Crusade campaign.
"We urge the free press of America to run these advertisements over their own
name, and to offer them to their advertisers for sponsorship," wrote Allan Brown
of the Bakelite Corporation, who coordinated the 1951 Crusade campaign.[42]

Freedom, as represented in the American way of life, was right. Tyranny,
exemplified by the iron grip of communism, was wrong. A sixty-second 1951
radio ad said, "Through your contributions to the Crusade for Freedom, Radio
Free Europe plans to bring more messages of hope to the prisoner peoples be-

This 1950 newspaper ad encouraged Americans to believe their donations to the Crusade for Freedom would help free Eastern Europeans living under communist rule. (Ad Council Archives, University Library, University of Illinois)

hind the Iron Curtain . . . to people now in chains who yearn for freedom . . . and a message of defeat to the Communist tyrants who now hold them under the iron heel of oppression."[43]

When a Czech passenger train successfully crossed the border and arrived in West Germany, the Crusade campaign made the incident the center of its third balloon leaflet effort—known as the "Winds of Freedom." On September 26, 1951, two thousand balloons carrying 2 million leaflets were released near Prague. The leaflets told the story, complete with pictures, of the train engineer and thirty-one refugees who had left their country.[44]

A 1952 Crusade letter to newspaper and magazine editors urging their support of the campaign openly acknowledged the goal of psychological warfare. "The outcome of the psychological war may not only determine whether or not we are plunged into a global shooting war, but the kind of world our children and grandchildren live in," wrote retired Rear Admiral Harold B. Miller, who had replaced Jackson as head of the National Committee for a Free Europe in 1952.[45] Jackson remained on the board.

At a January 18, 1952, meeting, the directors of the Crusade campaign decided to focus their 1952 effort more on fund-raising than on publicity and promotional events. To date, the first two campaigns had raised $3.5 million for the Radios.[46] The 1952 advertising messages continued to equate liberation with life in a better world. The headline in a 1952 Crusade print ad read, "Kids on Radio Free Europe Send Hope to Pals behind the Iron Curtain." The copy stressed keeping the hope of liberation alive. "Day and night Radio Free Europe is exposing communist lies and propaganda, and sustaining the hope of suppressed millions that someday they will live in a better world."[47]

In 1953 the Crusade For Freedom Organization merged with the American Heritage Foundation, another Ad Council client. The May 15, 1953, press release announcing the merger described the educational organization as dedicating itself to "persuade all Americans that only by active participation in the affairs of our nation can we safeguard our freedoms, preserve the liberties from which all these advantages flow, and continue to demonstrate to ourselves—and to the whole world—that the way of free men is best."[48] The merger would also provide additional cover, suggesting that the Crusade campaign was a grassroots efforts sponsored by American citizens, rather than the CIA.

As the campaign continued, the Ad Council copywriters would focus the messages on what individual actions Americans could take that would make a big difference in the struggle against communism. "You Mean I Can Fight Communism?" read the headline in a 1955 newspaper ad above the image of a woman. The copy promised that $1 would buy "100 words of truth beamed right through the Iron Curtain, Truth to smash Soviet lies, give hope and courage to the 70,000,000 enslaved people behind the Iron Curtain, Truth to stiffen their will to resist, to help keep the Kremlin off balance on its own home grounds."[49]

The 1956 campaign continued the escape theme and the idea of resistance, which was so much a part of Jackson's vision of the world. "Neither could fly . . . but they soloed to freedom," the headline of one print ad read. The ad explained how two Czech men had tied up a guard, stolen a plane, and flown to West Germany. "These two escaped but 70 million others remain captive behind the Iron Curtain. And these *are* the people at whom Radio Free Europe beams its daily broadcasts. Escape is not its aim. Radio Free Europe penetrates the Iron Curtain to spread truth . . . to strengthen hope and resistance."[50]

Encouraging such resistance eventually created a backlash against the campaign. After the Soviets crushed the Hungarian revolt in 1956, the campaign's liberation theme, which echoed the promises made in Radio Free Europe broadcasts that people living behind the Iron Curtain would one day be free, was interpreted as fomenting revolution. A November 20, 1957, Ad Council report documented a debate among it public policy committee members about whether to approve the campaign for another year. Although the campaign had been encouraging resistance to Soviet control for years, committee member Sarah Blanding, president of Vassar College, now had serious doubts about its goals. She "wondered if something could not be done to prevent giving the impression in [Radio Free Europe] broadcasts that things are going to happen which are impossible and which manifestly cannot happen."[51]

Others objected, citing the role Radio Free Europe played in informing the world of events in the satellite countries. If the Ad Council discontinued the campaign, "it would be a great shock to the people behind the Iron Curtain." The campaign was reapproved, with the request that Radio Free Europe should closely examine its operations.[52]

The Crusade for Freedom campaign continued to enjoy strong support from American businesses. Just how much was shown in the second major crisis the campaign experienced in 1968, when press reports revealed the CIA connection. At that point, the Free Europe Committee asked the Ad Council to drop its fund-raising appeals and instead offer an information booklet. That hardly diminished the interest from corporate donors. The current Ad Council president Robert Keim wrote in a July 8, 1968, letter: "During the 15 or 16 months since our last campaign ended, and in spite of the 'expose' having received considerable publicity in the press . . . contributions from industry have not diminished, we are told, and some companies even increased their contributions." The revised campaign strategy would "reacquaint the American public with Radio Free Europe" and motivate people to send for a booklet, "East Europe Today."

The Ad Council continued to run the Crusade campaign through 1970. In 1976 the Radios merged into one nonprofit entity called RFE/RL. It still broadcasts in twenty-one countries (including portions of central Asia and the Middle East) "where a free press is banned by the government or not fully established," according to its website.[53]

The Crusade for Freedom campaign demonstrates how the Ad Council and the U.S. government continued to derive benefits from their partnership in the aftermath of World War II. The campaign allowed Ad Council leaders to push an anti-communist theme in advertising since an economic system based on capitalism helped American businesses.

The ad copy also encouraged the kind of changes in Eastern Europe that were directly beneficial to U.S. interests. Campaign messages fueling hope among people living behind the Iron Curtain that they would one day be free bolstered the American government's Cold War liberation strategy abroad. In the struggle for hearts and souls, an epic battle of good versus evil was cast in language depicting the moral superiority of freedom and democracy over tyranny and communism. America, as the creator of an economic system that was expected to bring peace to all freedom-loving citizens, was depicted in the Ad Council's copy as a shining beacon of hope, undermining the Red menace.

Chapter 7

The Crying Indian

In America's Debate over Garbage and Pollution, Does the Campaign Shift Responsibility from Corporations to Individuals?

More than four decades ago, the Ad Council partnered with Keep America Beautiful to create a powerful visual image that dramatized how litter and other forms of pollution were hurting the environment, and how every individual has the responsibility to help protect it.

—*Ad Council website, August 2012*

In the twenty-first century, to be a great organization means recognizing that we have a responsibility to shareholders; but we also have a wider purpose, to be good stewards of the planet and to be good partners for our stakeholders in all the communities where we do business.

—*Indra K. Nooyi, chairman and CEO, PepsiCo*

Protecting the environment is a common concern in twenty-first-century America. But it wasn't always that way. Some of our earliest environmental activists, such as John Muir, founder of the Sierra Club, had their detractors. The original Earth Day was derided, in some circles, as a hippie idea. Fast-forward a few decades: schoolchildren now lecture their parents on the importance of ecology. Knowledge may be power, but it still takes powerful ad campaigns to galvanize the public to action. One of the most famous—"The Crying Indian"—did just that.

The campaign's sponsor, a nonprofit group called Keep America Beautiful, calls itself the nation's largest volunteer-based community action and education organization. Founded in 1953, the group is made up of companies that produce chemicals, plastics, throwaway bottles, and packaging. Keep America Beautiful's corporate sponsors include the American Chemistry Council, the Coca-Cola Foundation, the Dow Chemical Company, the Glad Products Company, McDonald's, Nestlé Waters, PepsiCo, and Waste Management Inc., among others. The group also partners with a number of state recycling organizations "to support our mission of engaging individuals to take greater responsibility for improving their community environments," according to its website. Although Keep America Beautiful worked regularly with the Ad Council between 1960 and 1985, its 1971 campaign featuring the "Crying Indian" was the one that captured the public's imagination.

Richard Earle, the Marsteller Inc. executive who wrote the second television spot for that campaign, calls the Crying Indian "a true public service icon" in his book *The Art of Cause Marketing: How to Use Advertising to Change Personal Behavior and Public Policy*. As Earle recounts, the trade publication *Advertising Age* selected the Crying Indian as one of the best commercials of the century. *Entertainment Weekly* and *TV Guide* considered it one of the fifty greatest commercials of all time.[1] On its website, the Ad Council said the ad "became one of the most memorable and successful campaigns in advertising history."

The use of an American Indian in the ad was a clever choice. The ad's emotional punch depended on the audience associating Indians with nature, simplicity, and an unspoiled environment. Once the audience identified with the Indian, the shock of seeing the devastated land would resonate.[2]

At the time of the campaign's launch in 1971, public attention was strongly focused on the civil rights of African Americans, American Indians, Mexican Americans, and other ethnic groups. Bruce J. Schulman, writing in *The Seventies: The Great Shift in American Culture, Society, and Politics*, observes that "in race relations, religion, family life, politics, and popular culture, the 1970s marked the most significant watershed of modern U.S. history. One year alone, 1973, witnessed the end of American intervention in Vietnam, the U.S. Supreme Court decision in *Roe v. Wade*, the exposure of the Watergate conspiracies, the Indian occupation of Wounded Knee, and the first Arab oil shock."[3]

While the advertising industry and communications media applauded the campaign's creativity, environmental and consumer watchdog groups cried foul. They argued that Keep America Beautiful had achieved an unpalatable

Entertainment Weekly and *TV Guide* considered this 1971 image of the Crying Indian to be one of the fifty greatest commercials of all time. (Hartman Center for Sales, Advertising & Marketing History, David M. Rubenstein Rare Book & Manuscript Library, Duke University)

feat in behavioral engineering with the Crying Indian and the campaign's accompanying slogan, "People Start Pollution. People Can Stop It." Groups including the Sierra Club, the National Audubon Society, and the National Wildlife Federation believed that the message put responsibility for littering and polluting the environment on the backs of individual citizens, shifting attention and debate away from the beverage companies' throwaway plastic bottles, the packaging industry's throwaway containers, and the use of polymers and resin by plastics manufacturers.

Because the Keep America Beautiful campaign focused on the environment, it received credit for tackling a difficult issue, even if the action messages focused on individuals and not corporations. In a letter accompanying the Ad Council's press release at the time of the campaign's launch, President Richard Nixon wrote, "It is especially gratifying to know that Keep America Beautiful

Inc. is launching such an intensive advertising campaign to give individual citizens the opportunity to contribute their best efforts in this crucial national endeavor."[4]

Despite the criticism, what people remembered about the campaign was what the advertising intended them to: the horrified Indian crying at the litter and devastation around him, and the message that people start pollution and people can stop it. The campaign also proved highly successful in reducing the environmental problems caused by litter. In its 2004 booklet, "Public Service Advertising That Changed a Nation," the Ad Council reported that the campaign had "helped usher in Earth Day and the Environmental Protection Agency, motivated 100,000 people . . . to request a booklet on how to reduce pollution, and helped reduce litter by as much as 88 percent by 1983."[5]

At the time of this writing in August 2012, Keep America Beautiful was poised to launch a new campaign with the Ad Council on recycling. From its perspective, individual willingness to recycle was "stagnant and showing a downward trend," said Robert Wallace, a Keep America Beautiful spokesperson.

Individual recycling can and does make a difference, but environmental groups say it is only one part of what is needed to solve America's growing garbage problem. Corporations and legislators also need to play a greater role. To understand why Keep America Beautiful campaigns have focused more on individual behavior than corporate responsibility, a brief history lesson is in order. It's necessary to examine how the group's emergence fit into the country's broader environmental movement, explain the goals of the constituencies the group represents, and analyze the strategy and messages in the ad campaigns.

The Postwar Economic Boom and the Rise of Environmentalism

When World War II ended, American optimism about the future prevailed against the initial gloom prompted by the use of the atomic bomb. Consumer product shortages and food rationing disappeared. Americans worked longer hours, had more money to spend, and greater choices about what they could buy. An abundance of everything signaled a future of seemingly infinite possibilities.

Birth rates soared, ushering in the baby boom generation. Fast-food restaurants such as McDonald's popped up. Consumer demand for automobiles created abundant jobs in the car industry. Hal K. Rothman, writing in *The*

Greening of a Nation? Environmentalism in the United States since 1945, describes how affordable housing—"about two years wages for the average family"—put home ownership well within reach of everyday workers: "Driving the new market for housing was an economic boom unparalleled in American history. To those who left the military with the federal and state benefits of wartime service, the world was truly their oyster; the option of government loans to finance housing, funds to support an education, and other mechanisms offered opportunities on a scale that no generation of Americans had ever before experienced. In an expanding economy, utilizing more and more natural resources, there appeared to be opportunities for everyone."[6]

With this great economic boom came the need for vast quantities of resources to meet production. Demand grew for lumber, gasoline, and packaging for new products. The war had advanced the spread of heavy industry—concentrated around cities such as Boston and Chicago during the prewar period—throughout the rest of the country. And with this vast manufacturing of new products and the growth of heavy industry came waste and pollution.[7]

America's dependence on coal switched to oil following the war. "Beginning in 1949," Rothman writes, "oil began an ascent that took its consumption in the United States from 5.8 billion barrels per year in 1949 to more than 16.4 billion in 1971."[8] Smog and carbon dioxide may have filled city skies and lungs, but citizens and manufacturers alike considered this a necessary price to pay for progress.

By the 1940s the conservation legacy built by John Muir, Teddy Roosevelt, and Gifford Pinchot was nearly dead as a force in American politics. In 1945, Rothman observes, conservation had "descended to its weakest level in the twentieth century."[9] Among the few remaining environmental groups with potential political clout was Muir's Sierra Club, characterized by Rothman as a "western-based, nature-oriented group dominated by genteel white, upper-middle-class members."[10] Other groups such as the Wilderness Society and the National Wildlife Federation claimed similar memberships. These groups did not have a tradition of aggressively advocating for environmental protection; they operated primarily as recreation outlets for their membership, who also benefited from America's economic progress. As a result, conservation was not a voice commonly heard in the postwar period by Congress, the federal government, or state and local municipalities.

In the early 1950s, Vermont farmers began a battle against throwaway glass bottles. Angered at the growing presence of bottles caught in farm equipment such as hay mowers or strewn in cow feed, where animals swallowed them with fatal results, the farmers successfully pushed for passage of a 1953 bill that banned the sale of throwaway bottles in the state.

Throwaway bottles had not become the norm in the United States until the postwar period. Until then, the refillable bottle was accepted by Americans and considered an important part of the distribution processes of some beverage manufacturers. In *War on Waste: Can America Win Its Battle with Garbage?* Louis Blumberg and Robert Gottlieb document how the refillable bottle in the beer market changed dramatically over a twenty-year period starting in 1945: "The introduction of the flip-top, non-refillable can by national breweries accounted for one major shift. Rather than differences in taste or price, this change was more a reflection of competition through product differentiation accomplished by packaging innovations and related advertising campaigns. Such changes, moreover, paralleled the decline of the local and regional breweries, often the last bastion of the refillable beer bottle."[11] After the arrival of plastic (polyethylene terephthalate, known as "PET") soft-drink bottles in 1978, refillable bottles declined rapidly.[12]

In the 1950s, when throwaway bottles started to capture a greater share of the market, the first "ban-the-can" and "bottle bill" movements appeared. With opposition mounting from the beverage container industry, Vermont's 1953 bottle bill expired in 1957. In response to growing concerns about choked landfills and air pollution from incinerators, however, bottle bills reappeared in the 1970s. This time the bills required a two- to five-cents deposit on beer and soft-drink bottles. Oregon and Vermont passed the legislation, but efforts in other states were unsuccessful. "By 1974, the industry lobbies had stymied efforts to pass laws in 15 states, almost all initiated by volunteer and grass roots groups rather than by public officials," Blumberg and Gottlieb report.[13]

In the late 1970s, Maine, Michigan, Iowa, Connecticut and Delaware enacted bottle bills. Although efforts to pass a national beverage container deposit law were thwarted by industry arguments that such a measure would kill jobs and raise prices, there was strong evidence that a national bill would help the environment and create tens of thousands of new jobs:

A series of studies, including an extensive model performed by EPA as part of the congressional reports required under the 1970 Resource Recovery Act, sharply disputed industry contentions. Basing their study on the experience of the Oregon and Vermont laws, EPA found that, after a five-year implementation of a national deposit law, there would be a 60 to 70 percent reduction of roadside bottle litter and a 20 to 40 percent reduction of all litter; that more than 7 million tons of municipal solid waste would be reduced, which would account for 5 percent of the total waste stream and 8.5 percent of all manufactured goods discarded; that there would be a reduction in energy use equivalent to 245 trillion Btu or 40 percent of the total energy required to supply all beer and soft drinks; that an annual savings of virgin raw materials would include 5.2 million tons of glass, 1.5 million tons of steel, and 500,000 tons of aluminum; that there would be a net national economic savings for supplying beverages of upwards of $2.5 billion; that it would cost about 2.5 cents *less* [sic] in consumer costs for each 12-ounce serving; and that there would be a net employment *gain* [sic] of more than 80,000 jobs, consisting of an increase in beverage industry employment of 165,000 jobs and a manufacturing loss of 80,000 jobs.[14]

But this argument was lost as worries over the tough economic climate sweeping the country took precedence. Schulman describes how the new term "stagflation" had entered the nation's lexicon in the early 1970s, "signifying a virtually inconceivable combination of galloping inflation with anemic growth and tenacious unemployment."[15] Toward the end of the decade, the economy worsened with the rise of inflation. As Schulman relates, "The cost of living leaped up at double-digit rates: interest rates reached 20 percent; the value of savings eroded; the prices of meat, milk, and heating oil rose out of sight."[16]

But economic worries took a backseat in the 1980s, when the decline in the number of available landfills, and the widespread decision by municipalities to no longer incinerate trash, prompted renewed public debate over what to do with America's growing amount of garbage. New York, Iowa, and Massachusetts passed deposit laws, which also required bottle manufacturers and distributors to help recycle cans and bottles. Efforts to pass a bottle bill in California were more contentious. Industry concerns resulted in state legislators scaling back the bill from requiring a five-cent deposit on returned bottles to a one-cent deposit. Loopholes such as exempting liquor and wine bottles were built into the bill, which provided no mechanism to encourage refillables.[17]

How Cultural Forces Shaped the Environmental Debate

The publication of John Kenneth Galbraith's *The Affluent Society* in 1958, Vance Packard's *The Waste Makers* in 1960, and Rachel Carson's *Silent Spring* in 1962 would prompt a national dialogue about the environmental consequences of unchecked progress. Galbraith, an economist and Harvard University professor, was well positioned to shape public debate about the environment.[18] In one of the most famous passages in his book, he wrote:

> The family which takes its mauve and cerise, air-conditioned, power-steered, and power-braked automobile out for a tour passes through cities that are badly paved, made hideous by litter, blighted buildings, billboards, and posts for wires that should long since have been put underground. They pass into a countryside that has been rendered largely invisible by commercial art. . . . They picnic on exquisitely packaged food from a portable icebox by a polluted stream and go on to spend the night at a park which is a menace to public health and morals. Just before dozing off on an air mattress, beneath a nylon tent, amid the stench of decaying refuse, they may reflect vaguely on the curious unevenness of their blessings. Is this, indeed, the American genius?[19]

Packard, a journalist and social critic, outlined the intent behind manufacturing strategies based on "planned obsolescence" and marketing strategies that encouraged the development of a "throwaway spirit." While manufacturers built in shorter life spans for their products to spur production and consumption, marketers sought to convince consumers that goods no longer in style should be replaced, even if they still functioned. As Packard explained:

> The technique of making products obsolete by designing them to wear out or to look shoddy after a few years has limited utility. This limit

on the usefulness of planned quality obsolescence inspired marketers to search also for other ways to render existing products obsolete. The safer, more widely applicable approach, many soon concluded, was to wear the product out in the owner's mind. Strip it of its desirability even though it continues to function dutifully. Make it old-fashioned, conspicuously non-"modern." As [Wall Street banker] Paul Mazur pointed out, "Style can destroy completely the value of possessions even while their utility remains unimpaired."[20]

In her book, Carson, a biologist by training who had worked for the U.S. Department of the Interior, built a case against the use of synthetic pesticides in agriculture. The production of inorganic compounds such as DDT to protect crops from pests had experienced a fivefold increase from 1947 to 1960.[21] In her opening chapter, Carson described "a strange blight" that crept over a fictional community, sickening animals and children: "There was a strange stillness. The birds, for example—where had they gone? Many people spoke of them, puzzled and disturbed. The feeding stations in the backyards were deserted. The few birds seen anywhere were moribund; they trembled violently and could not fly. It was a spring without voices. On the mornings that had once throbbed with the dawn chorus of robins, catbirds, doves, jays, wrens, and scores of other bird voices there was now no sound; only silence lay over the fields and woods and marsh."[22] Her warning that some of this was already happening in different parts of America prompted President John F. Kennedy to order a committee to investigate the concerns.

After his November 1964 election, President Lyndon Johnson made the environment a major focus of his administration, giving it equal importance to civil rights and the "war on poverty."[23] First Lady Claudia Alta "Lady Bird" Johnson helped focus public attention on the environment. She was a major impetus behind the Highway Beautification Bill passed by Congress on October 7, 1965, which regulated the number of billboards and junkyards along American highways. In announcing the successful passage of the bill, President Johnson said, "I want to make sure that the America we see from these major highways is a beautiful America."[24]

Lady Bird Johnson pushed for the creation of programs to improve the beauty of urban areas. To spruce up the nation's capital, she formed a committee of twenty citizens in early 1965 called the First Lady's Committee for a More Beautiful National Capital. Its members included philanthropists Laurance S. Rockefeller and Mary Lasker, and Katharine Graham, publisher of the *Washington Post*. Rothman notes that "by April 1966 four hundred thousand bulbs had been planted in parks, public squares, and the triangles that dotted the metropolitan area. Within two years, a full-scale local beautification program had become a fixture in the nation's capital."[25]

By the end of his administration, President Johnson's record on the environment had set the stage for the burgeoning environmental movement of the early 1970s. He signed nearly three hundred beautification and conservation initiatives, the most important of which addressed air and water pollution, solid-waste disposal, endangered species, and wilderness protection. During his presidency, the environment became a "principal concern of the federal government."[26]

As the baby boom generation had matured in the 1960s, Margaret Mead believed that young people who had grown up with the existence of the atomic bomb were more likely to understand the growing environmental crisis. She wrote, "They have never known a time when war did not threaten annihilation. When they are given the facts, they can understand immediately that continued pollution of the air and water and soil will soon make the planet uninhabitable and that it will be impossible to feed an indefinitely expanding world population."[27] Influenced by literature such as Jack Kerouac's 1958 novel *The Dharma Bums*, members of the counterculture movement preferred communing with nature to a soulless suburban existence. They were more than willing to join Ralph Nader in his attack on corporations that polluted the environment. Nader questioned the automobile industry's "power to pollute" in his 1965 book *Unsafe at Any Speed*. By the end of the decade, the focus on corporate polluters such as those backing Keep America Beautiful had mounted. The January 1969 leak at a Union Oil well off the coast of Santa Barbara, California, captured national media attention and heightened the focus on the "unchecked power of 'big oil.'"[28]

Corporate power was also linked to the environmental devastation caused by the Vietnam War, as the images on American televisions suggested that the United States was fighting a war against both nature and the Viet Cong:

American troops had sprayed one-eighth of the country with chemical defoliants. Though much of the herbicide spraying targeted forests, rice fields were targets too. The air war was just as devastating to the landscape. To many observers, the heavily cratered wastelands created by saturation bombing looked like the moon. Automated artillery fire also turned forests into biological deserts. Throughout the field of operations, the military used gigantic bulldozers to clear the terrain of potential cover for enemy troops. Even napalm was used to destroy vegetation. In the view of many scientists and activists, the United States was committing "ecocide."[29]

Earth Day on April 22, 1970, would symbolize a new form of environmentalism based on the growing activism that was sweeping the country, making the environment a part of the national legislative agenda for the coming decade. Gaylord Nelson, a Democratic senator from Wisconsin, proposed creating a nationwide day where people would host teach-ins about the environment. Media coverage prompted a flood of supportive letters. An estimated 20 million Americans began discussing the planet's ecological problems and demanding solutions from elected officials.[30]

There was particular interest in the environment among college students. In the fall of 1969, Earth Day organizers used eco-focused campus groups to organize the event. A November 1969 front-page story in the *New York Times* reported that the environment might soon overtake the Vietnam War as the number one issue on college campuses.[31] About 1,500 colleges held Earth Day teach-ins. As Adam Rome describes in his article "Give Earth a Chance: The Environmental Movement and the Sixties," people adorned with flowers and gas masks gathered in parks and in front of government and corporate offices. Demonstrators poured oil into the reflecting pool at Standard Oil headquarters in San Francisco. Protestors held up dead fish in New York to portray the polluted Hudson River. Business leaders and government officials spoke at events across the country. The purpose was to build "a movement to change the direction of society."[32]

Denis Hayes, a twenty-five-year-old hired by Nelson to coordinate the event nationally, told a Washington, D.C., Earth Day gathering what he considered the true meaning of the day to be: "I suspect the politicians and businessmen who are jumping on the environmental bandwagon don't have the slightest idea what they are getting into. They are talking about filters on smokestacks while we are challenging corporate irresponsibility. They are bursting with pride about plans for totally inadequate sewage treatment plants; we are challenging the ethics of a society that, with only 6 percent of the world's population, accounts for more than half of the world's annual consumption of raw materials."[33]

While the event did not produce the kind of radical change Hayes envisioned, it did attract national media coverage, and it prompted writers to produce Earth Day books calling for a more activist environmental agenda.

President Nixon also took significant initiatives on environmental issues. The Clean Air Act, passed in 1970, regulated the amount of hazardous pollutants that could be released into the air. Through an executive order, Nixon created the Environmental Protection Agency on December 2, 1970, and he called on Americans not to further abuse the land.[34]

Many businesses were feeling on the defensive, and Keep America Beautiful would come to their aid.

A Peek behind the Curtain

Environmental groups and critics believe that the public image Keep America Beautiful projects to Americans—that of a hardworking, grassroots organization dedicated to improving the environment—helps obscure the responsibility of the group's corporate sponsors, who benefit from keeping the public dialogue about garbage and pollution focused on individuals rather than on what companies can do to recycle or to reduce the amount of chemicals they use and non-biodegradable packages they manufacture. These same critics also argue that Keep America Beautiful's real purpose is to help defeat legislative attempts to stop the manufacturing of throwaway bottles and packages or to force companies to recycle more. To understand this criticism, it's necessary to examine the group's image based on its public documents and website, and assess the critiques of Keep America Beautiful that have been written by academic researchers and journalists.

Keep America Beautiful is listed as a 501c3 organization, according to its tax documents. Under the Internal Revenue Service's tax classification, this means that it is considered a charitable organization, "which may not attempt to influence legislation as a substantial part of its activities." Keep America Beautiful is also not a lobbying organization, and some limited activities to influence legislation are permitted charitable organizations under the tax code.[35]

As of September 2012, the group's slogan on its website encouraged people to "do something beautiful." One of its core beliefs listed at that time was "that each of us holds an obligation to preserve and protect our environment. Through our everyday choices and actions, we collectively have a huge impact on our world. It's really a simple concept, but one with far reaching effects."[36] Keep America Beautiful today considers its core issues to be "preventing litter," "reducing waste," and "beautifying communities." To achieve these goals, it "follows a practical approach that unites citizens, businesses and government to find solutions."[37]

Keep America Beautiful and environmental groups have not always been at odds. When Keep America Beautiful first started in 1953, its goal was to work with other nonprofit groups to help improve the environment. At the Keep America Beautiful website, a viewer reading under the headline "KAB—A Beautiful History" can learn that "Long before 'green' was fashionable, Keep America Beautiful formed in 1953 when a group of corporate and civic leaders met in New York City to discuss a revolutionary idea—bringing the public and private sectors together to develop and promote a national cleanliness ethic."[38]

The site's list of corporate donors illuminates the role businesses play in Keep America Beautiful. Lowe's Charitable and Educational Foundation, Philip Morris USA, and Waste Management each contributed $1 million or more to the group in 2011. Nestlé Waters North America and PepsiCo each gave between $500,000 and $999,999.

Keep America Beautiful was structured in the same manner as the beautification campaigns later started by Lady Bird Johnson, notes journalist and filmmaker Heather Rogers in her 2005 book *Gone Tomorrow, The Hidden Life of Garbage*.[39] And it involved community and church groups, the federal government, and the public education system in its mission: "Within its first few years KAB had statewide anti-litter campaigns 'in progress or planned' in thirty-two states, membership ballooned to more than 70 million, and the group enjoyed the active support of four federal departments and fifty national public interest groups. KAB was a fast success."[40]

While Keep America Beautiful viewed its birth as forging a public-private partnership to address protection of the environment, nongovernmental environmental groups such as Greenpeace considered it "a sophisticated green-washing operation."[41] Rogers agrees. She writes that the group's birth was a direct response to the Vermont legislature's passage of the 1953 bill banning the sale of all throwaway bottles in the state:

> KAB's founders were the powerful American Can Company and Owens-Illinois Glass Company, inventors of the one-way can and bottle respectively. They linked up with twenty other industry heavies, including Coca-Cola, the Dixie Cup Company, Richfield Oil Corporation (later Atlantic Richfield), and the National Association of Manufacturers, with whom KAB shared members, leaders, and interests. Still a major player today, KAB came out swinging, urgently funneling vast resources into a nationwide, media-savvy campaign to address the rising swells of trash through public education focused on individual bad habits and laws that steered clear of regulating industry.[42]

Rogers attributes the successful passage of state laws imposing fines on individuals for littering, with jail terms for repeat offenders, to Keep America Beautiful's growing influence: "Such solutions suited the KAB leadership, because they distracted the public from other options that might inconvenience industry, like production restrictions or forcing can, bottle, and beverage makers to reinstate the vastly less profitable refillable container."[43]

Keep America Beautiful spokesman Robert Wallace dismisses Rogers's thesis as "opinion." Yet other Keep America Beautiful documents reflect the pro-industry, anti-litter strategy. A 1963 short film, *Heritage of Splendor*, produced by the Richfield Oil Company for Keep America Beautiful, praised companies and berated litterers. Narrated by Ronald Reagan, the film featured idyllic scenes of mountains, streams, and grazing animals. Oil companies were called "conservation minded." The lumber industry was credited with raising "more wood than we use ... because we grow trees like a crop." The mining industry was applauded for "constantly developing more efficient ways to mine and develop our mineral ores."[44]

But the film reproached individuals who tossed out garbage on roadsides, in lakes, and on snow-covered ski paths. "How do we treat this important resource for recreation?" Reagan asked in the film. "We go away from home on a vacation and take a holiday from responsibility. We launch a fallout of litter."

All the packaging that went into the containers that people brought to picnics was seen in the film as a good thing. But the packaging turned bad in the hands of litterbugs. "Trash only becomes trash after it has first served a useful purpose," Reagan said in the film. "It becomes litter only after people thoughtlessly discard it."

Litter was depicted as a dangerous problem: viewers watched images of water skiers falling and cars crashing after encountering large pieces of trash. But there was hope: Keep America Beautiful was featured in the film as the kind of "responsible," civic-minded organization that would help Americans beat their litterbug habit.

Clearly, individual actions matter, and the Keep America Beautiful campaign performed a great service by heightening that awareness. But corporate actions also matter, and by ignoring industrial pollutants, Keep America Beautiful, whatever its merits, only addressed one side of the environmental issue. A cleaner America wasn't seen as a civic duty for American business, only for its customers.

The "People's Capitalism"

In the 1950s the Ad Council produced a series of pamphlets and campaigns that help explain its willingness to take on Keep America Beautiful as a client in 1960. At that time, cynicism about, and radical activism against, corporate interests were not yet as woven into the public psyche as they are today. Although trailblazers such as Galbraith, Packard, and Carson were sounding alarms, full public awareness that corporations contributed toward pollution and should also be held responsible for protecting the planet didn't come until the environmental movement reached maturity in the 1970s.

Back in Cold War America, free enterprise, production, and mass consumption were considered the keys to building the kind of national strength needed to combat the Red menace. The Ad Council's 1948 pamphlet, called "The Miracle of America," reflected its strong pro-business mentality. In the text Uncle Sam explained America's economic system to an average family: Americans enjoyed a high standard of living because of productivity. "And because we Americans produce so much better, we earn more and can buy more for every hour we work," Uncle Sam said.[45] The country was successful because its ability to generate goods and services was superior to other countries: "With only one-fifteenth of the world's population, and about the same proportion of the world's land area and natural resources, the United States has more than half the world's telephone, telegraph and radio networks; more than a third of the railways; more than three quarters of the world's automobiles; almost half of the world's radios; and consumes more than half of the world's coffee and rubber, two-thirds of the silk, a quarter of the coal and nearly two-thirds of the crude oil."[46]

In 1953 economist and Lehman Brothers banker Paul Mazur grew concerned that the U.S. pace of consumption was not matching its rate of production. Mazur had been a 1930s business partner of Edward Bernays, a nephew of Sigmund Freud and considered the "father of public relations." "We must shape a new mentality," Mazur concluded. "Man's desires must overshadow his needs."[47]

Ad Council campaigns in the 1950s reflected this horn-of-plenty economic outlook and went a step further by linking capitalism with America's democratic freedoms. In addition to the Crusade for Freedom campaign discussed in chapter 6, the Ad Council's "Future of America" campaign in 1954, "People's Capitalism" effort in 1956, and "Confidence in a Growing America" campaign in 1958 all tied the importance of political freedom with the benefits of mass production and consumption.

The thinking behind these campaigns was rooted in a series of roundtable discussions the Ad Council had sponsored from 1951 to 1953 with academics, economists, and other prominent opinion leaders. A 1956 council report described the result of these discussions: "The panel was unanimous on one point of towering significance: In America there has evolved a totally new kind of capitalism, which goes farther than any previous society toward 'achieving the good life' for the average man."[48]

To make Americans and the world aware that a capitalistic system provides the most benefits to its citizens, the council and the U.S. Information Agency launched the "People's Capitalism" effort. Instead of public service ads, this campaign featured a 7,000-square-foot traveling exhibition that showcased how Americans lived. It first opened February 13, 1956, in Washington, D.C., and later toured in Europe and Asia. This visual survey of American life in-cluded rooms from a 1776 colonial home and features from a modern 1950s home. The exhibition text noted: "Directly contrary to Karl Marx's predictions, in America the rich did not get richer and the poor poorer. America became a middle income nation."[49]

The Ad Council believed that large American businesses were the lynchpins that kept the U.S. economy humming. When it partnered with Keep America Beautiful in 1960, the council's officials viewed the group's anti-litter focus as a welcome effort by corporations to address the nation's growing environmental problems.

"Please, Please, Don't Be a Litterbug"

From 1961 to 1965, the Ad Council selected aluminum and packaging giant Reynolds Metals Company as the corporate sponsor of the yearly Keep America Beautiful campaign. It used Dancer Fitzgerald Sample, an agency that would be bought by Saatchi & Saatchi in 1986, to prepare the ads. As the campaign's June 1961 radio fact sheet outlined, the Ad Council instructed broadcasters how to inform their audiences:

> Present the image of America's natural and man-made beauties as marred by thoughtless littering that defaces the American scene everywhere, from the nation's Capitol [sic] to a quiet stream in the woods. Stress the cost in millions of dollars annually for cleaning up our highways, city streets, parks, beaches and other public places—the loss in fires caused by debris—the hundreds killed or badly injured through accidents resulting from litter on the highways—the danger to health and safety produced by rubbish. Point out that the outstanding factor in the litter nuisance is individual thoughtlessness and the habit of irresponsibility for the condition of public and private surroundings. Persuade Americans to replace the national litter habit with a feeling of pride in their streets and public places.[50]

The 1961 campaign featured the slogan "Keep America Clean and Beautiful." The tagline, "Every litter bit hurts," reinforced the focus on individual responsibility. The ads decried thoughtless behavior. In a one-minute radio spot, the announcer said:

> A scrap of paper is tossed from a car window . . . a cardboard carton lands beside it . . . a third bit of litter—a tin can—drops with a clunk . . . a fourth bit of litter—this time a banana peel—adds to the mess. One by one the litter bits grow—and *every litter bit hurts!* Hurts the beauty of America. Hurts the budget of America's taxpayers. *You* pay to clean up those mountains of trash! *Your* tax money—millions of dollars every year—go down the drain because, one by one, the litter bits pile up. Who's to blame? Millions of good citizens with the *bad* habit of *unconscious* littering. Carelessness . . . thoughtlessness—these are the underlying reasons for the overwhelming mess that litters the American scene. So—think before you throw. And put every litter bit in your car litterbag . . . the nearest basket . . . the proper container every time. That's how *you can always help keep America clean* and *beautiful!*[51]

By 1962 "Every litter bit hurts" and "Don't be a litterbug" had been added to the possible campaign slogans broadcasters were encouraged to use. Radio stations running the spots also sponsored events with anti-litter themes. Station WINN in Louisville, Kentucky, distributed ten thousand bumper stickers featuring a cleanup and beautification message, and gave away a $25 government bond to listeners each week. Station WDNC in Durham, North Carolina, dispensed ten thousand litterbags, including one to the state's governor. Station KOY in Phoenix handed out litterbags to every car entering the state. In Kansas City, Missouri, both the KMBC radio station and KMBC-TV aired the ads and sponsored a contest for the best suggestion to help keep the city clean. The stations donated 100 litter barrels that were placed at locations around the city.[52]

The 1962 campaign also featured the jingle "Please, please, don't be a litterbug." Six of the radio spots prepared that year included the jingle.[53]

The campaign escalated in 1963, with an edgy style designed to capture people's attention. The year's letter to broadcasters, written by David F. Beard, general director of advertising for the Reynolds Metal Company, warned that "The litterbugs are on the loose" in capital letters and continued: "and we're counting on you take up arms against them. The influence of your station is a big gun in the battle against thoughtless littering. For ammunition, the Advertising Council presents a new anti-litter campaign."[54]

The focus on blame was heightened. One 1963 radio ad said, "Just one piece of litter will do it . . . because bit by bit . . . every litter bit hurts. And most of the time, litter is caused by people who just don't think . . . people who forget that they're throwing their own money away . . . people who become litterbugs. So don't you be a litterbug. Think before you throw . . . and then put that litter in the nearest litter basket."[55] A full-page newspaper ad that same year showed a family at a picnic table. In the next image, the departing family members left the picnic table and surrounding area strewn with trash, while a nearby garbage can stood empty. The copy read, "Don't be a litterbug! Be a bug about litter."

The 1965 ads featured the character Susan Spotless, who served as a reminder to parents to teach their children anti-litter habits. "Well, look who's here," said the announcer in one 1965 radio ad. "It's Susan Spotless . . . dropping a bit of litter. Where? Into the litter-basket . . . where else? If we grown-ups remember—our kids won't forget to Keep America Beautiful."[56]

In 1967 corporate sponsorship of the campaign switched to Best Foods, a division of the Corn Products Sales Company. Its April 1967 letter to broadcasters touted the previous year's effort as "one of the most successful ever sponsored by The Advertising Council. Over $22 million in time and space was donated, with all the forms of media contributing substantially." The recommendations of what broadcasters should tell their audiences included the following suggestion: "Incorporate the fact that litter-prevention activities stimulate citizen pride in a community and inevitably promote and help motivate other cleanup and beautification projects."[57]

The 1968 and 1969 campaigns featured actor and songwriter Henry Gibson, best known for his appearances on *Rowan & Martin's Laugh-In*. He recorded the radio ads, and his poems appeared in the newspaper ads. The June 1969 letter to broadcasters quoted research by Public Opinion Surveys Inc., which noted that 64 percent of the audience said they had heard the Keep America Beautiful campaign on radio. The report referred to the findings as "an amazing performance for these campaigns in terms of advertising awareness."[58]

In keeping with the environmental messages promoted on Earth Day that year, the 1970 campaign marked a departure. Corporate sponsorship changed to the American Can Company. A new ad agency, Marsteller Inc., introduced the slogan "People start pollution. People can stop it." And the overarching message switched from anti-littering to anti-pollution. The Ad Council's August 1970 bulletin announcing the new effort explained that "environmental pollution is a threat to everyone. This campaign, which treats the vast problems of air, water, and ground pollution, has been broadened from the original Keep America Beautiful litter campaign. . . . And, unlike much anti-pollution advertising you may have seen, the main thrust of the program will be to point out ways people can help in the fight against pollution."[59]

The memorable image of the Crying Indian was introduced in 1971. The September letter to broadcasters from W. Howard Chase, the American Can Company's vice president of public affairs, said, "Our hope is to show all people—from cab drivers to corporate presidents—that pollution control is an individual responsibility."[60] In this campaign, the strategy broadened from presenting litter as costly or dangerous to positioning it "as the one pollutant that everyone can help eliminate."[61] Shifting from a focus on litter to the more general problem of pollution contributed to helping Americans realize that more needed to be done to protect the environment.

The fact sheet for the campaign included a new section called "The Environmental Crisis." While the focus remained on individual responsibility, the target audience was broadened to include individual occupations:

Everyone contributes to the pollution problem. Pollution can stem from many acts by individuals—things that most people do each day without even realizing it. People pollute as homemakers, as mothers, as students, as workers, as executives and as elected officials.

People pollute in many different ways; and the beginning of a solution to the problem can only be found when individuals start to examine their actions and face up to their own responsibility. There are many things that person can do to help stop pollution; and if each individual makes some effort, America may find that it has turned the corner in the war to save the environment.[62]

The famous television spot opened with an American Indian paddling a canoe down a stream, which became increasingly polluted with each stroke of his oar.

Viewers watched him observe the garbage floating in the water, the nearby factories spewing smoke, and the waves churning out trash along beaches. After he left his canoe to walk along a littered beach, someone tossed a bag of garbage at his feet. A tear rolled down his cheek as the announcer said, "Some people have a deep and abiding respect for the natural beauty that was once this country—and some people don't! People start pollution. People can stop it!"

The ad prompted viewers to send away for a pamphlet called "71 Things You Can Do to Stop Pollution," which targeted home owners and business leaders alike. For example, it recommended fourteen steps a business owner could take to fight pollution. "Industry has a responsibility for pollution control," the pamphlet read. "Probably the single most important thing the businessman can do is to factor ecological as well as economic considerations into his way of doing business." It encouraged "examining your own plant and production pollution problems" and taking the steps necessary to arrest them. It also recommended taking "an active role in efforts to restore rivers, lakes, and streams to their former natural state."[63]

Corporate responsibility was also directly addressed in some of the print ads. One magazine headline read, "Pollution Control: A Corporate Responsibility." The copy called on businesses to address the issue:

Pollution and pollution abatement have become important aspects of every business. They affect budgets, profit and loss, position in the community, corporate image, even the price of stock in some cases.

Pollution is now a problem that is receiving attention from astute businessmen. Water treatment plants, fume scrubbers and filtration systems, land reclamation, plant beautification, litter prevention, employee education programs, are all types of things industry is doing to help in the pollution fight.[64]

But critics had begun to castigate the focus on individual responsibility. "The damage done by litter is . . . inconsequential compared to the damage done by industrial pollution, but the Ad Council's slogan suggest[s] that individuals . . . are responsible," wrote Keenen Peck in a 1983 article in *The Progressive*.[65] In a 2002 article in *Advertising Age*, which examined the Ad Council's impact on its 60th birthday, John McDonough recalled the Crying Indian campaign: "While different versions of the '70s campaign spots showed smokestacks as well as garbage, critics argued that by placing responsibility for pollution on individuals rather than institutions, the campaign was a powerful political decoy devised by corporate interests to divert public attention from the real issues of industrial waste."[66]

It didn't help the campaign's image when press reports revealed the true heritage of the actor Iron Eyes Cody to be Italian and not "a full blooded Cherokee," as the Ad Council's press release announcing the campaign called him. In a June 2012 interview, Keep America Beautiful spokesman Wallace confirmed that Iron Eyes Cody was born Espera Oscar DeCorti. "He maintained to everyone, to our organization, and to Hollywood that he was a Cherokee," Wallace said. "That was one of the reasons Marsteller wanted him." Discussing the sense of betrayal many felt when they learned that Cody was not American Indian, Wallace said, "When people find out he was Italian, there is this feeling of being personally affected. There was such a deep connection to his nativeness and the themes of that ad."

Need for More Holistic Solutions

After the Crying Indian campaign launched, groups including the Sierra Club and the National Audubon Society asked Keep America Beautiful to join them in supporting bottle bills and making manufacturers find alternatives for wasteful packaging. The environmental groups wanted Keep America Beautiful to move beyond its focus on litter, and the U.S. Environmental Protection Agency (EPA) agreed. In a January 16, 1973, speech, Thomas Williams, then head of the EPA's Solid Waste Division, told his audience that the pollution problem could only be solved if all groups—industry, government, and environmental organizations—agreed on the scope of the issue, the need for two-way communication with the public, and the public's right to receive the full story. In his speech, entitled "A Litter Bit Is Not Enough," Williams argued, "I do not believe [the public's right to receive the full story] can be fulfilled if our major concern is to continue to be public education on the prevention of litter."[67]

The EPA's Williams criticized Keep America Beautiful's Clean Community System, which was "a community-based approach to litter prevention,"[68] where hundreds of well-intentioned communities across the nation worked to remove litter from their neighborhoods—as they still do today. In fact the Clean

Community System campaign was originally the idea of the U.S. Brewers Association, which had pushed hard for Keep America Beautiful to remain focused on litter and not support efforts to restrict packaging.[69] In a 1975 memo, Williams called the approach a public relations campaign used by the industry to "focus the attention of hundreds of communities on anti-littering campaigns. . . . When successfully inaugurated, it tends to abort any local efforts to institute beverage container deposit systems, placing emphasis on street-cleaning and other litter control activities . . . and tends to skew local spending for solid waste management in such a way as to encourage litter cleanup rather than the improved disposal or resource recovery systems."[70]

But Keep America Beautiful's corporate sponsors did not want to support beverage container deposit systems. As bottle bills gained popularity in several states, pressure from the packaging industry within Keep America Beautiful prompted a controversial response from William F. May, chairman of the board of the American Can Company. At a July 22, 1976, board of directors meeting, May called bottle bill supporters "communists" and urged a broad mobilization effort against four bottle bill referendums coming up that November.[71]

After Jack Anderson broadcast this story on his national television show, Williams recommended that the Environmental Protection Agency no longer be an adviser to Keep America Beautiful. The Urban League, the League of Women Voters, and the National Wildlife Federation also resigned. The incident revealed publicly that the pro-industry interests inside Keep America Beautiful were dominating its agenda.[72]

When Keep America Beautiful broadened its focus in the 1980s from litter to recycling, it took an important step toward finding more holistic solutions to the pollution problem. But again, the recycling focus was on what individual Americans could do. Meanwhile, Keep America Beautiful's financial backers expanded to include companies from the waste disposal industry, such as Waste Management Inc. and Browning Ferris. Its focus in the 1990s promoted the use of incineration and landfills to deal with America's growing garbage problem. Since incineration and landfills also hurt the environment, environmental groups and recycling advocates alike objected to Keep America Beautiful's approach.[73]

By the end of the 1990s, Keep America Beautiful's advertising messages reverted back to a focus on litter. In 1998 it released another Crying Indian ad.

Called "Back by Popular Neglect," the ad featured commuters leaving coffee cups and garbage at the bus stop. After the commuters got on the bus, the camera focused on the strewn garbage and a picture of Iron Eyes Cody, displayed on the window of the bus shelter. He was still crying.

In studying the Crying Indian campaign, scholars have agreed with the concerns raised by environmental groups. Finis Dunaway, in an article analyzing visual images in the American environmental movement, argues that "popular imagery" such as the Crying Indian stressed individual decisions and actions, and consequently ignored other explanations for the pollution problem.[74] Dunaway referenced scientist Barry Commoner to illustrate his point. In his 1971 book *The Closing Circle: Nature, Man, and Technology*, Commoner claimed that "decisions made by corporate and government leaders accounted for most of the nation's environmental problems." Dunaway argues that perspectives such as Commoner's "would be submerged by the proliferation of imagery that emphasized individual responsibility."[75]

In a written request for comment, the Ad Council was asked whether the messages in an environmental campaign should target both individuals and corporations alike if the United States hopes to solve its garbage problem. Its August 16, 2012, response focused on the importance of creating public service campaigns that prompt individuals to take action: "Ad Council campaigns are always issue-driven and each effort focuses on inspiring an individual action. Our campaign featuring the Crying Indian with KAB, along with our upcoming recycling effort is no different. We know that in order to confront the issue of reducing waste, we need to remember that it is a shared responsibility. However, ultimately the Ad Council model works best when we are able to provide consumers with awareness about an issue, and education on how they can adopt simple behaviors that change paradigms."

Regarding Keep America Beautiful, the Ad Council's statement read, "KAB takes no position on any legislation (including beverage containers). The organization does not lobby, nor does it challenge, counter or argue with any organizations that do take active legislative positions. Furthermore, it is not the role of the Ad Council to address policy or legislation to regulate corporations."

Despite the controversy, what the Crying Indian campaign did successfully achieve is putting concern about garbage and pollution into the minds and hands of everyone. Iron Eyes Cody's evocative tear did make this campaign one of the most memorable in the history of public service advertising. The Ad Council is right when it claims in its publicity documents that the campaign "did play a role in changing how America thought about litter and pollution."

At the same time, it's also important to understand what happens when the Ad Council directs the power of its public service advertising only toward what individuals should do to help clean up the environment. The shared responsibility of the role of other important actors like corporations and the government gets lost in the Crying Indian's message.

Chapter 8

Beyond Integration

Fighting for Historically Black Colleges

Here was a chance to make a profound difference for African-Americans in need at a time when America was struggling painfully with civil rights issues.

—*Ad Council brochure,* Public Service Advertising That Changed a Nation

The motto ["A Mind Is a Terrible Thing to Waste"], unchanged for more than three decades, has become part of the American vernacular, much like Maxwell House's "Good to the Last Drop," or Nike's "Just Do It!"

—*Marybeth Gasman,* Envisioning Black Colleges: A History of the United Negro College Fund

When Vernon E. Jordan Jr. came from Atlanta to New York in the spring of 1970 to run the United Negro College Fund, he knew that the organization, dedicated to raising money for black colleges, needed greater visibility. After a board member recommended that he see Ed Ney at the ad agency Young & Rubicam (Y&R), the two had lunch. Ney, who would become Y&R's chairman and CEO in 1971, recommended an Ad Council campaign.

The suggestion drew a blank stare from Jordan. "I'd never heard of the Ad Council, and I didn't know a damn thing about advertising," recalled Jordan, later a prominent adviser to President Bill Clinton and now a lawyer in private practice. Jordan served as cochair of the Ad Council's Advisory Committee on Public Issues from 2000 to 2002.

Jordan knew that the story of America's black colleges, with 45,000 students at the time, needed to be told. But his mission came when the United States was just emerging from the tumultuous 1960s and its battles over school integration in the wake of the historic 1954 Supreme Court decision in *Brown v. Board of Education*. Proposing an Ad Council campaign to help raise money for black colleges was bucking the integration tide.

There was another potential problem for the council. Education was traditionally one of its core issues. For several years, the council had conducted a campaign for the Council for Financial Aid to Higher Education, with the slogan "College Is America's Best Friend." To prevent undertaking fundraising campaigns for different groups, the Ad Council had concentrated on one umbrella organization that could distribute money to several organizations within its network. Jordan's request created a dilemma, since the council had turned down similar requests from women's college groups and land grant organizations.[1]

Mark Stroock, then Y&R's senior vice president of corporate accounts, recalled the struggle: "It was difficult to convince the Ad Council that this was a subject of national significance. They were very hard-nosed about accepting new accounts, and they threw in our face the idea—'You are asking for help for blacks when the whole country was on a kick for integration.' We had to argue quite heavily, and Vernon did a good job of preaching to the board."

In his passionate speech to the Ad council board, Jordan spoke of the history and future of African American educational institutions, including Clark-Atlanta University, Morehouse College, Spelman College, and Morris Brown College. He talked about the students at Tennessee's Morristown College and Fisk University. All these institutions, he told the Ad Council, helped Southern cities such as Atlanta play a positive role in the civil rights movement. "The presence of the Atlanta University Center in Atlanta made a difference in that city and in the South, [and] that led the South to the promised land," Jordan said. "These colleges prepared people to be teachers, doctors, and lawyers. By having these colleges, you help the country."

In her book *Envisioning Black Colleges: A History of the United Negro College Fund*, Marybeth Gasman describes how the council responded to Jordan's request for a campaign: "According to Jordan, the UNCF had to argue its case vigorously with the Ad Council to garner its support during the early 1970s because the UNCF was competing with many other worthwhile causes, including the Peace Corps and American Red Cross. The major obstacle was convincing the Ad Council that it needed to create a larger national campaign focused on the black community."[2] Gasman attributes the statement that the council had "never in its history taken on a major campaign in the black community" to her interview with Joe Taylor, the college fund's national campaign director at the time.

The Ad Council disputes that none of its previous campaigns had addressed race relations. It cites four campaigns as evidence: the 1965–66 Better Community Relations effort; the Equal Employment Opportunities campaign from 1965 to 1968, supporting the then new U.S. Equal Employment Opportunity Commission; the Crisis in our Cities/Urban Crisis effort mounted in 1968 and 1969, which had a race relations and Equal Employment Opportunity component focused on reducing inner-city poverty; and the 1970–77 Office of Minority Business Enterprise campaign, a federal government effort to create opportunities and provide financial resources for minority business owners.

The money that would be raised from the effort Jordan proposed to the Ad Council's board would be directly used to help educate and train black students in schools supported by the United Negro College Fund. Previous Ad Council campaigns such as the Better Community Relations effort encouraged everyday citizens to form human relations commissions in their home communities to deal with racial problems, unemployment, juvenile delinquency, and high school retention rates. The goal of the Equal Employment Opportunities campaign was to increase public awareness of the Equal Employment Opportunity Commission's work. The Crisis in Our Cities effort targeted businesses, helping them identify programs that could address urban social problems, especially in inner-city areas. The Minority Business Enterprise campaign used the business press to help the Office of Minority Business Enterprise raise venture capital from American businesses to support minority business owners.

Robert P. Keim, president of the Ad Council from 1966 to 1987, wanted the campaign, according to his memoir. Referring to the race riots that had taken place, Keim wrote: "The country was burning up, for godsake! Vernon Jordan addressed our Board as only a superb barrister could and of course won the day."[3]

Y&R soon went to work. The resulting "A Mind Is a Terrible Thing to Waste" campaign, with its TV, newspaper, magazine, and radio ads linking a lack of education with wasted potential, put the college fund on the map and spotlighted the significant role historically black colleges have played in American education and society.

The college fund traces the influence and visibility of its organization directly to its Ad Council campaign. "The impact of the campaign, whether measured in public recognition, support at the highest levels of national leadership, contributions to UNCF or in college graduates, was felt immediately and has continued over the decades since the first 'A mind is' campaign made its debut in 1972," the college fund said in a statement.

To understand how this campaign generated nearly $3.8 billion from 1972 to 2012 for America's thirty-eight historically black colleges directly supported by the college fund, it's necessary to explore key moments in the history of the civil rights movement that affected African American education. The campaign strategy and messages, which made this effort pivotal in helping more than 400 thousand black students graduate from college, will also be analyzed. Without the scholarships provided by the college fund, these students would not have been likely to receive higher education.

The Segregated South

On December 1, 1955, Rosa Parks was arrested for civil disobedience; by refusing to give up her seat on the crowded Montgomery, Alabama bus, she had violated a state law that required blacks to relinquish their seats to whites if the bus was full. Blacks were also required to sit at the backs of buses.[4]

The incident sparked an unprecedented 381-day boycott of the Montgomery bus system. The struggle for blacks to receive the full benefits of American citizenship was under way, and access to education would be at the heart of the battle.

"Jim Crow" was the label given to the racial caste system that existed in the Southern states between 1877 and the mid-1960s. The name came from a simpleton character created by a white performer who developed skits and songs to mock black people, appealing to the bigotry and hatred of blacks among white audiences.

The racist Jim Crow system institutionalized the idea that blacks were inferior to whites intellectually, culturally, and in every other way. "Newspaper and magazine writers routinely referred to blacks as niggers, coons, and darkies; and worse, their articles reinforced anti-black stereotypes," wrote David Pilgram, a professor of sociology at Ferris State University in Michigan. "Even children's games portrayed blacks as inferior beings."[5]

This occurred despite the fact that passage of the Thirteenth, Fourteenth, and Fifteenth Amendments to the U.S. Constitution had given blacks the same legal protections as whites. The Thirteenth Amendment abolishing slavery passed Congress on January 31, 1865, and was ratified by the states by December 6, 1865. The Fourteenth Amendment, ratified by July 9, 1868, granted citizenship to "all persons born or naturalized in the United States," which included former slaves who had been recently freed. The Fifteenth Amendment, ratified by February 3, 1870, gave black men the right to vote. But the Southern and border states would use the Jim Crow system and a series of tactics—from poll taxes to literacy tests—to prevent blacks from receiving their full rights as American citizens.[6]

As Kimberley Johnson argues in her book, *Reforming Jim Crow: Southern Politics and State in the Age Before Brown*, the education of blacks in the South provided "the starting point on which to ameliorate the worst aspects of the Jim Crow order."[7] Johnson credited Southern white reformers and large foundations such as the Rockefeller family's General Education Board and the Julius Rosenwald Foundation with building rural school programs for black children. (The Rosenwald Foundation built more than five thousand one-room schools, as well as teachers' homes.) While such historic efforts did operate within the institutionalized segregated education system, Johnson points out that the Southern black schools and colleges helped build a solid black middle class.

Access to education helped the black middle class understand the importance of organizations such as the National Association for the Advancement of Colored People (NAACP). Members of this black middle class, "mostly teachers but also social workers, doctors, lawyers, and others, would become the backbone of the NAACP's resurgence in the South, as well as the membership of dozens of local and national organizations that made up black Southern life 'behind the veil,'" Johnson writes.[8]

In the 1920s, Northern foundations, which had long played a strong role in supporting Southern universities, ushered in a new period of improved higher education for blacks in the South. At the beginning of the Jim Crow era, some foundations and state legislatures had forced many Southern black colleges to abandon courses based on the liberal arts in favor of classes that emphasized domestic service and manual labor.[9]Another sign of this was the shift in leadership from white to black at Howard University and Fisk University, Johnson observes.

Leaders of black educational institutions such as Benjamin Mays, the president of Morehouse College, near Atlanta; Horace Mann Bond, the president of Fort Valley (Georgia) State College; and Gordon Hancock, a professor at Virginia Union University in Richmond, all worked to reform the southern Jim Crow system. Hancock, with $10,000 from a Northern donor, founded the Torrance School of Race Relations at Virginia Union in 1931, the first of its kind. "Until its demise in 1938, the school promoted discussion and fact-finding concerning race relations," according to Raymond Gavins's article "Gordon Blaine Hancock: A Black Profile from the New South."[10]

Fisk University president Charles Johnson worked with the Roosevelt administration during the New Deal to create policies that would help poor Southern farm workers. He coauthored a report, *The Collapse of Cotton Tenancy*, that was instrumental in the passage of the Bankhead-Jones Tenant Farm Act in 1937.[11] The act created a system of mortgage loans to help rural families become farm owners.[12]

Southern black colleges represented what Johnson calls "the most visible vestiges of the political, civil, and social citizenship that had been stripped from African Americans in the wake of the rise of the Jim Crow order." The second Morrill Act of 1890 had provided federal funds specifically for black universities. As a result, it was impossible for the Jim Crow system to eliminate Southern black colleges. As Johnson explains, "Because the federal government and private foundations supported much of the funding for the maintenance of these colleges, state governments could not simply erase them, as they had done with so many other aspects of black citizenship. Because of the independence (albeit highly constrained) of black colleges ... these institutions became important sites of inter- and intraracial cooperation and organization as well as conflict."[13]

Southern black universities became instrumental in building a foundation for the coming civil rights struggle. They also provided what Johnson called a crucial "organizational and intellectual base to retreat to and regroup" for Southern African American leaders who lacked political power in the Jim Crow order.[14]

The first key step these leaders took was to move beyond the dominant model that had been established for black higher education, represented by Booker T. Washington's Tuskegee Institute. As Johnson writes, this "industrial education model, in which training in trades such as farming, blacksmithing, and domestic service was put forward as not only adequate but the limit for black higher education," had dominated thinking about black schooling until Washington's death in 1915.[15] But even white leaders interested in reforming black education realized that this model would not prepare black students to thrive in a modern society.

When the Great Depression hit, Northern religious organizations that had once supported Southern black universities began cutting back. "No southern state fully funded black institutions to the extent that they were entitled to under the Morrill Act," Johnson recounts, giving them on average only 43 percent of the money they should have received.

This disparity in funding helped lay the groundwork for the legal strategy that organizations such as the NAACP would use to demonstrate that separate was not equal. The Supreme Court had ruled in the 1896 *Plessy v. Ferguson* case that states could require people of different races to use "separate but equal" segregated facilities. But by the 1930s it was clear that the Southern states had not provided truly equal facilities to blacks. "Nowhere in the South did funding for African American education even come close to funding for whites," Johnson writes.[16]

In the end, Southern states would have to choose: either spend considerable money creating a separate higher education system for blacks that equaled what whites received, or desegregate the white state university system.

The Rise of the United Negro College Fund

The birth of the United Negro College Fund in 1944 would connect Southern black colleges with an expanded group of corporations and foundations in New York City. Frederick D. Patterson, then president of the Tuskegee Institute, believed that a cooperative fund-raising effort between Southern colleges and universities would yield better results than if each institution asked the same funders for money individually. The college fund was envisioned as a consortium that would help black colleges, "typically dependent on chance beneficence, to establish a permanent vehicle for raising money."[17]

Black Southern university leaders generally agreed with other black intellectuals who favored the liberal arts educational focus of W. E .B. Du Bois, rather than the Booker T. Washington self-sufficiency approach. But disagreements remained over what the best strategy should be to address the injustice suffered by blacks. Some Southern black college leaders wanted to reform the Jim Crow system from within, while other college leaders preferred the NAACP's activist approach as the only way to achieve permanent change.

Tuskegee's Patterson, who modeled his idea for the college fund after the March of Dimes, was considered a conservative who chose to work within the system. "He believed that funding black education was a method by which blacks could achieve full rights as citizens," according to Gasman.[18] But he faced an immediate crisis on his hands when he took over as president of Tuskegee in 1935. The institution was running a deficit of $50,000 a year.

Possibilities for foundation funding appeared bleak. Gasman argues that the "golden age of fundraising" had ended with the stock market crash of October 1929. Some wealthy donors had not yet recovered. Others, bitter about the Roosevelt administration's imposition of higher taxes on the wealthy, were not giving to causes as they once did. These wealthy donors believed that it was the role of philanthropy, rather than the federal government, to help needy causes. "When black college presidents approached wealthy individuals," Gasman relates, "their response was predictable: Roosevelt took our money, you go and ask him for your support. Don't come back to us."[19]

A 1943 U.S. Office of Education report confirmed Patterson's fears about the long-term financial viability of Southern black colleges. The report said that between 1930 and 1943, the overall income of Southern black colleges had decreased 15 percent, while income from private foundations had decreased 50 percent. Smaller well-known black schools such as Roger Williams University (Nashville), Mary Allen Junior College (Crockett, Texas), and the Howe Institute (Memphis) closed between 1930 and 1943. Others merged to improve their chances. Atlanta University became the graduate university of the Atlanta University Center, which also included Spelman and Morehouse.[20]

Patterson knew he still needed help from donors. He liked the March of Dimes model because it appealed to a broad population of average citizens rather than only focusing on a small number of wealthy donors. He called a meeting of other black college leaders and published his plan in the black-owned

Pittsburgh Courier. As he wrote in the *Courier* article, "The coming together of the private black colleges out of concern for our needs; the fact that we were not going to get the amount of money we had been receiving from our former sources; and the innovative fundraising practices of other organizations—all of these factors contributed to the formation of the UNCF."[21]

Eighteen presidents of Southern black colleges came to Patterson's meeting, but not everyone liked his idea. Gasman relates that Buell Gallagher of Talladega College in Alabama came to the meeting with a list of objections. Fisk University's Thomas Elsa Jones objected to the distance potentially placed between individual donors and the colleges, with the college fund in the middle. He used the Community Chest system—the precursor to today's United Way system—as an example: "The unification of the appeal is sometimes weakened by the distance that develops between the donor and the particular problem or institution which secures his interest."[22]

Patterson knew he still needed help from donors. His initial appeal to John D. Rockefeller Jr. of the General Education Board, founded in 1903 to aid education in the United States, was successful. Rockefeller and the Julius Rosenwald Fund would give the college fund $25,000. The college fund then created a distribution formula that would give more to member colleges that were financially weaker, while a set percentage of all money raised would go to all the member institutions, regardless of size. There was also a solicitation policy that would allow member colleges to seek donations for their individual institutions only during a specified time period. If presidents violated the solicitation policy, Patterson would explain the effect this way: "If you go to the donor ahead of the college fund, he may give you five thousand dollars or five hundred dollars, when he would give the college fund a hundred thousand dollars, because the cause is a bigger cause. Now, the only reason for you to have membership in the college fund is because you believe you can do better as a member of the Fund than you can by yourself. You're not bound. You come in here. You ask for membership. You get it. You can get out of it any time you feel that membership in the Fund is not valuable to you as what you can do for yourself outside the Fund."[23]

The college fund's early relationship with John D. Rockefeller Jr. and his General Education Board underscored the delicate balancing act the college presidents had to play as they fought to strengthen their institutions. They needed to win the approval of powerful white funders, without appearing too impatient in their quest to reform the Jim Crow system. An association with Rockefeller gave the college fund the credibility it needed in the foundation world to avoid being labeled too radical or even "communist" for simply trying to improve the plight of Southern blacks.[24] As Gasman puts it, Rockefeller's "involvement assuaged the fears of more conservative donors. In a time of legalized segregation and newly emerging fears of Soviet domination, these donors were less likely to question the black college curriculum, to accuse black colleges of Communist affiliation, or to worry about these institutions supporting radical solutions to the race problem; they knew Rockefeller Jr. was involved."[25]

For Rockefeller, the college fund represented a chance to improve the public image of the oil company built by his father John D. Rockefeller Sr., and to blunt criticism that the company was monopolistic. Rockefeller Jr. would not only give money; he was willing to write letters and speak publicly on behalf of the college fund.[26]

With this generous support came white paternalism. Rockefeller handpicked a group of white people to work at the college fund. He also recruited business leaders to head up fund-raising campaigns in cities. "Specifically," Gasman writes, "he sought individuals who, like himself, saw the UNCF as a solution that neither undermined capitalism nor involved government intervention."[27]

In working to obtain the support of the white fund-raising establishment, it was hard for black colleges to spark the kind of wholesale reform needed to eradicate the Jim Crow system. But the college fund would confront an even greater challenge in the wake of the Brown decision, the effects of which would challenge its very existence.

Brown v. Board of Education

When Rosa Parks sat down in her Montgomery bus in 1955, she symbolized resistance to more than six decades of daily indignities, large and small, that African Americans had suffered in the Jim Crow South.[28] The inferior education system for blacks was an indignity that lay at the heart of the *Brown v. Board of Education* decision. In deciding the *Brown* case, the Supreme Court overruled *Plessy v. Ferguson* by declaring that separating children in public schools on the basis of race was unconstitutional. The NAACP's argument, that "separate could never be equal in a political order that was based on explicit as well as hidden inequalities based on race and class," had prevailed.[29]

But this crucial civil rights victory created the very problem Vernon Jordan had to overcome in his quest for an Ad Council campaign. If the law now required schools to integrate, what purpose did a black college serve? As Gasman observes, "The UNCF and its member colleges faced a difficult task: supporting integration while also showing commitment to the continuation of their unique institutions."[30]

Worse, the Brown decision focused attention on the inferiority of black educational institutions, reinforcing the perception that black colleges were unnecessary, when in fact they provided critical educational opportunities for many black students. What *Brown* didn't do, as Derrick Bell argues in his 2004 book *Silent Covenants: Brown v. Board of Education and the Unfulfilled Hopes of Racial Reform*, was to grant educational equity to all of America's black children. "Traditional statements of freedom and justice for all, the usual fare on celebratory occasions, serve to mask continuing manifestations of inequality that beset and divide people along lines of color and class,"[31] Bell writes.

The college fund members wanted to provide as much educational equity as they could to black students. By the time of the *Brown* decision, the college fund had raised $14 million in its first decade between 1944 and 1954. These funds were used for training better teachers, updating classrooms and lab equipment, providing scholarships, and constructing new buildings. The fact that black colleges did provide unique opportunities for their students would give the college fund some of its chief ammunition to justify their need to continue.

Two cases, *Sipuel v. Board of Regents* in 1948 and *Sweatt v. Painter* in 1950, established that "the traditions and culture that made up the college environment were important."[32] Ada Sipuel was denied entrance to the University of Oklahoma law school because of her race. Similarly, Heman Sweatt was denied admission to the law school at the University of Texas based on his skin color. In Sipuel's case, the Supreme Court ruled that, based on the Fourteenth Amendment, states had to provide a graduate education for blacks that was equal to what whites received. The University of Oklahoma responded by hiring three black lawyers to serve as faculty and then roping off an area in the state capitol building that they called the "Negro law school." The Supreme Court later declared this practice unconstitutional.[33]

Although Sweatt had lost his case at the state level, the Supreme Court ruled that the University of Texas had to admit all students regardless of race. Gasman relates that the Sweatt case in particular was important for the later *Brown* decision because the Supreme Court had now said that "separate but equal" was not equal. The Sipuel and Sweatt cases also declared that the role of the educational environment, such as the facilities, faculty, and college traditions, all factored into what was considered an equal education. Black students needed to learn the same material as whites and have access to the same type of institutional support.[34]

For the college fund, these court decisions supported the argument that "the unique traditions of black colleges [provided] an educational environment that was, for some students, more suitable than that of predominantly white institutions."[35] Since Sipuel and Sweatt had been handpicked by the NAACP as good test cases, these students were academically prepared. But, as Gasman notes, the college fund had to grapple with whether some black students could operate on a level playing field in predominantly white institutions if their educational background was not equal: "The UNCF leaders began to ask themselves what would happen when the larger segment of the black student population, which came from unequally funded secondary schools and consisted of first-generation college students, moved into predominantly white institutions. Would they receive an equal education? Was it possible that a separate, identically funded environment could better provide an equal education—one that was caring, black-centered, and successful at raising the expectations of black students?"[36]

The college fund had a legitimate argument for the continued existence of black colleges, but it would now have to accelerate the pace of its fund-raising if it hoped to modernize the schools' curricula and facilities. John S. Lash, writing in "The Umpteenth Crisis in Negro Higher Education" in 1951, stressed that "in a word, the Negro colleges must accomplish in a comparatively brief time what the courts have decreed has not been accomplished in some fifty years: they must bring themselves into substantial equality with erstwhile 'white' institutions."[37]

Tuition became a big issue for black students trying to attend predominantly white colleges, and it would become one of the college fund's principal arguments in asking for money to support black colleges. As Lash noted:

It is clear that there will be an increase in the cost of higher education for the Negro student in the integrated university. Furthermore, it is clear that the increased costs will tend to limit the number of Negro students. Undoubtedly, a difference of several hundred dollars a year will be prohibitive for many Negro parents, particularly since there is nothing in the proposed pattern of integration which will raise their standard of living. The fact that the Negro higher education has been held inferior may be explained in part by the more fundamental fact that it has been in a sense at least, a bargain-basement education, available to comparatively large numbers of students at a comparatively cheap price.[38]

Following the passage of the 1964 Civil Rights Act and the 1965 Voting Rights Act, enrollments at black colleges increased—with 100,000 students participating.[39] Southern black students played a key role in helping the burgeoning civil rights movements shift from courtrooms to the marches, freedom rides, boycotts, voter registration drives, and sit-ins carried out on the streets in the Southern states. "The involvement of college students brought enthusiasm and optimism to the movement—younger, more impatient activists who escalated the civil rights struggle and broadened its base," observes Raymond D'Angelo in *The American Civil Rights Movement: Readings and Interpretations.*[40]

Changes were also taking place at the college fund. In 1966 Steven J. Wright, who had served as president of both Fisk University and Bluefield State College in West Virginia, took over as the college fund's president. Wright was determined to move beyond the paternalistic fund-raising model established by Rockefeller. But difficulties remained. Wright clashed with advertising giant David Ogilvy, who was then chairman of the college fund's mostly white board of directors. According to Wright's account in Gasman's book, he disagreed with Ogilvy over who had the authority to hire the college fund's staff. "I don't think that a chairman of the board ought to be involved in choosing the personnel that's going to work with you if you are going to be the chief administrative officer. . . . I made it very clear [to him]," Wright said.

Wright eventually left because of the disagreements. When Vernon Jordan, a Howard University Law School graduate, arrived in 1970, he was seen by the college fund's board as "young, energetic, and willing to fight for a cause."[41] He took over at a time when growing signs of the difficult economy to come were already present.

Forest Long's Lasting Achievement

Jordan's professional and personal connections helped him establish a relationship with the Y&R ad agency before he approached the Ad Council. Alex Kroll had just become creative director of Y&R in 1971 when the council asked Y&R to tackle the college fund campaign. At age thirty-three, he had been handed responsibility for unifying all of Y&R's advertising across the agency's global domain. Managing a client's expectations, especially after the tumultuous 1960s, when companies relied on ad creators to explain to them "what the flower children really wanted," as Kroll said, was part of the job. So was dealing with artistic temperaments.

The college fund assignment was challenging. "How do you make an appeal that was not just about black, or brown, or white skin, but about something else that was unarguable—that every kid deserved the chance to fulfill his or her potential?" Kroll wondered. He knew that the black colleges were in rough financial shape, but he knew little about their history. It was Y&R copywriter Forest Long, and fellow Y&R colleague Paul Rubenstein, who visited ten black colleges, where they met with college presidents and attended classes.

On that research trip, Long was struck by what he saw and heard. "These kids wouldn't have gone to college if it hadn't been for UNCF," said Long, who was quoted in the Ad Council publication *Public Service Advertising That Changed a Nation.* "It was these schools or no education. That made quite an impression on us. Then we came back and started thinking about what we could do."

Kroll describes Long as a tall, lanky, reticent, "Gary Cooper" type, who developed a passion for giving young black people the chance to get a college education. Long was familiar with an ad campaign Y&R had created in the late 1960s for the New York Urban Coalition. It had featured cinema verité spots that focused on issues affecting blacks in New York City, such as the lack of job opportunities and substandard housing. The slogan for the effort—"Give jobs. Give money. Give a damn."—influenced Long.

When Long thought he had the right slogan for the college fund campaign, he made an appointment to see Kroll. The storyboards Long brought to the meeting, early sketches of what the eventual 1972 "Don't Waste a Mind" TV ad would be, showed the face of a black man slowly fading away. Long presented his ideas slowly to Kroll, punctuating each comment with a lengthy, thoughtful pause. Nearing the end of his presentation, he raised his voice, nearly shouting the slogan he wanted: "A mind is a hell of a thing to waste."

Kroll disliked the swear word. "There was something in Forrest that wanted to take the profanity from the 'Give jobs. Give money. Give a damn.' campaign up a notch," Kroll remembers. "I told him I liked the commercial and the essence of the message. But there was something about the word 'hell' that seemed trashy and not serious. It was something you would say in a bar, and I thought it would be offensive to faculty, alumni, students, and potential contributors. It was a little demeaning."

Long remained seated while Kroll explained his objection. When Kroll finished speaking, Long slowly stood up. Without a word, he dropped the storyboards on the floor and left the office. "I was stunned," Kroll recalls. "I didn't know if he had resigned from the agency, or quit the account. I had to pick up the storyboards myself." At the time, Kroll didn't realize just how much Long had come to care about the cause he was writing advertising copy for. The rejection of even a single word mattered a great deal to him.

Meanwhile, the college fund didn't like the profanity either. Joseph Taylor, the college fund's campaign manager at the time, recalled the debate over it in Gasman's book: "We sat right up there on that fifth floor [at Y&R] and argued the whole afternoon on one word. . . . Somebody said, we had at that time, too many presidents who were ministers and they would object to the word 'hell.'"[42]

The day after Long left Kroll's office in anger, he requested a second meeting. When the copywriter arrived, he said only one word to Kroll: "Terrible." Fearing that Long was about to go into another "adolescent snit"—his description of Long's behavior the day before—Kroll asked: "What's terrible?" Long took a deep breath, his impatience evident. Finally, he said: "A mind is a terrible thing to waste."

"Okay," Kroll said. Long had his slogan.

The slogan would endure for the next forty years. The line would be repeated by presidents in speeches and mangled by vice presidential candidate Dan Quayle in 1988. When Mel Brooks used it in his 1993 movie *Men in Tights*, Kroll knew that the line had entered America's lexicon. And he credited the college fund with having the good sense to never change it.

In its publication *Public Service Advertising That Changed a Nation*, the Ad Council noted that when the campaign first launched, "no one dared imagine how many young lives would be radically altered for the better. By sticking to a singular message that every deserving child should go to college, more and more African-American teens are able to realize their dreams."[43]

The slogan, accompanied by strong visual messages, made the United Negro college fund a household name. Before the campaign, the organization "was not well known outside the black intellectual and white business communities," Gasman reminds us.[44] Surveys done by the college fund in 2012 found that 91 percent of all Americans and 98 percent of all African Americans recognized the slogan. More than half of Americans and 86 percent of African Americans associated the phrase with the United Negro College Fund.

Making the Miracle Happen

As the image of a black man's face faded in the powerful 1972 TV spot "Don't Waste a Mind," the voice-over said, "There are people born every day who can make peace, cure disease, create art, abolish injustice and end hunger, but if they don't get an education, they may never get a chance. A mind is a terrible thing to waste." At the end of the ad, the words "Give to the United Negro College Fund" appeared on the screen.

What the 1972 campaign did, according to Gasman, was to help all Americans understand what blacks experienced and how they viewed the world: "UNCF leaders' willingness to consider words like 'terrible' and 'hell' in their ads attests to the seriousness that they wished to convey to the American public: black realities, stark choices."[45]

When the 1973 campaign launched, the advertising messages focused on America's untapped brainpower. "We cannot afford to deny any qualified person the opportunity of college training," wrote Chester Fisher, vice president and director of urban and environmental affairs for insurance company

Metropolitan Life, to newspaper advertising directors. Metropolitan Life was the corporate sponsor assigned to the effort.[46] The advertising fact sheet accompanying Fisher's letter outlined the stark need: "Seventy percent of the students at the UNCF colleges come from families making $5,000 a year or less."[47]

By positioning the black colleges as national assets, the very argument Vernon Jordan had made to the Ad Council, the campaign aimed to make Americans aware that everyone had a stake in the future of black children. The fact sheet advised media advertising directors to "explain that this is an urgent campaign aimed at benefiting the total American Society and not just one element of it . . . a flow of trained professional people of all colors is needed to meet the challenges of our times." It also recommended stressing "the advantages of achieving an integrated society."[48]

The advertising in 1973 took a two-pronged approach. Some ads focused on what black students could achieve with a college education, while others appealed to wealthy donors. One print ad told the story of Harvard Stephens. "He was born in a one-room house in Newell, Alabama. The youngest of nine children locked in a cycle of poverty and ignorance that has shrouded black America for 200 years." The ad informed readers about how he had graduated from Talladega College and then went on to medical school.

A second print ad, equally poignant, was aimed at well-off parents who could afford to give their children riding lessons or straighten crooked teeth. This ad said:

> If you can afford to give your children the best, and often most expensive, things in life, you're lucky.
>
> Take riding lessons. A two-year-old gelding, stable fees, riding habit, and lessons can easily cost $2,000. And that blue ribbon at the horse show would probably be worth every penny it cost.
>
> But there are some families that aren't so lucky. Families whose incomes are so low that meat on the table is a rare luxury. Families who watch their children approach college age with the certain knowledge that there will be nothing for them after high school but marriage, babies, and forty years of labor.
>
> Barring a miracle.

The United Negro College Fund is trying to make the miracle happen. We support 40 private, predominantly black colleges that help 45,000 students break out of the urban ghettos and rural backwaters of this country into 20th century America.

We know there's a place for them. We know we can help them find it. All we need is money.

$2,000 will turn a kid into a crackerjack rider. But it will also send a kid to college for a year.

Please. Send a check for $1.00, $20.00, $100.00 to the United Negro College Fund.

A Mind Is a Terrible Thing to Waste.[49]

The 1975 campaign added testimonials. One radio spot recounted the story of Norman Francis, then president of Xavier University. A college fund scholarship had made all the difference in his life. "Education is the bridge between opportunity and despair," Francis said in the ad.[50]

Reminding Americans of the nation's racist past became an important theme in the 1976 effort. As one radio spot explained, rampant discrimination had also occurred in Northern states:

In 1833, Prudence Crandall, a young Quaker, opened a school for Black girls in Connecticut. The villagers tried to burn it, they refused to sell her food or medicine. They made it legal to punish outsiders . . . still, Black children from Boston, New York, and Philadelphia came to the school. Then the state passed a law prohibiting the establishment of Negro schools. Miss Crandall disobeyed and was sent to jail. The law didn't stop Blacks from learning. And it didn't stop others from helping, despite the danger. Thanks to a continuing tradition of support for Black education, the United Negro College Fund has been able to help Black students change the course of their lives at UNCF schools. Supporting Black education won't cost your life or liberty anymore. Today, it just costs money.[51]

INVEST IN AMERICA'S GREATEST NATURAL RESOURCE.

Liabilities? Or, assets? Investing in the United Negro College Fund can help make the difference. Because some of these high school students won't be able to go to college on their own.

Your investment in UNCF helps support 41 private, four-year colleges and graduate schools. Colleges that enroll as many as 48,000 students. And when they graduate, those students return to the community with fresh ideas about old problems. With skills that make companies as well as communities work. And with a real chance to improve their standard of living. So, everybody benefits.

Invest in the United Negro College Fund by sending your check to: Box B, United Negro College Fund, 500 E. 62nd Street, New York, N.Y. 10022. So your dollars can make America's greatest resource even greater.

No one can do it alone.
GIVE TO THE UNITED NEGRO COLLEGE FUND.
A mind is a terrible thing to waste.

A Public Service of This Magazine & The Advertising Council **Ad Council**

This 1978 "Invest in America's Greatest Natural Resource" newspaper ad helped spotlight the significant role historically black colleges played in American education and society. (UNCF)

One print ad continued the theme by featuring a woman representing Prudence Crandall, who was dressed in early nineteenth-century clothing, her hands bound behind her back with a rope.

By 1980 the campaign had raised $19 million for the college fund.[52] To reach the $2 million fund-raising goal set for 1981, the advertising featured musicians Billy Davis Jr. and Marilyn McCoo, previously the lead vocalists in the 5th Dimension. In one thirty-second radio spot, the couple alternately sang and talked about how the college fund had "helped thousands of blacks fulfill their potential in walks of life where they couldn't walk before."[53]

The role American businesses played in supporting the college fund was featured in the 1984 campaign. One print ad, directed at readers of business newspapers and magazines, showed a smiling young African American wearing his college graduation cap and gown. The headline read: "Why General Motors, Ford, and Chrysler Put Thousands Every Year toward the Development of New Ideas."

Powerful TV ads such as the 1987 "Bus" spot drove home the point that the difference between opportunity and despair for many young African Americans was a college fund scholarship. The ad opened with the image of a bus coming down the road, and a mother rejoicing that her son had just been accepted to college. "But tuition's so high, Mama," the son said. "There's a way," the mother replied. "There's got to be a way." The son caught the bus that took him on his college journey. But at the end of the spot, another young man was left standing alone, watching the departing bus. The announcer said, "The fact is, for each one we reach, there's another one we can't. Not without funds. And, if we can't reach them, chances are nobody can."[54]

Over the years, several American presidents would recognize the significance of the college fund. According to a college fund statement, John F. Kennedy donated $500, the proceeds of the Pulitzer Prize money for his book *Profiles in Courage*, to the college fund and invited member colleges to meet with him. Barack and Michelle Obama contributed $260,000 to the college fund, which included $125,000 from Obama's Nobel Peace Prize.

Perhaps most important, the campaign served as a catalyst to create "a huge change in America's attitudes toward race and education," as the college fund said in a 2012 statement: "Forty years ago, when the first campaign was released, the idea that African Americans should—or even could—go to college was not widely held. Today, African Americans attend almost every college and university. . . . the country is led by an African American president and first lady, both of whom have built remarkable careers on the best education America has to offer. The huge increase in contributions to UNCF suggests that forty years of 'A mind is' campaigns, [and] hundreds of millions of impressions, played an important role in the growing acceptance of the idea implicit in the phrase."[55]

Looking back through the years, Y&R's Alex Kroll believes copywriter Forest Long had "tapped into something deeper than some of us understood." He had tapped into America's heart, and opened its mind.

Chapter 9

Fighting Back

McGruff Shows Americans How to Take a Bite Out of Crime

You want a friend in Washington? Get a dog.

—Harry S. Truman

The call came in over the police car's radio. "Car 38, we have a 10-60 in progress," the dispatcher said. Adman Jack Keil, seated in the back of a New York City police cruiser that night in September 1979, was on a ride-along to discover what police officers thought about a potential public service advertising (PSA) campaign to fight crime.

Fear of crime was at an all-time high in the United States. Citizens said in surveys they were ready to help, but would the police let them? Up until now, officers had discouraged public assistance. But without the cooperation of officers on the street, Keil knew the campaign would be doomed from the start.

The two officers in Car 38 weren't happy about having an ad executive assigned to their shift—so they decided to have some fun. "We have a crime in progress," one officer said as he steered the cruiser down Central Park West without any lights or siren. At Sixty-Eighth Street, the officer turned the wrong way down a one-way street. When the cruiser veered up on the sidewalk with no crime scene in sight, Keil was on to the officers' game. The public safety dispatcher radio code for a 10-60 refers to a lock-out, hardly the "crime in progress" that the officer pretended it was.

Given that treatment, Keil braced himself for the scorn the officers would likely heap on the idea of using advertising as a crime prevention tool. "Do you resent the public helping the police fight crime?" he asked. He expected the officers to dismiss such efforts as inexperienced do-gooders impeding the pros.

He was wrong. "If the public does not help, we're lost," one officer said. The cops were concerned themselves about crime growth and needed the country's help to stop it. In Keil's mind, this realization validated the need for what would become the Ad Council's Take a Bite Out of Crime campaign, featuring an affable cartoon character named McGruff. No other research done on the campaign would be more important than what Keil learned that night.

Rampant Crime

McGruff the Crime Dog took more than a bite out of crime; he made a cultural impact still felt today. He was first introduced in February 1980 for a crime prevention campaign that continues to run thirty-three years later. The famed PSA was created to reassure a cynical and scared public that the government took their fears seriously. By any measure, the campaign was an extraordinary success. The McGruff spot isn't remembered for its catchy jingle or tagline; it's a potent reminder that a PSA can change lives in a positive way. Consider: in 1984, a Justice Department crime survey found that burglaries and theft had hit their lowest level in the twelve-year history of the survey. FBI figures at the same time noted a 7 percent drop in serious crimes.[1]

McGruff addressed a national concern that had been festering since the mid-1960s. May 1965 marked the first time a majority of polled Americans listed crime as the top problem facing the nation. President John Kennedy had been killed by a sniper's gunfire, and the assassinations of Martin Luther King Jr. and Robert Kennedy would follow before the decade drew to a close.

President Lyndon Johnson responded to the polls by creating the President's Commission on Law Enforcement and the Administration of Justice, which spent $2.5 million over the next two years and made its recommendations in a February 1967 report titled "The Challenge of Crime in a Free Society." Echoing the policy approaches of Johnson's "Great Society" anti-poverty and education initiatives, the commission called for gun control legislation, improved training of police officers, better education for citizens, and more research about crime.[2]

Some of these recommendations were included in the Safe Streets and Control Act of 1968, which created the Department of Justice's Law Enforcement Assistance Administration (LEAA)—a way to give local police agencies federal money to improve law enforcement activities. A decade later, funds from the LEAA would be used to start the crime prevention campaign. The bulk of

What business does a handsome dog like me have with a top cat like you?

My name's McGruff, and it's my business to help prevent crime. I think it should be your business, too—to teach your employees how to protect themselves. Just send for my business kit —it'll help you develop a program that teaches your employees how to make their homes burglar-proof, make their neighborhoods safer, even how not to get mugged. And, while you're at it, get in touch with the cops—they can help you out. So now you're probably wondering (like a top cat businessman should), what's in it for you. That's easy. When your company works harder for your people, your people work harder for your company.

So take the time, and...

TAKE A BITE OUT OF CRIME

McGruff, Crime Prevention Coalition,
20 Banta Place, Hackensack, NJ 07601
Please send me lots of information on
Crime Prevention.

Name:_____

Company:_____

Address:_____

City:_____ State:_____ Zip:_____

A message from the Crime Prevention Coalition, this publication and The Ad Council. © 1980 The Advertising Council, Inc.

This 1980 newspaper ad helped introduce McGruff the Crime Dog to a nation eager to fight crime. (National Crime Prevention Council) the $300 million given to LEAA in the first year increased the number of police officers in communities and gave them equipment—from assault rifles to small mechanical robots—to help fight crime. The law also permitted wiretappings and established the first major restrictions on handgun purchases.[3]

With the election of President Richard Nixon, crime prevention shifted from a focus on the societal causes of crime to an approach centered on individual responsibility. Nixon promised to reverse what he considered the soft approach to crime control practiced under Democratic presidents by pushing for mandatory minimum sentences, fewer pretrial releases for multiple offenders, and the appointment of judges who would be tough on crime. The 1968 Republican platform included a section on crime control: "We must re-establish the principle that men are accountable for what they do, that criminals are responsible for their crimes, that while the youth's environment may help to explain the man's crime, it does not excuse that crime." Nixon replaced Johnson's War against Poverty with a War against Crime.[4]

But the new president could not change social realities. Crime rates continued to rise, becoming one of three key issues dominating national concern throughout the 1970s. The trend in crimes per 100,000 people, measured by the FBI, had been climbing steadily from 363.5 in 1970 to nearly 549.5 in 1979. Roughly one-third of the 9.7 murders per 100,000 people in 1979 were committed by a person the victim had never met. The random nature of many crimes only intensified the fear.[5]

The Democratic administration of Jimmy Carter focused more on the environment, nuclear arms control, and human rights than crime. This opened the door for California governor Ronald Reagan, the Republican nominee in the 1980 presidential election, to attack Carter as being weak on crime. With Reagan as president, a get-tough-on-crime mood swept the country, fueled in part by escalating fears that the mayhem was unstoppable.[6] An eight-day killing spree by two nineteen-year-old friends John Lesko and Michael Travaglia in western Pennsylvania over the end-of-year holidays in 1979 captured headlines. Dubbed the "kill for thrill" case, Lesko and Travaglia murdered four people—including a police officer—between December 31, 1979, and January 3, 1980, for money, for a vehicle, and for their idea of sadistic fun.[7]

With President Reagan's push for law and order, government leaders increasingly favored protecting crime victims and punishing offenders. One sign of the more conservative attitude toward crime came in Supreme Court Chief Justice Warren Burger's speech to the American Bar Association in February 1981. When Burger, appointed by President Nixon, stepped to the microphone, he let loose a tirade against violent offenders. Calling society "impotent," he asked the crowd of lawyers, "Why do we show such indignation over alien terrorists and such tolerance for the domestic variety? Are we not hostages within the borders of our own self-styled enlightened, civilized country?" His recommendation to battle "the reign of terror in American cities" called for a greater emphasis on deterrence, including "swift arrest, prompt trial, certain penalty, and—at some point—finality of judgment."[8]

His audience, and the nation, seemed to agree. A *Time* magazine report noted that the lawyers interrupted the speech eight times to applaud. A *New York Times* editorial said the speech hit a nerve with "an entire generation of citizens who dread the city streets and, in their fear, feel deprived of elementary rights." David Armstrong, then president-elect of the National District Attorneys Association, praised Burger for "exposing the cracks in our system before they get worse and the system breaks apart."

A steady dose of media coverage about crime followed. A week before President Reagan was shot, a March 23,1981, cover story in *Time* warned that "crimes are becoming more brutal, more irrational, more random—and therefore all the more frightening."[9] *Newsweek*'s cover feature that same day reported how "Americans are experiencing crime—and their fear of it—as a national epidemic."[10] *U.S. News and World Report* published a special report on July 13, 1981, called "The People's War against Crime," which described how "harried Americans . . . fed up with being victimized by crime . . . are doubling up their fists and fighting back."[11]

Within this volatile climate, the street-smart hound dog McGruff was introduced. In a clear, concrete campaign, he told Americans what they could do to fight back through simple measures, such as locking doors and reporting any suspicious activities. The country, already primed to receive such advice, embraced him.

No Fear Messages

To appreciate McGruff's effectiveness, it's important to understand his complicated genesis. Take a Bite Out of Crime was an unusual campaign by Ad Council standards. As America's first national crime prevention effort, which included about $300,000 in taxpayer money from the Department of Justice the first year, it would likely receive considerable public scrutiny. To demonstrate its accountability, Justice insisted that an independent group should evaluate the effectiveness of the effort, something that had not been undertaken for previous Ad Council campaigns. The campaign's second sponsor—what would become the National Crime Prevention Council—didn't exist at the time the McGruff character was created in 1979.

The Ad Council had rejected the idea of a national crime prevention campaign when the Justice Department first came knocking in 1977. Included in FBI director Clarence Kelly's proposal had been the use of fear messages: Americans would be told that the world was a bad place and that they should buy deadbolt locks to stay safe. The Ad Council thought this "Fortress America" approach would be ignored by an already frightened public, and it sent the FBI back to the drawing board. As a member of the council's Public Policy Committee responsible for deciding on campaigns, Leo Perlis, then director of the AFL-CIO's Community Services Division, heard Kelly's proposal and became intrigued with the idea.

Perlis met with Kelly; Milton Rector, then head of the Newark, New Jersey–based nonprofit National Council on Crime and Delinquency (NCCD); and Ferris Lucas, a board member of the National Sheriffs' Association. A crime prevention campaign coalition soon formed, with members agreeing that NCCD should manage it but that sponsorship should be brief. NCCD, which preferred concentrating its efforts on incarcerated juveniles, was less interested in crime prevention. Former staff member Faye Warren explains that the crime prevention campaign needed a coordinator located in Washington, D.C., near the Justice Department.

But Robert Keim, the Ad Council's president and CEO at the time, tells a different story in his book *A Time in Advertising's Camelot: The Memoirs of a Do-Gooder*: "The idea of their [NCCD] paying the out of pocket costs went over like a lead balloon, although they reluctantly agreed to lend their name to the project, at least initially, with Carl Loeb standing in the wings as a financial angel."[12]

Loeb, an NCCD board member, chemist, and philanthropist, had grown discouraged by what he deemed Rector's more liberal approaches to criminal justice issues, and he prompted an organizational shake-up. He left the board, taking with him two other board members and two staffers, including Warren and Berkeley M. (Mac) Gray, a former police officer. Loeb kicked in $250,000 of his own money and secured a $750,000 grant from the Justice Department to start the National Crime Prevention Council (NCPC) in the spring of 1980. NCPC's initial mission would be to direct and manage the McGruff campaign.

The Ad Council had already assigned the creative responsibilities for the campaign to Dancer Fitzgerald Sample (DFS), the ad agency that had worked on Keep America Beautiful's anti-litter campaigns from 1961 to 1965. On February 8, 1979, at the Pierre Hotel in New York City, twenty-one directors and thirteen guests attended the Ad Council's board of directors meeting. The directors represented a cross-section of ad agency, corporate, and publishing heavyweights such as William Littleford, president and CEO of *Billboard* magazine, and Carlo Vittorini, president and CEO of *Parade* magazine. Guests included Louis E. Martin, President Carter's special assistant on issues affecting minorities and women, and the Department of Defense's John Holdridge, the former U.S. ambassador to Singapore.

At the board meeting, headed by chairman John Kelley of NBC, members heard research results compiled by DFS through focus group interviews held in Hartford, New York City, New Orleans, Minneapolis, San Francisco, and Los Angeles. The bottom line: Americans believed little could be done about crime; the police should prevent it, but the public would not pay higher taxes to put more officers on the street.

The research clearly showed that the public already feared crime, confirming the Ad Council's previous assessment that the heavy-handed approach first suggested by the Justice Department in 1977 was the wrong way to go. DFS had boiled down the research to one central strategy for the campaign. "Emphasize that individual actions can reduce crime," the research stressed, according to a council memo about the meeting. "Offer easily accessible opportunities for people to participate."[13]

The meeting ended with a promise from Kelley to present a campaign preview to the board March 15.

The Birth of McGruff

At DFS, the task of turning the communication strategy into compelling ads fell to Keil, the agency's executive vice president and creative director. Part raconteur, part artist, Keil had landed in the ad business via Hollywood and Broadway, after he had failed to sustain an acting career. He had learned how to create ads from Cameron Hawley, the acclaimed author of the novels *Executive Suite* and *Cash McCall*, after he took a job in the ad department at the Armstrong Cork Company. Hawley, who equated creativity with risk, pushed his charge to stretch his imagination. After joining DFS in 1964 as a copywriter, Keil promoted products such as Cheerios, Life Savers, and Toyota vehicles. He eventually wrote two influential books about creativity in the ad business: *The Creative Mystique* in 1985 and *How to Zig in a Zagging World* in 1988.

Now Keil needed something clever about crime prevention. On a Monday in February 1979, Keil passed his boss, Stuart Upson, in the office corridor. Upson, a firm believer in advertising's ability to improve society, would retain his position as chairman at Saatchi & Saatchi after its buyout of DFS, and he also became chairman of the Ad Council's board in 1990.

"How is the campaign going?" Upson asked. "It's coming along," Keil replied. "Fine," Upson said. "I would like to see something next Tuesday."

Even today at age ninety, Keil recalls the panic that set in. "I had nothing," he remembers. "The greatest stimulus to creativity is fear, and I had to get going."

McGruff's genesis occurred during the Los Angeles–to–New York red-eye flight Keil took that Wednesday. Stuck in a Kansas City airport at 3 a.m. after his flight had to make a sudden landing, Keil started thinking about Smokey Bear, a character he loved. "An animal could work," he told himself. "I thought about an elephant stomping on crime. Oh no. . . . A lion, the King of beasts. That won't work." Suddenly he sat up and said out loud, "Take a bite out of crime." Dogs bite, so Keil had his animal. Sketching furiously on an envelope, he drew a Snoopy look-alike wearing a Keystone Cop hat.

Back in New York that Thursday morning, Keil presented his idea to his creative team. "They liked my campaign but said my version of the dog stinks," he recalled. "They told me, 'He is a funny little dog, and nobody will listen to him.'" Stung, Keil fired back: "OK, wise guys, you have twenty-four hours to come up with a dog."

Five teams—each made up of a copywriter producing the words and slogans and an art director sketching the images—worked around the clock. "The phrase when they throw everyone on [an assignment] and you are up to your neck in competition is a 'gang bang,'" said Sherry Nemmers, a twenty-one-year-old copywriter at the time, who is credited with turning Keil's rough concept of a dog into a fully developed character. "Everyone was so secretive. When you are coming up with an idea, the first time that you have it in your head, it is totally yours. The minute you open up your mouth to your partner—who is like a marriage partner—it's no longer yours."

Nemmers (now a writer and creative director at her own New York–based consultancy, Brand Ideas) remembers pacing outside of Keil's office the next morning, thinking "I don't want to let this idea out" as she waited to show him her dog. Inside, Keil was rejecting version after version. A wimpy-looking mongrel who became a wonder dog? No. An aggressive-looking deputy dog? No. A golden retriever "Sarge" dog? No. A J. Edgar Hoover bulldog, complete with a cop's hat and badge? No.

Finally Nemmers and art director Ray Krivascy got their chance. "She comes in with this sketch of a dog in a raincoat, and he was tired," Keil recounted. "He had seen the world, and he had epitomized all the detectives we had seen from Raymond Chandler to Dashiell Hammett and even Columbo." (At the time, actor Peter Falk was playing the bumbling but cunning detective Columbo, who favored a tousled trench coat and cigars, in the popular and long-running TV series.)

In the pitch, Krivascy showed the sketches as Nemmers talked. "He is a shaggy-looking hound dog wearing a rumpled trench coat with raspberry stains from a peanut butter and jelly sandwich," she said. "He is wearing crepe soles and his shoes squeak when he walks. He has bad posture and is a little hunched over. He has a raspy, growly voice. He is a goofy guy—a little like Columbo and Peter Sellers combined—but very approachable. He is like talking to your Dad, and he is very casual when he has figured something out. He is holding a cigar, and he brushes off the ashes from his coat as he is talking and saying something very smart."

Smitten, Keil exclaimed, "That's him! That's the nuts" (his expression for something terrific).

A talking dog as a national spokesman to fight crime would prove to be a hard sell with the buttoned-up crowd at the Department of Justice. The Columbo-like cigar would not survive scrutiny by the Ad Council, which couldn't condone smoking in its PSAs. But Nemmers didn't know any of that yet. Eyes wide and heart pounding, she turned and gave Krivascy a hug, something she says doesn't happen in advertising today when a team nails a pitch. "Nobody acts that un-cool."

In the Trenches

Keil jokes that commercial advertising's reputation as a career is considered "slightly above a used-car salesman." Advertising still carries the taint of the déclassé profession that J. Walter Thompson ad agency consultant James Webb Young had encountered in the 1940s before he helped create the Ad Council.

Public service advertising, however, gets more credit. When William O'Barr, a professor of cultural anthropology at Duke University, interviewed Priscilla Natkins, the Ad Council's executive vice president and director of client services, for a 2006 article in *Advertising & Society Review*, her humorous remarks reflected the different perceptions. "Is your background in marketing?" O'Barr asked. "I used to be in the ad agency world," Natkins replied. "So you just came here?" O'Barr asked, referring to the Ad Council. "And cleansed my soul," Natkins said. "Strike that from the record!"[14]

Sherry Nemmers also felt the strong "do-good" attraction of making PSAs. A Vassar graduate who had majored in English and creative writing, she had worked less than a year at Grey Advertising before joining DFS in 1977. She thought she would stay in advertising another year at most before jumping to publishing, but McGruff changed all that. She would work on the campaign until she left Saatchi & Saatchi in 1991. "That campaign was my baby," Nemmers reflected. "McGruff and I grew up together."

Keil told Nemmers she must produce a series of three sixty-second, thirty-second, twenty-second, fifteen-second, and ten-second spots for TV and radio. The campaign also had to include subway and bus posters and print ads of various sizes. When she wasn't out on a shoot, the work would chain her to a typewriter for the next nine months.

The campaign introduced Nemmers to many career firsts; in fact, it was her first ad campaign ever. She had never worked with animation before, and she made her first foray into acting when her arm and hand appeared in the first TV spot, locking the door behind McGruff as he entered a house. Locking a door was easy, and she didn't want to spend money on an actor. But she was not prepared for the need to place her arm flat against the wall at the correct angle, or to twist her right hand backward. It took her eleven takes to get it right.

To film the TV spots, Nemmers chose tough neighborhoods in Detroit, Hartford, and Clifton, New Jersey. The crew set up the equipment at 8 p.m.; filming began at 11 p.m. and continued until dawn. Once while shooting, the crew witnessed a man jumping over a fence with a TV in his arms.

"Crime was something you could reach out and touch, and being on those shoots made me so acutely aware of it," Nemmers remembered. "These cities were being vandalized. It was tangible and real. We were in one of the most violent periods, an economically depressed period that was unruly and undisciplined. We didn't have money for police, so crime really was out of control."

The McGruff name came from a national contest placed on the back of cereal boxes, a clever marketing strategy to nurture public support for the character. The most common suggestion from the more than three thousand entries was "Sherlock Bones." But the prize went to a New Orleans police officer. McGruff debuted in the spot "Stop a Crime" in February 1980, with Keil doing the voice-over for the dog. (At first, the ad team wanted Peter Falk's Columbo voice, but Keil worried that the actor's cadence, often punctuated by long pauses between words, would be too slow for TV spots.)

In the spot, from the perspective of a person inside the house, viewers see the front door slowly creak open before McGruff walks in, pointing a flashlight around. "You know what I think?" he says in his raspy, growly voice. "I think you forgot to lock your door. A lot of people do that. They forget. It's too bad, because all crime needs is a chance. Don't give it a chance." After sniffing some brownies on a table, McGruff tells viewers where they can write for a booklet on crime prevention tips, and he ends the spot with, "Lock your door."

Nemmers wanted the dog to taste a brownie, but the crime prevention coalition considered that theft. Technically, opening an unlocked door and entering someone's home as McGruff does is trespassing, but everyone decided they could live with that to make the point.

Two more spots, "The Gilstraps" and "Mimi Marth," followed; they focused on the importance of community involvement in stopping crime. McGruff opens the first spot by saying the Gilstraps are not really moving but are being robbed, as viewers watch men pack a truck with possessions from their home. The neighbors, knowing the Gilstraps are out of town, call the police. The scene then shifts to a patrol car parked a block away, where two officers are eating while seated in their car. (Nemmers had the officers snacking on doughnuts but had to switch to hot pastrami sandwiches after vehement protests from the crime prevention coalition about the stereotype.) The cops arrive and arrest the offenders. At the end, McGruff says, "You know what it takes to stop a crime? Your help and your neighbors."

To show how neighborhood watch groups could make a difference, Nemmers chose Mimi Marth, a resident of Hartford, for a spot of the same name. Marth sees a guy stealing a bike and uses her walkie-talkie to report the theft to police. "This is Mimi Marth, part of the eyes and ears patrol of Hartford, Connecticut," McGruff says in the spot. "There's 126 of them, regular people like you and me, working against crime."

Each of the spots had to include what the Ad Council calls "a fulfillment strategy": at the end of each PSA, there must be a phone number, P.O. box number, or web address where people can get more information. The Justice Department sent out booklets to those making inquiries, with simple tips on how to prevent crime.

The impact was immediate. In the first few months of the campaign, the public requested 300,000 copies of the booklet *Got a Minute? You Could Stop a Crime*. By 1981 more than a million copies had been sent out as a result of the PSAs.

Nemmers credits McGruff with raising awareness about how to stop crime and popularizing the neighborhood watch movement. "This is the power of advertising in a positive way," Nemmers said. "We were able to do something that made such a huge difference in people's lives. People were empowered. This campaign was a huge contribution the Ad Council made to society, because it cleaned up neighborhoods practically overnight."

A Hard Sell

The McGruff campaign was originally intended to be part of the Justice Department's Law Enforcement Assistance Administration (LEAA), created during the Johnson administration to provide money to local police agencies for crime fighting.

By 1979 the LEAA had come under fire from critics who alleged that its block grants were wasteful, and President Carter ordered it shut down. The dismantling task fell to Robert Diegelman, then head of the Justice Department's Office of Justice Assistance, Research and Statistics. He decided to save the crime prevention campaign, however, because he thought a world-weary, street-savvy McGruff would help the public address America's growing crime problem. Knowing how critical his superiors had become of the LEAA, Diegelman started writing monthly reports to his boss, Assistant Attorney General for Public Affairs Robert Smith, about how the campaign would feature an animated figure.

In February 1980, a few days before the Ad Council launched the campaign at a press conference held at the National Press Club in Washington, D.C., Diegelman received a call: he must report to Attorney General Benjamin Civilleti's office at 7:30 a.m. the next morning. One of 500 senior-level officials at Justice, Diegelman had never met with the attorney general before. This meeting couldn't be good.

The Ad Council already had heard rumblings that the Crime Dog wasn't a hit at Justice. "The Department of Justice was under fire by Congress to do something about preventing crime," former president Keim writes in his memoir. "At our yearly Washington Conference during the White House Cocktail Party wrapping things up, the Acting Attorney General told me he had to appear before a Congressional sub-committee on their request for supplemental funds for crime prevention activities and he'd have to tell them that a hound dog was going to be the campaign voice and image. He was beside himself and was about to back out. 'Sir,' said I, mustering up my courage, 'we're giving you another Smokey Bear that will do for preventing crime what Smokey does to prevent forest fires. Tell the committee that. They'll love it.' I spilled this out with more bravado and conviction than I really felt."[15]

Diegelman met with Civilleti and Smith in the attorney general's private study that next morning. Civilleti got right to the point: "Why has the LEAA gotten into a campaign that is spending good money on a talking dog?"

"I would say I judged the question as being a hostile one," Diegelman said when he recounted the story. "I had launched into a whole explanation of the campaign when Smith jumps in and says 'Why didn't we know anything about this?'"

"For the last year, I sent you a progress report every month," Diegelman replied. "You never said it was going to be a talking dog," Smith said. "You just said it was going to be an animated figure." "Would it have made any difference if it were a talking fish?" Diegelman retorted.

The conversation deteriorated further when Civilleti ordered Diegelman to cancel the campaign. Diegelman explained that this was not possible, because the advertising had already been distributed to TV and radio stations. "This campaign is going to run whether we tell them to do it or not," Diegelman said. "In that case, Mr. Diegelman, I strongly suggest that I not see you present at the press conference," Civilleti replied.

Diegelman knew his career was on the line. "I might be dumb, but I am not suicidal. I said, 'Thank you very much sir, I will not attend.' I left the meeting and called the Ad Council with my regrets."

Thinking he had no chance of getting any future funding for the campaign, Diegelman aided Carl Loeb by putting $750,000 toward the creation of the National Crime Prevention Council. McGruff's successful debut and the NCPC's future ability to create merchandise around the character helped solve the fund-raising problem. Today NCPC still receives money from the Justice Department to support the campaign.

Measuring Impact

In 1979 Garrett O'Keefe, then a professor of mass communications at the University of Denver, received a $900,000 grant from a separate Justice office, the National Institute of Justice, to evaluate the effectiveness of the crime prevention campaign. At the time, he was surprised to learn that no previous Ad Council campaign had undergone the rigorous type of social science evaluation he and his research team planned for McGruff.

Nearly half of the public service ads in the 1970s had addressed health or personal safety by focusing on alcohol and drug abuse messages, nutrition, preventive health care, and traffic safety. Other issues included community service, educational opportunities, and concerns about the environment. A 1973 study in the *Journal of Broadcasting* had noted that nearly two-thirds of all televised PSAs ran between 7 a.m. and 6 p.m. on weekdays. Television networks and radio stations preferred PSAs that featured local market concerns and messages, disseminated by reputable organizations with no hidden commercial agendas, according to a 1981 survey in *Public Relations Review*.[16]

When public relations firm Needham Porter Novelli surveyed television public affairs directors in 1985, its study ranked the factors influencing the likelihood of a PSA airing. Of primary importance was whether an ad dealt with an issue of local interest, followed by subject matter and then good production quality. Public affairs directors gave extra consideration to spots when a local sponsoring group called a station to promote the PSA. Stations preferred receiving thirty-second spots provided in one- or two-inch videotape format rather than 16mm film.[17]

The Needham Porter Novelli survey also found that broadcast public affairs directors in 1985 chose PSAs about drunk driving, missing children, child abuse, cancer, and diabetes. That same year ABC ran more than a thousand PSAs about alcohol and drug abuse, with about 47 percent of those airing during prime-time television viewing hours, 32 percent during the daytime, and 21 percent late at night.

Kathleen Reid, in a study completed for a 1993 symposium of the International Visual Literacy Association, states that PSA campaigns play "a primary role in contemporary society to promote more active citizen involvement in varying dimensions of society."[18] But studies assessing a PSA campaign's ability to persuade large audiences by evaluating audience response to the messages didn't crop up until the 1970s. Toward the late 1980s and early 1990s, research examining the content of the verbal and visual messages was added to the mix.

Given McGruff's likability, O'Keefe said he expected his research to show some positive results, but he did not anticipate the magnitude of the effects. "Media response to the campaign was excellent," he wrote in a 1985 study published in the academic journal *Social Science and Modern Society*. "More than $100 million of time and space had been donated by mid-1981, making McGruff one of the most popular Ad Council campaigns."

O'Keefe also reported that about "1 million booklets had been distributed free-of-charge in response to the ads. Another 250,000 had been sold through the Government Printing Office. More than 100 requests had been received for negatives to use in reprinting the booklets locally. The Department of the Army printed 300,000 McGruff booklets for use in their programs. A host of national, state and local programs have either been enhanced or initiated as a result of campaign activities."[19]

O'Keefe and his team had surveyed 1,200 adults in 1980 to determine their response to the campaign, and later surveyed another 426 adults in three cities to discover any behavior change. Some 48 percent, or 573 adults, said they recognized the spots, and nearly a quarter of the 426 adults in the later survey had taken some action, such as locking their doors or joining neighborhood watch groups. The upbeat character of McGruff played a role in the positive results. "The dog character tested very positively in terms of citizens' evaluations," O'Keefe wrote in the 1985 study. "It appears to be in continuously high demand as a logo for neighborhood and statewide crime prevention efforts. Over 200 copyrights have been issued for such uses of McGruff, and it is in the process of being marketed as a doll figure aimed at general consumers. The character may well approach the general popularity of Smokey Bear as a campaign symbol."

O'Keefe also concluded that the audience would likely tune out any fear messages: "Had the PSAs included more in the way of particular information about how people are victimized, or the consequences of victimization, those cues may well have triggered fear in ways that would have interfered with the persuasive impact of the message."

On its website, the Ad Council points to other measures of success as well. When a 1984 Justice Department crime survey found that burglaries and theft had hit their lowest level in the twelve-year history of the survey, the department attributed the decline in part to "greater citizen involvement," a major theme in the campaign. McGruff was the impetus, but Americans had collectively taken a bite out of crime.

The Crime Dog Takes a Back Seat

O'Keefe's study recommended the continued use of McGruff in the TV spots, but Jack Calhoun, the first president and CEO of the NCPC, hired in 1983, had other ideas. Calhoun's prior work as the commissioner of the Massachusetts Department of Youth Services in 1976, and later as commissioner of the U.S. Administration on Children, Youth and Families, appointed by President Carter in 1979, prompted him to address family issues and the roots of crime. Calhoun believed that the first three McGruff spots ("Stop a Crime," "The Gilstraps," and "Mimi Marth") had adequately focused on individual and property protection, but now it was time to dig deeper and explore the larger community issues affecting crime. "At some point, I have to step out from my locked house and barred windows," Calhoun said.

Under Calhoun's direction in the mid-1980s, the McGruff campaign addressed the issue of child kidnapping before tackling the escalating problems of drugs and gun violence, through messages designed to protect children and teenagers. Calhoun believed that a cartoon character had the potential to appear "frivolous" in such serious contexts. McGruff's role therefore diminished in the harder-hitting TV spots, much to the dismay of people on Calhoun's staff such as Warren and Gray, who, as Calhoun describes it, believed the hound dog "got shunted into the background as a Good Housekeeping seal of approval."

In the sixty-second "Real Situations" PSA, McGruff appears about twenty seconds into the spot, after Brian tempts a young Mike to try marijuana, and then once at the end, following several scenes featuring kids resisting the temptation. In the thirty-second versions of "Teddy Bear" and "Blanket," two spots dealing with the tragic consequences of gun violence, only McGruff's picture and the slogan "Take a Bite Out of Crime," appear at the end.

Calhoun's approach was justified after O'Keefe again measured the campaign, this time focusing on the 1991–92 period, when the objective was "to convince people that they must work together in community efforts to help defeat crime and drug abuse—specifically, violent crimes against children and teens," as O'Keefe writes in his 1996 book *Taking a Bite Out of Crime: The Impact of the National Citizens' Crime Prevention Media Campaign.* Eighty percent of the citizens surveyed could recall the PSAs. Half the sample recognized PSAs like "Teddy Bear" after only a few months of play, when it had taken the initial spots such as "Stop a Crime" and "The Gilstraps" longer to reach a similar level of recognition. O'Keefe suggests the "more graphic nature" of that later spots "may well have contributed to their accelerated awareness levels."[20]

A More Modern McGruff

In 1993 the campaign shifted direction again when McGruff's nephew Scruff appeared in a separate effort to teach children between the ages of five and nine. Nemmers had left Saatchi & Saatchi the year before, finding the radical shift decreasing McGruff's presence difficult to accept. A children's activity book featuring Scruff appeared in 1993. By 2001, the campaign shifted back to teens. The new PSAs encouraged teens to get involved in the safety of their community, while adults received messages promoting their involvement in delinquency prevention programs.

By the thirtieth anniversary of McGruff in 2010, it was time to give the Crime Dog a new look. (By this time, the NCPC no longer worked with the Ad Council, because of limited financial resources to maintain a national campaign, but it continued to produce smaller McGruff efforts on its own.) "He was something of an anachronism, and he didn't really fit because he referred to a detective archetype that no longer had any meaning for young people," says Pat Giles, a Saatchi & Saatchi creative director who was assigned to change the character for an online video in 2010. "They didn't know Columbo."

The media landscape had also changed dramatically. Today children are used to avoiding commercials, and they don't place much value in PSAs, Giles observes. When the National Crime Prevention Council decided to create an anti-bullying campaign around McGruff to celebrate his thirtieth anniversary, the target audience—school-aged children—were largely online and wanted to be entertained. Giles said he and his partner, John Sullivan, begged NCPC to let them give McGruff a deeper story. With their backgrounds in animation from the Disney Channel and Nickelodeon respectively, the creative team built an imaginative cartoon world of dogs, using flash animation. The resulting fifty-second Internet video called "Samantha's Choice" features a more modern McGruff, willing to take off his rumpled trench coat to reveal a neat white shirt and black tie underneath. "Most people don't recognize me without my coat on," he chuckles after teaching animated dog children some anti-bullying tricks.

The challenge for Giles and Sullivan was to update McGruff while being respectful of the character. This was no easy task, given the significant concerns at the NCPC that they would somehow redesign McGruff or make him unrecognizable. The creative team also wanted to soften McGruff so that kids would feel more comfortable around law enforcement figures. "Pop culture can make villains out of cops," Giles points out. "Anthropologically, this is a leftover from the 1960s, where the baby boomers still rule the world and the cop represents 'the man.' These are not very positive portrayals of authority to kids."

Like Smokey, McGruff endures as a pop icon. The U.S. Post Office issued a McGruff stamp in 1984. In 1986 the Crime Dog appeared on a special episode of the ABC TV show *Webster*, giving Webster and his classmates advice on how to deal with bullies. Folksingers Peter, Paul and Mary adapted part of their song "Where Have All the Flowers Gone?" for a McGruff PSA in 1997, showing the impact of gun violence on the victims and their families. In 2011 NCPC president and CEO Ann Harkins said that 83 percent of adults still recognize the Crime Dog, 80 percent of kids say they would listen to his advice, and 72 percent think he is cool. "It's all about the message," Harkins says. "McGruff still speaks to your safety."

Lessons Learned

O'Keefe's published analysis includes a list of advertising techniques that made McGruff so successful, from using commercial advertising research and planning strategies in the campaign's design and execution, to segmenting the public into target audience groups with messages tailored specifically for them. The repetition of the messages, high production quality, and use of entertaining characters and stories also helped the effort.

Initially, O'Keefe never expected to write such a list. He recalls feeling the same skepticism that law enforcement officials expressed when they had first heard about an animated crime dog. "We got some sketches early on, and I thought, 'Oh God, what are these guys going to do with this?'" he remembers. It was only when he saw the actual animation and could examine how the character, in combination with the voice, gave McGruff some remarkable authority that he thought it could work. "It came out of a creative mind, and that's great," O'Keefe says. "Doing research [to create the character] would have probably screwed it up."

McGruff became a cultural hallmark of empowerment against crime. His message changed how people viewed the issue in their neighborhoods. Curbing violence was no longer just the responsibility of police officers. Citizens who participated in neighborhood watch groups came to believe they also played a role in solving the problem. The willingness of police officers to wear a McGruff costume helped reinforce the crime prevention message. There are four thousand McGruff costumes in existence today.

Jack Keil often donned the costume, once appearing with Dick Cavett. But his favorite on-air experience happened on the local NBC affiliate in Washington, D.C., where he appeared as McGruff with the NCPC's Mac Gray. Here's how he tells the story:

> Mac was talking about crime. Then I said, "You bet, Mac. You tell them."
> Surprised, the interviewer said: "I didn't know the dog talked. Tell me, dog, how did you get into the business?"

"Well, it is a funny thing. I used to be the pet of a detective and he took me around to these crimes. One day, he was sick, and we a got a call. I ended up going on the call."

"What happened to the detective?" the interviewer asked.

"I go home every night, feed him, and take him for a walk."

Looking back over thirty years, Keil is still amazed to remember how "an idea in the Kansas City airport created a whole industry fighting crime."

Chapter 10

Public Service Ads and the Public Interest

The power to decide what messages are of social importance and must have wide distribution (and which are not) is a considerable power.

—Erik Barnouw, The Sponsor: Notes on a Modern Potentate

U p until the mid-1980s, radio and television broadcasters were required to demonstrate that their stations operated in the public interest in order to renew their licenses. Airing public service advertisements (PSAs) was one way broadcasters could fulfill their public interest obligations. In 1984 the Federal Communications Commission (FCC) dropped its rules requiring stations to show how their programming content benefited local communities. Since then, critics have increasingly argued that stations can now set their own standards about what kind of content is considered in the public's best interest. How many PSAs are aired by broadcasters when there are no federal requirements to make them do so is a critical issue that affects the Ad Council and every non-profit organization in the United States that struggles to obtain critical airtime. Some studies, undertaken by public health groups and others, have shown a decline in the number of PSAs television stations have aired since the FCC changed the rules in 1984.

The Kaiser Family Foundation's *Shouting to Be Heard* studies are one example. Since 1991 the nonprofit foundation has produced policy reports and research to fulfill its mission of providing an independent and nonpartisan voice in the nation's discussions about major health care issues. The reports help inform health policy experts and journalists who write about health issues.

Kaiser considers PSAs a central component in public education campaigns that can raise awareness and change behavior about public health issues from alcohol and drug abuse to drunk driving and AIDS. It issued two reports, the first in 2002 and the second in 2008, to provide some data about the state of PSAs on television. As the second Kaiser report notes, some consumer advocates believe that broadcasters should again be required to dedicate a certain amount of airtime to PSAs in exchange for their use of the airwaves. Attempts to push such proposals since the late 1990s have not gained any traction with Congress or the FCC.

On January 24, 2008, when Kaiser issued its second report, the study's findings about the state of public service ads on television was grim. The networks had devoted only seventeen seconds an hour—one-half of one percent of all airtime—to public service ads. (The report was based on a composite week of programming collected from September 25 to December 3, 2005.) There was also no significant change in the time given to PSAs since Kaiser last studied the issue in 2002.[1]

That day Kaiser had invited Martin Franks, CBS's executive vice president for policy, planning, and government relations, to a panel discussion about the study's findings. How Franks responded offers an important window into how broadcasters regard this issue. When it was his turn to speak, Franks took the position that the report's methodology was flawed because it only measured the frequency of public service ads and not the number of viewers who might have seen the spot. "Unfortunately, I didn't find the footnote [in the report] that dealt with the quality in terms of the time," Franks said. "Nothing about gross ratings points, nothing about the reach, and with affection and respect, I think that's a major flaw in the report." Consider, Franks said, a public service spot CBS had aired during the 2007 Super Bowl, which was counted the same way as every other public service ad in the Kaiser report. The network had partnered with Big Brothers Big Sisters of America to prepare the thirty-second spot featuring the coaches of the teams competing in the big game that day. Lovie Smith, former coach of the Chicago Bears, and his mentor Tony Dungy, former coach of the Indianapolis Colts, discussed the importance of mentoring young people. More than 93 million viewers watched the game, according to Nielsen Media Research.

"It blew up the Big Brothers Big Sisters switchboard and website," Franks said. "There was extensive news coverage of it, and in your report, I believe, that would show as one PSA (public service ad)."

Reach matters, but the Super Bowl comes only once a year. And the networks make no promises that they will air public service ads every year during the Super Bowl. According to the Kaiser report, just six seconds an hour were being devoted to public service ads in prime time. Among all the donated public service ads in the report, 46 percent ran from midnight until 6 a.m. For broadcast stations, 60 percent of the PSAs ran after midnight.[2]

During the panel discussion that day, Vicky Rideout, then Kaiser's vice president and director of its program on entertainment, media, and health, emphasized the study's finding that too few PSAs run during prime time: "Prime time is when you get the most audience, and midnight to 6 a.m. is when you get the least, and that's why we look at the proportion of spots in prime time versus overnight."

By picking on the report's failure to mention the national reach of the Smith–Dungy public service ad that ran one time on Super Bowl Sunday, Franks had just exercised a shrewd public relations tactic: if the news is unwelcome, attack the credibility of the report. By doing so, Franks would at least be guaranteed a sound bite or a quote from the journalists who were covering the event. And his employer, CBS, would look like it considered airing PSAs during prime time an important part of its public service duties by offering free air time during the Super Bowl—where advertising space now runs more than $4 million for a thirty-second spot—for an ad on behalf of Big Brothers Big Sisters.

At the time, the Ad Council also considered the report's methodology flawed. It was disappointed that the study had examined only one week of television content and had surveyed a limited number of cable networks and broadcast affiliates. The council thought the Kaiser report painted a far bleaker picture of the state of public service advertising, one that was not reflected by its own more holistic measuring methods. Because the Ad Council's model depends on the time broadcasters donate to PSAs, any criticism suggesting that television networks don't air enough public service ads is considered a sensitive one by the council's staff.

To understand what happened to PSAs on the airwaves after 1984, when the federal government dropped its requirement that broadcasters must air the spots, it's necessary to examine the history of broadcast regulation, how the networks currently decide what PSAs should be aired, and how the Ad Council measures its own PSA reach.

Broadcast Networks and Public Service Ads

When it comes to deciding which PSAs run and where, networks give priority to social issues their own audiences care about, their own public service spots promoting their programs, the needs of their advertisers, and the state of the national economy. ("CBS Cares" and NBC's "The More You Know" are two examples of efforts by the networks to create PSAs featuring their actors and programs.) The public sees more PSAs during recessions than they do during a robust economy.

The Ad Council must closely control the creative content of each spot to avoid offending or running afoul of the network standards and practices departments, which monitor and reject any ad that is too political, that is too overtly sexual, or that smacks of advocacy.

Dennis Wharton, a spokesperson for the National Association of Broadcasters (NAB), says stations are particularly sensitive to messages that can be offensive. "A TV station will tailor a message that is not going to offend anybody," he observes. "Pick a social issue—breast cancer, literacy campaigns, mental health issues—there are endless messages that can be designed not to offend."

Broadcasters set their own rules for reviewing programming and advertising content. They are subject to federal scrutiny only when it comes to indecency standards, which apply from 6 a.m. to 10 p.m. Janet Jackson's "wardrobe malfunction" during the 2004 Super Bowl game, and shock jock Don Imus's 2007 "nappy-headed hos" comment about the Rutgers University women's basketball team on his *Imus in the Morning* CBS radio and MSNBC cable television show, are two recent examples that have prompted Federal Communications Commission (FCC) scrutiny.[3]

Even broadcasters say that the ad clearance rules can be arbitrary and subjective. Before he became president of the NAB, Edward Fritts served on a committee to review the association's Code of Broadcasting. After spending a week going through a network ad clearance process, he was struck by what he had learned. "The ad for Huffy bicycles showed somebody trail riding and jumping, but we rejected it because the rider wore no protection for his elbows and knees and no helmet," Fritts recalls. "But we accepted an anal itch cream because it only showed the package three times."

PSAs have faced even stricter and more subjective reviews from the networks. When NBC rejected three spots for the White House's anti-drug abuse campaign in 1999, the network criticized them for depicting parents in a negative light. Created by the agency Ogilvy & Mather, the spots showed parents chatting on the phone, watching television, or sending e-mails when they could have spent that time talking to their kids about drugs.[4]

At the time, Rosalyn Weinman, then NBC's executive vice president for broadcast content and East Coast entertainment, questioned why the ads singled out those three activities when parents do dozens of things every day. "Why not tell parents to shampoo less or play less golf?" she asked in an *Adweek* article, arguing that the spots made parents feel guilty when the message could have been more encouraging.[5]

But Shona Seifert, then Ogilvy's executive group director, who managed the federal Office of National Drug Control Policy (ONDCP) account, claimed that NBC was concerned about upsetting other advertisers. "Each ad suggests parents spend less time with a product or service they advertise," Seifert said. "They are nervous that AT&T and computer companies would have a problem with our ads."[6]

Rideout, who left Kaiser in 2010 to open her own consulting practice, calls what the Ad Council must produce to get network ad clearance on controversial issues such as sex education "a tiptoe-around-the-topic type of ad." When Rideout first went to work for Kaiser in 1997 the foundation had recently completed a three-year campaign with the Ad Council about how to talk to kids about sex. She encountered a staff that was not happy with how much the campaign had cost or how much airtime it had received. "A campaign aimed at teens on adolescent health issues like sexually transmitted diseases and HIV is very hard to do through the Ad Council model, because such an ad would be sent to every network in the country, and if it was too hard hitting or controversial, and if it shocked a large segment of the audience, it would not work," Rideout said.

Rideout concluded that the Ad Council model wasn't the right fit for the topic of teens and sex, and sought an alternative. Since no other national model existed, she had to create one. The Kaiser staff knew that teens were watching MTV shows such as *The Real World*. The obvious answer was a Kaiser partnership with MTV. So Rideout met with MTV's Stephen Friedman in 1998 on the first day of his new job as the youth-oriented cable network's head of strategic partnerships and public affairs. (He was later promoted to president of MTV in 2011.)

Kaiser was the first to approach MTV about forging a public service partnership, and Friedman thought the idea made sense for the network, for Kaiser, and for the cause. He agreed to run several thirty- and sixty-second PSAs per week in prime day slots, and to air three half-hour shows that would feature HIV in the content. In return Kaiser paid the production costs and worked with MTV to create the public service ads and consult on the shows. The foundation also paid for an 800 toll-free number at the time and later, the development of the campaign's website. Kaiser then took what later became its Know HIV/AIDS effort to BET (Black Entertainment Television), then to UPN (United Paramount Network), which no longer exists, and finally to the parent company, Viacom.

Kaiser's successful track record with the other Viacom properties enabled it to secure a deal with the parent company by which it invested $600,000 a year and in return received about $200 million in media time and space. Viacom not only ran the PSAs, which were created by the ad agencies DDB (Seattle) and Crispin Porter + Bogusky (Miami), but also embedded HIV content across all its media properties and contributed about $1 million in cash to the effort.

The Kaiser partnership with Viacom launched in 2003 and ran for five years. To heighten awareness about the issue within the African American community, Kaiser aired PSAs and worked with Viacom to integrate HIV/AIDS messages into Showtime's *Soul Food* and UPN shows such as *Girlfriends, One on One, Half and Half*, and *The Parkers*. The five shows included nine episodes on HIV, reaching an estimated audience of 36.8 million. The effort also included nonfiction shows on BET, including *Rap City, 106 & Park*, and *The Naked Truth*.[7]

In an October 2004 survey titled "Assessing Public Education Programming on HIV/AIDS," Kaiser found that more than eight in ten African American adults and more than nine in ten of the target audience of eighteen- to twenty-four-year-olds reported seeing at least one of the PSAs or shows. Forty-five percent of all African American adults and 75 percent of younger African

Americans eighteen to twenty-four said they had watched one or more of the episodes. The report was based on a national telephone survey of 800 African Americans eighteen or older, conducted from March 15 to May 11, 2004, and on interviews with more than 2000 adults.[8] "When a media partner is committed to donating quality airtime to a public education campaign—and to using a variety of programming formats—the exposure can be significant," the report found.[9]

Rideout understands that this media partnership model has its own limitations. Media companies are not willing to take on more than one such partnership at a time, and not every cause matches the issues a network may be interested in. "It can't work for every issue all the time," she says. "It was a great alternative for Kaiser at the time, but it is a limited-use model."

Paid public service models require substantial funding, which can't always be sustained over time. The White House's anti-drug abuse campaign, a partnership between ONDCP and the nonprofit Partnership at Drugfree.org, garnered $200 million in taxpayer money when it launched in 1998, but Congress eliminated funding for the campaign in 2011. The American Legacy Foundation's anti-smoking campaign, called Truth, received $300 million a year from the tobacco industry under the terms of the Master Settlement Agreement forty-six states made with Philip Morris, R. J. Reynolds, Brown & Williamson, and Lorillard in 1998, but that funding ended in 2003.

Such paid campaigns are considered effective, according to the University of Michigan's "Monitoring the Future" study for the anti-drug abuse effort and articles published in the *Journal of Public Health* about the American Legacy Foundation's anti-smoking campaign. But they can also decrease the inventory of airtime broadcasters make available to other nonprofit efforts.

The Ad Council's model still allows for the greatest number of causes to have their voices heard, Rideout argued. "You can critique the Ad Council model all you want, but it is a vital, if imperfect, model," she said. "I am not sure I could design a better one without a whole lot of public funding or a different regulatory structure for broadcasters."

To understand why broadcasters are no longer required to air PSAs, it is important to review the historical forces that have shaped the public interest standard in broadcast regulation.

Public Service Ads and the Public Interest

The Radio Act of 1912 permitted the U.S. Department of Commerce and Labor to grant radio licenses to citizens on request. This approach worked until the number of people operating over the airwaves created enough signal interference that listening to a program without interruption became almost impossible by the 1920s.[10]

The country needed a system free of signal interference, but debate erupted over two distinctly different approaches. Politicians, educators, labor activists, and religious groups wanted a common carrier system, which would allow anyone to buy airtime. These groups feared that a broadcast licensing system would trample their free speech rights, preventing their voices from being heard over the public airwaves.[11] Existing broadcasters wanted to keep their own editorial control and create a way to link their individual stations into national networks. They asked Congress for a licensing system that would grant their stations full free speech rights.[12]

In its analysis of the public interest standard in television broadcasting, the Advisory Committee on Public Interest Obligations of Digital Television Broadcasters (also known as the Gore Commission), established by President Bill Clinton in 1997, portrayed these two enduring arguments as contrasting visions of free speech. The licensing system stemmed from one vision of free speech, often associated with Justice Oliver Wendell Holmes, who viewed the First Amendment as guaranteeing the "free marketplace of ideas." Under this scenario, "a free trade in ideas" will "yield the most freedom, the closest approximations to truth, and the greatest common good."[13] The Gore Commission, which was charged with determining the public interest obligations of broadcasters in a digital world, equated the common carrier argument with James Madison's vision of the First Amendment as a way to "ensure political equality, especially in the face of economic inequalities, and to foster free and open political deliberation." In this scenario, free speech serves "the civic needs of a democracy."[14]

The Radio Act of 1927 and the Communications Act of 1934 resolved the conflict but not the tensions between the two views, which still influence broadcast regulatory policy today. The Radio Act of 1927 established a five-person Federal Radio Commission to grant and revoke licenses. It defined the airwaves as a public resource that broadcasters were licensed to use but not to own. It set the foundation for broadcasters acting as public trustees of the air-waves: "The station itself must be operated as if owned by the public. . . . It is as if people of a community should own a station and turn it over to the best man in sight with this injunction: 'Manage this station in our interest.' The standing of every station is determined by that conception."[15]

The Communications Act of 1934 created a seven-person Federal Communications Commission. It banned a common carrier system and gave broadcasters the licensing system they wanted. As a compromise with the common carrier proponents, the act imposed a general requirement that broadcast licensees operate in the "public interest, convenience and necessity." In return for receiving an exclusionary licensing system, the broadcasters had to operate in the public interest. The act also paved the way for the Fairness Doctrine, which required that equal time be given to the presentation of both sides of a controversial issue.[16]

The forces restricting individual citizens from obtaining access to the airwaves today are a function of the limitations of the predigital electromagnetic spectrum, where only so many stations could operate without creating signal interference, and the government-imposed licensing system.[17]

As circumstances changed, Congress gave the FCC broad authority to develop and revise the definition of a broadcaster's public interest obligations. The commission's authority, however, is limited by First Amendment principles. The FCC can't censor broadcasters, and it can only regulate programming content in the most general way. It can step in if it perceives that the broadcast industry is not performing in a way that meets the public's needs, but it can't directly dictate editorial content. Under this legal framework, which differs from the regulatory apparatus for other media, the government grants exclusive free-speech rights to licensees and not individuals. Congress and the courts have justified this special treatment by mandating that licensees serve as public trustees of the airwaves.

Following the quiz show scandals of the 1950s and the paying of bribes to air certain songs, the FCC decided that it should further define the public interest standard and establish programming guidelines. The commission's 1960 Programming Policy Statement listed fourteen "major elements usually necessary to the public interest." Opportunity for local self-expression was among the fourteen, and public service ads counted as a way for stations to serve local communities.[18] In 1971 the FCC created a rule, based on the concept of "ascertainment," which required broadcasters to seek out the needs of the local community. Broadcasters had to consult with the public and community leaders to develop suitable local programming and PSAs.[19]

In a 1969 Supreme Court case, *Red Lion Broadcasting Co. v. the Federal Communications Commission*, broadcasters challenged the FCC's public interest requirements and the Fairness Doctrine in particular. Red Lion operated south central Pennsylvania radio station WGCB. On November 27, 1964, WGCB aired a fifteen-minute broadcast featuring the Reverend Billy James Hargis as part of a *Christian Crusade* series. Hargis, in discussing a book by Fred J. Cook, *Barry Goldwater: Extremist of the Right*, said that Cook had been fired by a newspaper for making false charges against city officials; that he had worked for a communist-affiliated publication; that he had defended Alger Hiss and attacked J. Edgar Hoover and the Central Intelligence Agency; and that he had written his book "to smear and destroy Barry Goldwater."[20]

After hearing the broadcast, Cook believed he had been personally attacked and demanded free airtime to respond, but the station refused. Cook took his complaint to the FCC, which concluded that the Hargis broadcast had been a personal attack and that Red Lion had failed to meet its equal time obligation under the Fairness Doctrine. The regulations under the doctrine required the station to send a tape, transcript, or summary of the broadcast to Cook and to grant him equal airtime to respond. The Court of Appeals for the District of Columbia Circuit upheld the FCC's decision.[21]

In deciding the case, the Supreme Court ruled that it was constitutional for the FCC to limit a broadcaster's First Amendment rights based on the scarcity of broadcast spectrum. If there wasn't enough available spectrum for everyone to have their own broadcast station, then "those fortunate enough to have a broadcast license must accept government restrictions on its use." The FCC's legal foundation for its subsequent indecency policy stems from the Red Lion case. The case upheld the constitutionality of the public interest standard and the Fairness Doctrine.[22]

In 1976 the FCC conducted a specific inquiry on PSAs. The San Francisco–based nonprofit Public Media Center filed a petition with the FCC asking for a quantitative rule that would require broadcasters to air a specific number of PSAs. The center complained that broadcasters gave little consideration to PSAs and often scheduled them for unfavorable hours when few viewers watched. When they did air PSAs, the center claimed that broadcasters frequently favored ads by local citizen groups and charities, and also gave special consideration to Ad Council PSAs. The petitioners asked the FCC to require broadcasters to air a minimum of three PSAs, totaling at least ninety seconds of airtime, every two hours throughout the day. They asked the FCC to limit the number of PSAs a licensee or network could accept from a single group such as the Ad Council, and to require a certain percentage of PSAs to come from local groups. The Federal Trade Commission, the United Church of Christ, the Southern California Committee for Open Media, and the Council on Children, Media, and Merchandising all supported the Public Media Center's petition.[23]

The groups supporting broadcasters in opposing the petition included nonprofits that benefited from Ad Council PSAs, such as the United Negro College Fund. Broadcasters, supported by the United Way, the Boy Scouts of America, and the President's Council on Physical Fitness and Sports, argued that PSAs were part of a broadcaster's editorial discretion established by statute and the First Amendment, and that there was no "evidentiary basis for the FCC to act." The FCC agreed at first and denied the petition. But it later reconsidered and decided to conduct the study that the Public Media Center had requested. The FCC justified its change of heart by noting that "Congress, as well as governmental agencies such as the Federal Trade Commission and the Department of Health and Human Services are interested in the employment of public service ads in answering public needs."[24]

The FCC based its study on broadcasters' public service ad logs, which are still maintained today as part of the licensing renewal process. It asked when PSAs had aired, how much time had been given to them, what the subject was, who the sponsoring organization was, how the ads had been selected, and how the PSAs had served the public interest. The results showed that the average television and radio station aired one to two PSAs per hour, and about 200 per week—the equivalent of 1 to 2 percent of all airtime. Stations ran a range of ten- to sixty-second spots, with the majority running thirty seconds. The FCC concluded that PSAs were "not necessarily aired in graveyard hours," but neither were they "centered in drive and prime-time periods." Broadcasters reported that local public service was the determining factor in selecting the ads. In the end, the only action the FCC took was to help broadcasters receive more credit for airing PSAs in the "other" programming category of their annual reports and in their renewal application forms.[25]

The new deregulatory approach to the broadcast industry in the 1980s eliminated some of the rules affecting PSAs. The FCC removed its formal ascertainment requirements in 1984, meaning that broadcasters no longer had to seek out the opinion of community leaders before developing programming or deciding which public service ads to air. But it still allowed broadcasters to count PSAs toward their statutory public service programming obligations.

Public service ads did not capture FCC interest again until 1997, when the current FCC chairman Reed Hundt said PSAs on the four major networks had "dried up and disappeared like rain in the desert."[26] Hundt based his comment on the results of the 1997 Television Commercial Monitoring Report, known in the industry as the "clutter report," prepared annually by the Association of National Advertisers and the American Association of Advertising Agencies. The report noted that the four major networks (ABC, CBS, NBC, and Fox) averaged 5.2 seconds of PSAs per prime-time hour in 1995, which was down from twelve seconds per hour in 1993. The report said that PSA airtime remained flat at 5.2 seconds in May 1996 and increased to 6.2 seconds in November 1996.[27]

Hundt asked the National Association of Broadcasters to provide a report on PSAs and network promotions for the previous ten years, which would include statistics on time devoted to the spots and the dollar equivalents of paid ads. He also asked broadcasters whether they thought they had any obligation to run PSAs as part of their license renewal.

At the time, broadcasters counted toward their PSA commitment their own campaigns prepared in house, which promoted their shows as well as a cause. NBC's "The More You Know" campaign is an example of this practice. Ad Council president Ruth Wooden questioned whether these campaigns should count as PSAs, since they featured and promoted network stars and shows rather than a separate public service organization. Nevertheless, the practice of counting such campaigns as public service ads continues today.[28]

In a speech to broadcasters at their April 1997 convention in Las Vegas, Hundt urged broadcasters to develop a voluntary code for public service ads: "If PSAs cannot be guaranteed in the traditional ways of the past, what new practices need to be developed that would keep this wonderful medium on the side of all the public service goals that PSAs have so nobly and successfully served?" Alex Kroll, then chairman of the Ad Council, told broadcasters at the convention that their response to PSAs was "anemic." "Why isn't there a national uprising from people to do something about it?" asked Kroll, the chairman emeritus of the ad agency Y&R (Young & Rubicam), who had helped develop the United Negro College Fund's Ad Council campaign.

Kroll suggested that broadcasters should devote sixty seconds a night to PSAs focused on helping inner-city kids. Hundt echoed this sixty-second request in his speech. But broadcasters refused, earning a stinging rebuke from *Advertising Age*, the industry trade publication. Its May 19, 1997, editorial called their decision "a big mistake . . . that will win them no friends and could cost them dearly in Congress." At the time broadcasters were lobbying lawmakers and regulators to keep the old analog spectrum while expanding into the multi-billion-dollar new digital spectrum; to avoid establishing a family viewing hour; and to prevent any requirement that would force them to give free airtime to political candidates.[29] "In the midst of all these delicate negotiations, how can the NAB seriously propose that broadcasters thumb their nose at running traditional, non-marketing-driven PSAs?" the editorial asked. "Every viewer (and legislator) can see that prime-time is stuffed with self-serving promotions. Is there nowhere in this enormous clutter that an actual non-commercial public service announcement might fit?"[30]

Broadcasters refuted the criticism and fought back. The theme of Edward Fritts's speech at the 1997 convention was how to keep Big Brother out of their business. "The FCC chairman [Hundt] has called for a new era of quantifiable public interest programming requirements—according to Washington dictated standards," Fritts said. "I say to you today that you know more about public interest in your communities than anyone in Washington ever will."[31]

Fritts also wrote Hundt a letter questioning the FCC chairman's interest in PSAs: "Your focus on PSAs as a unique measure of public service is indeed difficult to understand in light of the Commission's outright rejection of educational PSAs" counting toward broadcasters' program obligations for children. Hundt responded by threatening to open up a public inquiry.[32]

Before stepping down as chairman in 1997, Hundt unsuccessfully fought Office of National Drug Control Policy head Barry McCaffrey over the White House's deal with broadcasters (known as "the media match") to air one free

PSA promoting its anti-drug abuse campaign for every paid spot. "It's a shame," Hundt later said about the media match. "The public shouldn't . . . be in a position where it has to buy the right to use its own medium."[33]

In December 1999 the FCC inquired whether broadcasters should improve how they made information about public service ads available to the public. This was part of an overall review of whether to institute new public interest rules for broadcasters after the transition to digital broadcasting.[34] Broadcasters spent $300,000 to commission an independent report of its community service, undertaken by Alexandria, Virginia–based Public Opinion Strategies. The April 2000 report noted that radio and television broadcasters had spent $8.1 billion on community service between August 1, 1998, and July 31, 1999, up from $6.8 billion in 1998, the last time the NAB had conducted such a report. The figure was based on a survey sent to 11,147 radio and television stations, to which 5,677 responded. The report defined community service as airtime for PSAs, as well as a "broadcasters' fundraising efforts for charities, charitable causes, needy individuals and disaster relief activities." It reported that $5.6 billion of the total spent on community service came from donated airtime for PSAs: "The average television station ran 142 PSAs per week," and "the average radio station ran 152 PSAs per week."[35]

Fritts called the $8.1 billion figure "honest, conservative and unassailable," but that hardly stopped the critics. Some argued that PSAs were just one part of a broadcaster's public interest obligations, and that the networks needed to do more in other areas. The Benton Foundation, a nonprofit media and telecommunications watchdog group, released a report that found that twenty-four television stations had devoted only 0.3 percent of their programming in a two-week period to local public affairs programming. "PSAs alone do not fulfill the broadcasters' responsibility to serve the civic, educational and cultural needs of their communities," said Benton president Larry Kirkman.[36]

Other groups, such as the Alliance for Better Campaigns, wanted broadcasters to air five minutes of political discourse about candidates every night in the thirty nights leading up to an election. Its March 2000 study with the Annenberg Public Policy Center found that ABC, CBS, and NBC aired an average of only thirty-six seconds each night of candidate-specific discourse between the February 1 New Hampshire primary and the March 7 Super Tuesday primary. While the networks did average close to five minutes a night of "political coverage," the study argued that the coverage focused on campaign strategy and the "horse race" rather than political issues.[37]

The voices clamoring for more free airtime in the name of public interest prompted the nonprofits that benefited from Ad Council campaigns to protect what time broadcasters did devote to PSAs. Once again, the beneficiaries backed the broadcasters. The National Crime Prevention Council's executive director Jack Calhoun, sponsor of the McGruff campaign, noted that "broadcasters have helped drive crime rates to their lowest levels in 30 years" by running $128 million worth of public service ads for the group in 1999.[38]

But Erik Barnouw, writing in *The Sponsor: Notes on a Modern Potentate*, argued that other actors such as advertisers and ad agencies also played roles in determining what messages were aired. In his study of the sponsor's role in American television, Barnouw wrote that "the power to decide what messages are of social importance and must have wide distribution (and which are not) is a considerable power. That it had become part of the domain of sponsors and advertising agencies, who already controlled most network time by purchase, seemed odd to some observers, and even preposterous. But sponsors and agencies had not in the first instance sought a role in the matter. Because of their dominance of the most valuable time—including prime time—the role had been virtually thrust upon them. It was a case of power gravitating toward power. Soon it was taken for granted."[39]

The Gore Commission

The 1996 Telecommunications Act gave networks a sizable segment of the broadcast spectrum to help with the transition to digital broadcasting. The commission was charged with spelling out the public interest in broadcasting and making recommendations that also considered a broadcaster's rights of free speech.[40] After deliberating from October 1997 to April 1998, the Gore Commission issued ten recommendations. Among the most significant called for the FCC to adopt a set of public interest obligations for broadcasters that would cover community outreach, public affairs programming, public service ads, and closed captioning. The commission also recommended that Congress establish a trust fund to create a permanent source of funding for public broadcasting, and that broadcasters should voluntarily provide five minutes each night for candidate discourse in the thirty days prior to an election.[41]

The FCC and Congress have not implemented these recommendations. To date, there is no trust fund for public broadcasting, nor have broadcasters provided any free airtime for political speech. And there are no public interest obligations. When the subject of public interest obligations do come up, various constituencies have different agendas about what the requirements should be, and they all fight for free airtime. Former NAB president Fritts says he believes that broadcasters have an obligation to run public service ads, but that they must be considered part of a broader public interest mix that includes raising money for charitable causes and providing disaster relief and recovery efforts. The question of how many PSAs broadcasters should air and when has long been debated with little agreement, and there is not likely to be a change anytime soon.

As with most complicated issues, determining whether public service advertising is in jeopardy depends on which side of the debate you stand. Based on the Kaiser Family Foundation report, broadcasters are airing fewer PSAs, and a rapidly changing communications landscape altered by digital media has contributed to the problem. Even if broadcasters dispute the Kaiser report, the NAB's last community service report in 2006 showed a $1 billion decline in donated PSAs from the $8.1 billion figure in 2000. Previous NAB reports showed earlier declines.

The Ad Council views the issue differently. It uses a method that monitors PSAs year-round on all broadcast affiliates, across more than 210 broadcast markets. Based on this approach, the council found a 129 percent increase in the number of its PSAs on broadcast TV from 2007 to 2011, and a 10 percent increase in the number of times a person had been exposed to a TV public service message. Given the economic climate during the same time period, the council also found a 4 percent decline in the dollar value of the ad placements—the amount the council would have had to pay if it had purchased the airtime.

In a statement, the council said, "The Ad Council looks at broadcast TV PSAs as one part of an integrated, comprehensive approach that relies on all forms of media (radio, print, out of home, Web, social media). While the 2008 Kaiser study states that 46 percent of all PSAs air overnight, the Ad Council has found that year after year on average 70 percent of Ad Council PSAs air in desirable day parts."[42]

Digital communication has radically changed media habits. The rise of the Internet, social networking sites, and video on demand has transformed the way we consume media. Now citizens can produce it. As broadcasters watch their viewer numbers decline, they are devoting less free airtime to PSAs. The creators of public service campaigns can no longer rely exclusively on traditional communication vehicles such as television to reach their intended audiences.

To deal with these trends, the Ad Council now focuses on developing integrated public service campaigns that run across all media. Digital communication is an increasingly important part of that mix.

Epilogue

Looking to the Future

In the digital age, when marketers want to draw attention to a particular project or campaign, they create a microsite—a dedicated web address about a specific issue. Microsites are typically one part of a broader communications campaign that includes advertising in broadcast, print, and other traditional mediums. Marketers will use thirty-second broadcast TV spots or print ads to help drive attention to the microsite, which has become—in the case of public service advertising—the Internet equivalent of the 800 toll-free number or pamphlet previously used to give the public more information about a social issue.

The Ad Council and many other for-profit and nonprofit organizations seeking public attention often use microsites in their marketing efforts. The microsite the Ad Council created for the Save the Children campaign discussed in chapter 1 shows how broad social issues can be framed to benefit particular causes. At www.everybeatmatters.org, the campaign creators (which included the Ad Council, the nonprofit group Save the Children, and the ad agency BBDO) made the sound of a child's heartbeat the central motif of the final campaign, which launched in September 2012. The microsite demonstrates how the council combined the use of both interactive media, and social media to foster deeper engagement with all audiences in an increasingly fragmented media landscape. And it is an important example of how the Ad Council sees its future.

Not that long ago, organizations could shout their messages across three dominant broadcasting networks, but they never really knew whether the people they wanted to reach were listening. They could—and still do—place ads on TV programs they thought their audiences were watching. They could—and still do—buy print ads in magazines they thought their audiences were reading.

But the communication was one-way. What the Internet provided was a new opportunity to have an interactive conversation with the public, especially younger audiences.

"You can't just have a TV and radio and print ad for someone who is fifteen to twenty-two," said Barbara Shimaitis, the Ad Council's senior vice president of interactive services. "The thinking now is, who is the target audience? What is the message we are trying to do? What are we trying to communicate to them? And what is the best way to reach them?"

The Save the Children microsite is sleek and sophisticated in a way that reflects the Ad Council's ability to draw on the best digital talents in the ad industry. The image of a healthcare worker placing a stethoscope on the chest of a smiling baby draws people into the site. Four buttons enable viewers to watch a video, download music, give money, and read a story about the Colorado-based band OneRepublic. The band used the heartbeats of children in Malawi and Guatemala, captured by healthcare workers using a special stethoscope, to create the song "Feel Again."

In one video on the microsite, OneRepublic singer Ryan Tedder talks about how he integrated the heartbeats into the song. "These kids—a number of them had heartbeats that ranged from 130 to 140 beats a minute," he said. "From a musical perspective, it was the perfect tempo." Susan Ridge, Save the Children's vice president of marketing, said in the video that the song was intended to break through the psychic barriers people maintain to manage a complex world. "The lyrics are really a message to say, 'Look folks, we can get numb to things in the world, right?'" she explains. "There are a lot of situations that overwhelm us, but we don't have to feel that way. Feel again."

Social media features on the site enable viewers to share the message with their friends, family, and other networks. Viewers can "tweet the heartbeat" and create a self-portrait using the heartbeats.

The launch of the Every Beat Matters site was seamless. But it doesn't always work that way. Digital technology brings both rewards and headaches, from site design problems to coping with inappropriate comments posted on YouTube or Facebook. There are both pluses and minuses to interactivity.

When the Ad Council updates a classic icon such as Smokey Bear, it underscores its belief that the future of public service advertising lies in the ability to "activate an online dialogue about our social issues." It has elaborated on the approach in a recent statement: "Social media and digital strategies are providing the opportunity to activate an online dialogue about our social issues, broaden the reach of the messages, and deepen the public's level of interaction with our causes. Through programs on Facebook, Twitter, and other platforms, we now have a channel for continued communication and engagement with the public on an ongoing basis. All of our campaigns have a social or digital component, and over 75 percent of our partners have a more formal social media program conducted by the Ad Council, and, oftentimes, an external agency."[1]

In 2008, when the council reintroduced Smokey with a more modern look, it added social media to the communications mix. To reach young adults between eighteen and thirty-four, it launched Smokey's Facebook page, where thousands of fan photos have been posted. In 2009 it introduced viral marketing tools called widgets for the bear's sixty-fifth birthday in August. One widget included a five-question quiz, "How well do you know Smokey Bear?" The second widget, "Wildfire Awareness," included buttons that viewers could click to read related news and link to Smokey's Twitter feed. The council further expanded the bear's social media reach in 2010 to include games, puzzles, and other viral marketing tools such as apps and memes. Smokey also now has profiles on YouTube and Flicker.

The That's Not Cool campaign, undertaken in 2009 with the Family Violence Prevention Fund to address digital dating abuse, marked the first time the council had selected a digital ad agency—the Interpublic Group's R/GA—to prepare all the elements in the communications campaign, including traditional ads for TV, radio, and billboards. In a 2010 interview with *MediaPost*, R/GA's Nick Law said, "Marketing in the digital space creates more opportunities around changing behaviors. It is a lot easier and a lot more effective to use social media to rally people around a cause. It goes to actually helping people."

The Ad Council periodically updates its well-known historical campaigns online, such as the long-running recycling campaign with Keep America Beautiful. This campaign's focus is no longer based solely on creating memorable slogans or icons but rather on integrating its messages across all media platforms to reach the right audience.

In 2012, eighteen-year-olds in a college classroom could still complete the following sentences: "A mind is . . . ," "Only you can . . . ," "Friends don't let friends . . . ," and "Loose lips. . . ." But since the majority of Americans no longer watch only three networks, can the Ad Council continue to create timeless campaigns and slogans that will become embedded in American culture? Are we losing an important part of our cultural experience when we hypertarget demographics and platforms?

Barbara Shimaitis says that, while the Ad Council would welcome the next memorable image or slogan that captures lasting public recognition, it is no longer the priority. What matters more in the digital world is reaching audiences where they live, and changing behavior for the good.

Ad Council CEO Peggy Conlon agrees: "What the Internet is teaching us is [that] conversations are as relevant as they ever were because they are more intimate, more personally relevant, and more actionable."

The PSA campaigns examined in this book were all more than memorable ad images and slogans. They demonstrated how the personalities, financial interests, and prevailing social attitudes of the day impacted the final advertising product. They illustrated the Ad Council's influence in determining what social issues are important and what public service messages Americans see. They have reflected the ability of America's broadcasting system to control what content gets on the airwaves and to protect its own advertisers—even if that protection has occasionally conflicted with social causes. They have shown how other powerful actors, including the federal government and corporations, can use public service to promote their policy agendas or deflect their responsibility for helping to solve major social problems such as pollution.

These powerful campaigns have mirrored the sweeping social and political forces that have shaped the United States from World War II until today. How the nation grappled with the war itself, the nation's land management policies, women's empowerment, the atomic bomb, communism, the environment, racism, and crime can be traced through the various Ad Council campaign messages. The campaigns have shaped public acceptance of consumption as a welcome sign of progress, promoted understanding that women could successfully perform the same jobs as men, championed capitalism as the dominant economic system, and fostered awareness that the environment is everyone's responsibility.

The Ad Council's influence has spanned generations and changed our world for the better. But change is never easy. The council has had to juggle competing interests and dictates with creative expression over its seven decades of history. It's a delicate balancing act, and as the organization heads purposefully into the second decade of the twenty-first century, it remains an important vehicle for social change. It's also a potent reminder that the most impactful ad campaign doesn't need the biggest budget, but rather the most inspired message.

Acknowledgments

I would like to thank my faculty colleagues, students, family, and anyone who has ever talked to me about this book—whether they wanted to or not. My graduate assistants Lauren Adams, Julie Black, Katelyn Chesley, Francesca Ernst, Sara-Kathryn Ferrell, Lauren Fliegelman, Lauren Reed, Jenny Wang, and Gail Ziegler dug tirelessly through databases to unearth research gems. Faculty colleagues W. Joseph Campbell and Christopher Simpson slogged through academic papers based on some chapters in this book. Smithsonian Books Director Carolyn Gleason recognized the value of showcasing the Ad Council's place in American history. Editor Duke Johns helped make the prose sing.

I would also like to thank the Ad Council's staff for their willingness to grant the kind of access and time that made this project possible. My special gratitude goes to a few people who guided me throughout the writing of this book. Without the valuable insights of Maria Ivancin, Fern Siegel, Leonard Steinhorn, and Rodger Streitmatter, this book would not have been possible.

Lastly, I dedicate this book to my family. Thank you, Josephine, Richard, Grant, and Bryson for supporting me during every weekend I spent writing.

Notes

Prologue

1. Ad Council, minutes of meeting of Advertising Council, February 5, 1942, Section 13/2/201: Box 1, Ad Council Archives, University of Illinois, Urbana.

Chapter 1. What Is the Ad Council?

1. Ad Council Campaign Review Committee meeting, New York, November 16, 2011 (attended by author).
2. Interview with Ruth Wooden, September 5, 2012.

Chapter 2. Advertising's Gift to America

1. James Webb Young, address to the Association of National Advertisers and the American Association of Advertising Agencies, Hot Springs, Va., November 14, 1941, Section 13/2/300: Box 1, Ad Council Archives, University of Illinois, Urbana.
2. Inger L. Stole. "Consumer Protection in Historical Perspective: The Five-Year Battle over Federal Regulation of Advertising, 1933 to 1938," *Mass Communication and Society* 3 (2000): 351–72.
3. Richard A. Harris and Sidney M. Milkis, *The Politics of Regulatory Change: A Tale of Two Agencies* (New York: Oxford University Press, 1989), 148.
4. Roland Marchand, *Advertising the American Dream: Making Way for Modernity, 1920–1940* (Berkeley: University of California Press, 1985), xvii.
5. Stole, "Consumer Protection," 354.
6. Stuart Chase and F. J. Schlink, *Your Money's Worth: A Study in the Waste of the Consumer's Dollar* (New York: Macmillan, 1927), 42.
7. Maurice Mandell, "A History of the Advertising Council" (PhD diss., Indiana University, 1953), 42.
8. Stole, "Consumer Protection," 355.
9. Ibid., 355, 352.
10. Ibid., 356.
11. Ibid., 359.
12. Ibid., 364.
13. Ibid., 365.

14. Inger L. Stole, "'The Salesmanship of Sacrifice': The Advertising Industry's Use of Public Relations during the Second World War," *Advertising & Society Review* 2, no. 2 (2001), http://muse.jhu.edu/journals/advertising_and_society_review/v002/2.2stole.html.

15. Ibid.

16. "War on Advertising as Monopoly Breeder Is More Than Talk," *Printers' Ink*, August 30, 1940, 9.

17. L. D. H. Weld, "$5 Million Campaign Suggested to Educate Public about Advertising," *Printers' Ink*, July 18, 1941.

18. Mandell, "History of the Advertising Council," 47.

19. Ibid., 48.

20. Ibid., 49–50.

21. Young, address, November 14, 1941.

22. Mandell, "History of the Advertising Council," 55.

23. Ibid., 56.

24. Ibid., 62.

25. John Orr Young, *Adventures in Advertising* (New York: Harper & Brothers, 1949), 96–97.

26. Harold B. Thomas, *The Background and Beginning of the Advertising Council* (New York: Advertising Council, 1952), 17.

27. Ibid., 18.

28. Ibid.

29. Ibid., 18–21.

30. Ibid., 22.

31. Ibid., 24.

32. Ibid., 25.

33. Ad Council, minutes of meeting of Advertising Council, January 14, 1942, Section 13/2/201: Box 1, Ad Council Archives, University of Illinois, Urbana, 2.

34. Ad Council, minutes of meeting, February 5, 1942, 6.

35. Franklin Delano Roosevelt, State of the Union address, January 6, 1942, http://www.presidency.ucsb.edu/ws/index.php?pid=16253.

36. Ad Council, By-Laws of the Advertising Council, February 18, 1942, Section 13/2/201: Box 1, Ad Council Archives, University of Illinois, Urbana.

37. Ad Council, minutes of the Sponsor Members and Board of Directors of the War Advertising Council, May 28, 1943, Section 13/2/201: Box 1, Ad Council Archives, University of Illinois, Urbana.

Chapter 3. Smokey Bear

1. Ad Council, *Public Service Advertising That Changed a Nation* (New York: Ad Council, 2004), 3.

2. Edmund Morris, *Theodore Rex* (New York: Random House, 2001), 229.

3. Ibid., 231.

4. Ibid.

5. Theodore Roosevelt, speech, May 19, 1903, Sacramento, Calif., http://theodore-roosevelt.com/images/research/txtspeeches/454.txt.

6. U.S. Forest Service, "Multiple-Use Sustained-Yield Act of 1960," accessed September 23, 2012, http://www.fs.fed.us/emc/nfma/includes/musya60.pdf.

7. Pete Dunne, *Prairie Spring* (New York: Houghton Mifflin Harcourt, 2009), 149–50.

8. John L. O'Sullivan, "Annexation," *United States Magazine and Democratic Review*, July/August 1845, accessed on May 25, 2012, 5–10.

9. Harold K. Steen, *The U.S. Forest Service: A History* (Seattle: University of Washington Press, 1976), 13.

10. Ibid.

11. U.S. Forest Service, *The U.S. Forest Service: An Overview*, (Washington, D.C.: U.S. Forest Service, 2008), 2.

12. Steen, *U.S. Forest Service*, 27–37.

13. Timothy Egan, *The Big Burn: Teddy Roosevelt and the Fire That Saved America* (Boston: Houghton Mifflin Harcourt, 2009), 9.

14. George Everett, "Mark Twain's Big Sky Tour: Twain's Mastery Delighted Audiences, Disarmed Soldiers, Condemned the Corrupt," *Montana Pioneer*, March 2010, http://www.mtpioneer.com/2010-March-mark-twain.html.

15. Egan, *Big Burn*, 18–19.

16. Ibid., 37.

17. Ibid., 42.

18. Ibid., 69.

19. Ibid., 70.

20. William Clifford Lawter Jr., *Smokey Bear 20252: A Biography* (Alexandria, Va.: Lindsay Smith Publishers, 1994), 7.

21. Steen, *U.S. Forest Service*, 75.

22. Ibid.

23. Egan, *Big Burn*, 98.

24. U.S. Forest Service, "The 1910 Fires," accessed June 26, 2012, http://www.foresthistory.org/ASPNET/Policy/Fire/FamousFires/1910Fires.aspx.

25. Egan, *Big Burn*, 240.

26. Ibid.

27. U.S. Forest Service, "The Weeks Act," accessed June 26, 2012, http://www.foresthistory.org/ASPNET/Policy/WeeksAct/index.aspx.

28. Steen, *U.S. Forest Service*, 189.

29. Ibid., 213.

30. Ibid., 214–17.

31. Lawter, *Smokey Bear 20252*, 28.

32. Ibid., 29.

33. Ellen Earnhardt Morrison, *Guardian of the Forest: A History of the Smokey Bear Program* (New York: Vantage, 1976), 2.

34. Ibid., 3.

35. Lawter, *Smokey Bear 20252*, 29.

36. William V. Mendenhall to Sigurd Larmon, April 28, 1942, U.S. Forest Service, Record Group 95, Smokey Bear Campaign Historical Correspondence 1942–84, Box 1, National Archives, College Park, Md.

37. Ibid.

38. Sigurd Larmon to William V. Mendenhall, U.S. Forest Service, Record Group 95, Smokey Bear Campaign Historical Correspondence 1942–84, Box 1, National Archives, College Park, Md.

39. Jeanne M. Knapp, *Don Belding: A Career of Advertising and Public Service* (Lubbock: Texas Tech University, 1983), 16.

40. Ibid.

41. U.S. Forest Service, "Highlights of Wartime Forest Fire Prevention Campaign," June 22, 1942, Record Group 95, Smokey Bear Campaign Historical Correspondence 1942–84, Box 1, National Archives, College Park, Md.

42. Ibid.

43. Arnold B. Larson to Dr. John Shea, U.S. Forest Service, Record Group 95, Smokey Bear Campaign, Historical Correspondence 1942–84, Box 1, National Archives, College Park, Md.

44. U.S. Forest Service, record of meeting with Advertising Council on Forest Fire Prevention Campaign, June 3, 1942, Record Group 95, Smokey Bear Campaign, Historical Correspondence 1942–84, Box 1, National Archives, College Park, Md.

45. W. I. Hutchinson to Dana Parkinson, May 16, 1942, Record Group 95, Smokey Bear Campaign, Historical Correspondence 1942–84, Box 1, National Archives, College Park, Md.

46. Ibid.

47. Claude Wickard to Miller McClintock, May 26, 1942, Record Group 95, Smokey Bear Campaign, Historical Correspondence 1942–84, Box 1, National Archives, College Park, Md.

48. E. W. Loveridge to Richard F. Hammatt, "Assignment to Wartime Forest Fire Prevention," June 16, 1942, Record Group 95, Smokey Bear Campaign, Historical Correspondence 1942–84, Box 1, National Archives, College Park, Md.

49. Lawter, *Smokey Bear 20252*, 31.

50. Robert D. Baker, *The National Forests of the Northern Region: Living Legacy* (College Station, Tex.: Intaglio, 1993), 160.

51. U.S. Forest Service, "Wartime Forest Fire Prevention Campaign: Region 1," September 23, 1942, Record Group 95, Smokey Bear Campaign, Historical Correspondence 1942–84, Box 1, National Archives, College Park, Md.

52. Richard F. Hammatt to Don Belding, September 12, 1942, Record Group 95, Smokey Bear Campaign, Historical Correspondence 1942–84, Box 1, National Archives, College Park, Md.

53. U.S. Forest Service, "Report on Wartime Forest Fire Prevention Campaign: California Region," Record Group 95, Smokey Bear Campaign, Historical Correspondence 1942–84, Box 1, National Archives, College Park, Md.

54. Lawter, *Smokey Bear 20252*, 33.

55. U.S. Forest Service, "Wartime Forest Fire Prevention," December 18, 1942, Record Group 95, Smokey Bear Campaign, Historical Correspondence 1942–84, Box 1, National Archives, College Park, Md.

56. Richard F. Hammatt to Ervin Grant, August 17, 1944, Record Group 95, Smokey Bear Campaign, Historical Correspondence 1942–84, Box 1, National Archives, College Park, Md.

57. Richard F. Hammatt, "Special Art for Wartime Forest Fire Prevention Campaign through OWI Art Pool," August 9, 1944. Record Group 95, Smokey Bear Campaign, Historical Correspondence 1942–84, Box 1, National Archives, College Park, Md.

58. Ibid.

59. Lawter, *Smokey Bear 20252*, 42.

60. Ibid.

61. Ibid., 43.

62. Jake Kosek, *Understories: The Political Life of Forests in Northern New Mexico* (Durham, N.C.: Duke University Press, 2006), 186.

63. Ibid., 188.

64. Ibid., 193.

65. Ibid.

66. Ibid.

Chapter 4. The Rosie Legend and Why the Ad Council Claimed Her

1. Sherna Burger Gluck, *Rosie the Riveter Revisited: Women, the War, and Social Change* (Boston: Twayne Publishers, 1987), 4.

2. Ibid., 9.

3. Maureen Honey, *Creating Rosie the Riveter: Class, Gender, and Propaganda during World War II* (Amherst: University of Massachusetts Press, 1984), 22–23.

4. Ibid., 26.

5. Ibid., 27.

6. Ibid., 29.

7. War Manpower Commission, "The Employment of Women in War Production," May 1942, Record Group 211, Records of Raymond Rubicam, Box 1, Employment Reports File, National Archives, College Park, Md., 24.

8. Franklin Delano Roosevelt, broadcast, October 12, 1942, http://www.ibiblio.org/pha/policy/1942/421012a.html.

9. War Manpower Commission, "The Public Looks at Manpower Problems," January 5, 1943, Record Group 211, Records of Theodore Repplier, Box 1, Figures, Facts, and Surveys File, National Archives, College Park, Md., 15.

10. War Manpower Commission, "Manpower Campaigns," Fall 1942, Record Group 211, Records of Raymond Rubicam, Box 1, Campaigns on Manpower File, National Archives, College Park, Md.

11. Honey, *Creating Rosie*, 29–30.

12. Leonard Steinhorn, *The Greater Generation: In Defense of the Baby Boom Legacy* (New York: St. Martin's Press, 2006), 94.

13. Betty Friedan, *The Feminine Mystique* (New York: W. W. Norton, 1963), 16.

14. James J. Kimble and Lester C. Olson, "Visual Rhetoric Representing Rosie the Riveter: Myth and Misconception in J. Howard Miller's 'We Can Do It!' Poster," *Rhetoric & Public Affairs* 9 (2006): 544.

15. Ibid., 545.

16. Ibid., 543–46.

17. Emily Yellin, *Our Mothers' War: American Women at Home and at the Front during World War II* (New York: Free Press, 2004), 44.

18. Michael Osborn, "Rhetorical Depiction," in *Form, Genre, and the Study of Political Discourse*, ed. Herbert W. Simons and Aram A. Aghazarian (Columbia: University of South Carolina Press, 1986), 90.

19. Robert N. Bellah et al., *Habits of the Heart: Individualism and Commitment in American Life* (Berkeley: University of California Press, 1985), 39.

20. S. Paige Baty, *American Monroe: The Making of the Body Politic* (Berkeley: University of California Press, 1995), 8–9.

21. National Archives, Records of the Office of War Information, Administrative History, accessed July 8, 2012, http://www.archives.gov/research/guide-fed-records/groups/208.html#208.1.

22. War Manpower Commission, memo to Ken Dyke from Paul V. McNutt, September 29, 1942, Record Group 211, Records of Raymond Rubicam, Box 1, Campaigns on Manpower File, National Archives, College Park, Md., 18.

23. Honey, *Creating Rosie*, 32–33.

24. War Manpower Commission, meeting with J. Walter Thompson Company on Women's Campaign, January 8, 1943, Record Group 211, Office Files of Mary B. White, Box 1, Campaigns: J. Walter Thompson File, National Archives, College Park, Md.

25. J. Walter Thompson Company, "Recruit Women for War Industry and Civilian Jobs as well as the Armed Forces," n.d., World War II Advertising Collection, Box 1, David M. Rubenstein Rare Book and Manuscript Library, Duke University, Durham, N.C.

26. Leila J. Rupp, *Mobilizing Women for War: German and American Propaganda, 1939–1945* (Princeton, N.J.: Princeton University Press, 1978), 138.

27. Ibid., 138–39.

28. Ad Council, "How Industry Can Help the Government's Information Program on Womanpower," October 1943, Section 13/2/207: Box 1, Ad Council Archives, University of Illinois, Urbana.

29. War Manpower Commission, "Manpower Campaigns," 4.

30. Ibid., 7.

31. Ibid., 6.

32. Ibid., 11.

33. War Manpower Commission, "Women Workers Will Win the War: Plan for a Campaign to Get Women in Critical War Areas in War Work or Essential Civilian Jobs," Record Group 211, Office Files of Mary B. White, Box 3, Plan Book—Original Copy, Revised File, National Archives, College Park, Md., 9.

34. War Manpower Commission, "Answers to Questions Women Ask about Work," Record Group 211, Office Files of Mary B. White, Box 1, Campaigns: J. Walter Thompson File, National Archives, College Park, Md.

35. William E. Berchtold to Mary Brewster White, February 5, 1943, J. Walter Thompson, Record Group 211, Office Files of Mary B. White, Box 1, Campaigns: J. Walter Thompson File, National Archives, College Park, Md.

36. J. Walter Thompson, "Should Your Wife Get a War Job?" January 11, 1943, Record Group 211, Office Files of Mary B. White, Box 1, Campaigns: J. Walter Thompson File, National Archives, College Park, Md.

37. War Manpower Commission, "New Britain Industry Needs Women Workers," November 7, 1942, Record Group 211, Publicity Materials Relating to Women's Mobilization, Box 1, National Archives, College Park, Md.

38. J. Walter Thompson Company, "Last Night I Listened to the Clock," 1944, World War II Advertising Collection, Box 2, David M. Rubenstein Rare Book and Manuscript Library, Duke University, Durham, N.C.

39. Frank W. Fox, *Madison Avenue Goes to War: The Strange Military Career of American Advertising, 1941–45* (Provo, Utah: Brigham Young University Press, 1975), 13.

40. J. Walter Thompson Company, "Put It There, Sister!" June 1944, World War II Advertising Collection, Box 2, David M. Rubenstein Rare Book and Manuscript Library, Duke University, Durham, N.C.

41. Ibid.

42. Office of War Information, Record Group 208, Box 1, Press Releases, National Archives, College Park, Md.

43. Office of War Information, Record Group 208, Box 3, Magazine Covers File, National Archives, College Park, Md.

44. War Manpower Commission, "Radio Department: Erwin, Wasey & Company," Record Group 211, Records of Theodore Repplier, Box 2, Radio Announcements File, National Archives, College Park, Md.

45. Ibid.

46. War Manpower Commission, "Series of Ten One-Minute Radio Announcements, Women's Campaign," February 12, 1943, Record Group 211, Office Files of Mary B. White, Box 1, Campaigns: Women's Campaign Kit File, National Archives, College Park, Md.

47. Ibid.

48. Women's Advisory Committee chairman Margaret A. Hickey to a meeting of the War Manpower Commission, speech, March 1, 1943, Record Group 211, Office Files of Mary B. White, Box 3, Promotion Exhibits File, National Archives, College Park, Md.

49. Ibid.

50. Robert P. Keim, *A Time in Advertising's Camelot: The Memoirs of a Do-Gooder* (Madison, Conn.: Long View Press, 2002), 4–5.

51. Ad Council, "Ad Council's Response: Rosie the Riveter," August 16, 2012.

Chapter 5. "A Keg of Dynamite and You're Sitting on It"

1. Kai Bird and Martin J. Sherwin, *American Prometheus: The Triumph and Tragedy of J. Robert Oppenheimer* (New York: Vintage Books, 2005), 332.

2. Letter from William Higinbotham to Theodore Repplier, February 14, 1946, 13/2/305, Box 1, File Atomic Energy 1946, Ad Council Archives, University of Illinois, Urbana.

3. Robert J. Oppenheimer, "Atomic Weapons," *Proceedings of the American Philosophical Society* 90 (January 1946): 9.

4. Emergency Committee of Atomic Scientists, Albert Einstein fund-raising letter, December 11, 1946, Box 13/2/305, Box 2, File Council Campaigns 1946–1948, Ad Council Archives, University of Illinois, Urbana.

5. Megan Barnhart, "Selling the International Control of Atomic Energy: The Scientists' Movement, the Advertising Council, and the Problem of the Public," in *The Atomic Bomb and American Society: New Perspectives*, ed. Rosemary Piehler and Kurt Mariner (Knoxville: University of Tennessee Press, 2009), 104.

6. Harry S. Truman, statement announcing the bombing of Hiroshima, August 6, 1945, http://www.pbs.org/wgbh/amex/presidents/33_truman/psources/ps_hiroshima.html.

7. Paul Boyer, *By the Bomb's Early Light: American Thought and Culture at the Dawn of the Atomic Age* (New York: Pantheon, 1985), 12.

8. Sydnor H. Walker, ed., *The First One Hundred Days of the Atomic Age: August 6–November 15, 1945* (New York: Woodrow Wilson Foundation, 1946), 12–35.

9. Norman Cousins, *Modern Man Is Obsolete* (New York: Viking Press, 1945), 7.

10. Alice Kimball Smith, *A Peril and a Hope: The Scientists' Movement in America, 1945–47* (Chicago: University of Chicago Press, 1965), 54.

11. Eugene Rabinowitch, "Five Years After," *Bulletin of the Atomic Scientists* 7, no. 1 (January 1951): 3–6.

12. Walker, *First One Hundred Days*, 45–46.

13. Susan Caudill, "Trying to Harness Atomic Energy, 1946–1951: Albert Einstein's Publicity Campaign for World Government," *Journalism Quarterly* 68 (1991): 253–62.

14. Cousins, *Modern Man Is Obsolete*. 22.

15. Raymond Swing, *In the Name of Sanity* (New York: Harper & Brothers, 1945), 1.

16. Boyer, *By the Bomb's Early Light*, 33.

17. Ibid., 39.

18. Harold Urey, "The Atom and Humanity," *Science* 102 (November 2, 1945): 435–39.

19. Walker, *First One Hundred Days*, 34.

20. Emergency Committee of Atomic Scientists, "A Statement of Purpose," November 17, 1946, 13/2/305, Box 2, File Council Campaigns 1946–1948, Ad Council Archives, University of Illinois, Urbana.

21. War Advertising Council, minutes, Public Advisory Committee meeting, June 5, 1946, 13/2/201, Box 3, Ad Council Archives, University of Illinois, Urbana.

22. War Advertising Council, "Report on Major National Problems," 13/2/207, Box 4, Ad Council Archives, University of Illinois, Urbana.

23. Ad Council, "Radio Fact Sheet," October 14, 1946, Emergency Committee of Atomic Scientists Papers, Box 7, Folder 8, Special Collections Research Center, University of Chicago.

24. Harry S. Truman, news conference following the signing of a Joint Declaration on Atomic Energy, November 15, 1945, Harry S. Truman Library and Museum, http://www.trumanlibrary.org/publicpapers/index.php?pid=196&st=nuclear&st1=atomic.

25. Ad Council, "Report to Public Advisory Committee on the Atomic Energy Campaign," January 8, 1947, Emergency Committee of Atomic Scientists, Box 7, Folder 8, Special Collections Research Center, University of Chicago.

26. Ibid.

27. Letter from Michael Amrine to William Higinbotham, January 16, 1947, Federation of American Scientists Papers, Box 4, Folder 5, Special Collections Research Center, Special Collections Research Center, University of Chicago.

28. Ad Council, "Business Steps Up Its Candle Power: The 5th Year of the Advertising Council," March 1, 1947, 13/2/305, Box 1, Federation of American Scientists Papers, Box 4, Folder 5, Special Collections Research Center, University of Chicago.

29. Ad Council, "Report to Public Advisory Committee."

30. Emergency Committee of Atomic Scientists, memo to trustees, October 5, 1946, ECAS Papers, Box 1, Folder 7, Special Collections Research Center, University of Chicago.

31. Ibid.

32. Letter from Theodore Repplier to Joseph Schaffner, October 10, 1946, Emergency Committee of Atomic Scientists Papers, Box 7, Folder 8, Special Collections Research Center, University of Chicago.

33. Letter from William Higinbotham to Joseph Schaffner, November 20, 1946, Federation of American Scientists Papers, Box 15, Folder 4, Special Collections Research Center, University of Chicago.

34. Letter from Allan Wilson to Joseph Schaffner, January 13, 1947, Emergency Committee of Atomic Scientists Papers, Box 7, Folder 8, Special Collections Research Center, University of Chicago.

35. Letter from G. Edward Pendray to Albert Einstein, January 14, 1947, Federation of American Scientists Papers, Box 4, Folder 5, Special Collections Research Center, University of Chicago.

36. Letter from William Higinbotham to Albert Einstein, January 17, 1947, Federation of American Scientists Papers, Box 15, Folder 4, Special Collections Research Center, University of Chicago.

37. Letter from Joseph Schaffner to Albert Einstein, January 21, 1947, Emergency Committee of Atomic Scientists Papers, Box 7, Folder 8, Special Collections Research Center, University of Chicago.

38. Caudill. "Trying to Harness Atomic Energy." 255.
39. Emergency Committee of Atomic Scientists, Albert Einstein fund-raising letter, December 11, 1946.
40. Albert Einstein, "Only Then Shall We Find Courage," *New York Times*, June 23, 1946.
41. Letter from Allan Wilson to G. Edward Pendray, February 6, 1947, Box 13/2/305, Box 2, File Ad Council Campaigns 1946–1948, Ad Council Archives, University of Illinois, Urbana.
42. Letter from Allan Wilson to Joseph Schaffner, February 27, 1947, Emergency Committee of Atomic Scientists Papers, Box 7, Folder 8, Special Collections Research Center, University of Chicago.
43. Harry S. Truman, special message to the Congress on atomic energy, October 3, 1945, Harry S. Truman Library and Museum, http://www.trumanlibrary.org/public papers/index.php?pid=165&st=hope&st1.
44. Bird and Sherwin, *American Prometheus*, 328.
45. Ibid.
46. Boyer, *By the Bomb's Early Light*, 54–55.
47. Andrei Gromyko, speech, United Nations Atomic Energy Commission, June 19, 1946.
48. Andrei Gromyko, speech, United Nations Security Council, March 5, 1947.
49. Ad Council, Gromyko speech and the atom memo, March 7, 1947, Box 13/2/305, Box 2, File Ad Council Campaign 1946–1948, Ad Council Archives, University of Illinois, Urbana.
50. Harry S. Truman, special message to the Congress on Greece and Turkey, March 12, 1947, Harry S. Truman Library and Museum, http://www.trumanlibrary.org/pub-licpapers/index.php?pid=2189&st=&st1=.
51. Letter from Joseph Schaffner to Theodore Repplier, April 8, 1947, 13/2/305, Box 2, Council Campaign File 1946–1948, Ad Council Archives, University of Illinois, Urbana.
52. Letter from Allan Wilson to Joseph Schaffner, April 15, 1947, Emergency Committee of Atomic Scientists Papers, Box 7, Folder 8, Special Collections Research Center, University of Chicago.
53. Letter from Hans Bethe to Joseph Schaffner, April 29, 1947, Emergency Committee of Atomic Scientists Papers, Box 1, Folder 7, Special Collections Research Center, University of Chicago.
54. Statement of receipts and disbursements, April 30, 1947, Emergency Committee of Atomic Scientists Papers, Box 4, Folder 6, Special Collections Research Center, University of Chicago.
55. Ad Council. "Report to Public Advisory Committee."
56. Ibid.
57. Ibid.
58. Boyer, *By the Bomb's Early Light*, 37.

Chapter 6. The Struggle for Men's Souls

1. Robert P. Keim, *A Time in Advertising's Camelot: The Memoirs of a Do-Gooder* (Madison, Conn.: Long View Press, 2002), 129.
2. Christopher Simpson, *Blowback: America's Recruitment of Nazis and Its Effects on the Cold War* (New York: Weidenfeld & Nicolson, 1988), 227.
3. Stacey Cone, "Presuming a Right to Deceive: Radio Free Europe, Radio Liberty, the CIA, and the News Media," *Journalism History* 24, no. 4 (Winter 1998–99), 148–56.
4. Frances Stonor Saunders, *The Cultural Cold War: The CIA and the World of Arts and Letters* (New York: New Press, 1999), 17.
5. George Catlett Marshall, speech, Harvard University, June 5, 1947, accessed February 6, 2012, http://www.oecd.org/document/10/0,3746,en_2649_201185_1876938_1_1_1_1,00.html.
6. Harry S. Truman, address before a Joint Session of Congress, March 12, 1947, http://avalon.law.yale.edu/20th_century/trudoc.asp
7. Rebecca Boehling, "The Role of Culture in American Relations with Europe: The Case of the United States's Occupation of Germany," *Diplomatic History* 23 (1999): 65–66.
8. Saunders, *Cultural Cold War*, 28.
9. Ibid., 30.
10. Ibid., 3.
11. Giles Scott-Smith, "The 'Masterpieces of the Twentieth Century' Festival and the Congress for Cultural Freedom: Origins and Consolidation, 1947–1952," *Intelligence and National Security* 15 (2000): 121–43.
12. Sig Mickelson, *America's Other Voice: The Story of Radio Free Europe and Radio Liberty* (New York: Praeger, 1983), 13.
13. Christopher Simpson, *Science of Coercion: Communication Research and Psychological Warfare, 1945–1960* (New York: Oxford University Press, 1994), 38.
14. Ibid., 39.
15. Saunders, *Cultural Cold War*, 38.
16. Josef Joffe, "America's Secret Weapon: A Study of How the CIA Sponsored Modern Art Exhibitions and Literary Journals during the Cold War," review of Saunders, *Cultural Cold War*, *New York Times*, April 23, 2000, http://www.nytimes.com/books/00/04/23/reviews/000423.23joffet.html.
17. Simpson, *Science of Coercion*, 39.
18. Saunders, *Cultural Cold War*, 39.
19. Mickelson, *America's Other Voice*, 17.
20. Saunders, *Cultural Cold War*, 131.
21. Ibid., 132.
22. Mickelson, *America's Other Voice*, 52.
23. Simpson, *Blowback*, 219.
24. Ibid., 228.
25. Blanche Wiesen Cook, "First Comes the Lie: C. D. Jackson and Political Warfare," *Radical History Review* 31 (1984): 42–70.

26. Ibid., 46.

27. Henry R. Luce, "The American Century," *Life*, February 17, 1941, 61–65.

28. Cook, "First Comes the Lie," 44.

29. Ibid., 47.

30. Simpson, *Blowback*, 102.

31. Kenneth Osgood, *Total Cold War: Eisenhower's Secret Propaganda Battle at Home and Abroad* (Lawrence: University Press of Kansas, 2006), 44.

32. Ned O'Gorman, "'The One Word the Kremlin Fears': C. D. Jackson, Cold War, 'Liberation,' and American Political-Economic Adventurism," *Rhetoric & Public Affairs* 12 (2009): 397.

33. James Webb Young, speech to the Advertising Council of Rochester, January 15, 1951, Section 13/2/207: Box 9, Ad Council Archives, University of Illinois, Urbana.

34. Ibid., 2.

35. Cook, "First Comes the Lie," 47.

36. Ad Council, "Talks in the Treaty Room," memo, Section 13/2/306: Box 1, Ad Council Archives, University of Illinois, Urbana.

37. Crusade for Freedom fact sheet, 1951, Frank Altschul Papers, Box 165, File 489, Rare Book and Manuscript Library, Columbia University, New York.

38. Ad Council, Crusade for Freedom print ads, "The Big Truth Is the Best Answer to the Big Lie of Communism," October 5, 1950; "If Communism Triumphs, Democracy Will Die," October 5, 1950; and "Join the Crusade for Freedom and Back Your Country's Cause," October 5, 1950; Section 13/2/207: Box 130, File 502, Ad Council Archives, University of Illinois, Urbana.

39. Letter from Lucius D. Clay to Charles P. Taft, February 21, 1951, Personal Office File, Charles P. Taft Papers, 1816–1983, Manuscript Division, Library of Congress, Washington, D.C.

40. Ad Council, Crusade for Freedom print ad, "The Commissar Lies, I Heard the Truth from Radio Free Europe!" January 1951, Section 13/2/207: Box 130, File 551, Ad Council Archives, University of Illinois, Urbana.

41. Ad Council, Crusade for Freedom print ad, "Mr. Jankowski, Your Son Escaped, He Is Safe in Cleveland," September 1951, Section 13/2/207: Box 130, File 551, Ad Council Archives, University of Illinois, Urbana.

42. Memo, Allan Brown to advertising managers, 1951, Ad Council Archives, Section 13/2/207: Box 130, File 551, Ad Council Archives, University of Illinois, Urbana.

43. Crusade for Freedom radio ad, 1951, Box 165, File 483, Rare Book and Manuscript Library, Columbia University, New York.

44. "Czech Refugees Send Freedom Balloons Aloft," *New York Herald Tribune*, September 27, 1951, Frank Altschul Papers, Box 165, File 484, Rare Book and Manuscript Library, Columbia University, New York.

45. Memo, Harold B. Miller to "gentlemen," January 1952, Ad Council, Section 13/2/207: Box 10, Advertising Council Historical File 1942–1997, Ad Council Archives, University of Illinois, Urbana.

46. Letter from Lucius D. Clay to Howard P. Taft, February 14, 1952, Personal Office File, Charles P. Taft Papers, 1816–1983, Manuscript Division, Library of Congress, Washington, D.C.

47. Ad Council, Crusade for Freedom print ad, "Even a Boy Can Fight Communism with Truth," January 1952, Section 13/2/207: Box 130, File 551, Ad Council Archives, University of Illinois, Urbana.

48. Crusade for Freedom press release, May 15, 1953, Personal Office Files, Charles P. Taft Papers, 1816–1983, Manuscript Division, Library of Congress, Washington, D.C.

49. Ad Council, Crusade for Freedom print ad, "You Mean I Can Fight Communism?" January 1955, Section 13/2/207: Box 130, File 551, Ad Council Archives, University of Illinois, Urbana.

50. Ad Council, Crusade for Freedom print ad, "Neither Could Fly but They Soloed to Freedom," January 1956, Section 13/2/207: Box 130, File 551, Ad Council Archives, University of Illinois, Urbana.

51. Ad Council, report on Public Policy Committee Meeting, November 20, 1957, Section 13/2/209: Box 1, Report of Public Policy Committee Meeting, 1956–1957, Ad Council Archives, University of Illinois, Urbana.

52. Ibid., 3.

53. RFE/RL, "Fast Facts," accessed June 15, 2012, http://www.rferl.org/info/FAQ/777.html.

Chapter 7. The Crying Indian

1. Richard Earle, *The Art of Cause Marketing: How to Use Advertising to Change Personal Behavior and Public Policy* (New York: McGraw-Hill, 2000), 2.

2. Kevin C. Armitage, "Commercial Indians: Authenticity, Nature, and Industrial Capitalism in Advertising at the Turn of the Twentieth Century," *Michigan Historical Review* (Fall 2003): 71–95.

3. Bruce J. Schulman, *The Seventies: The Great Shift in American Culture, Society, and Politics* (New York: Free Press, 2001), xii.

4. Ad Council, Anti-Pollution Campaign press release, Ad Council Collection, Box 28, David M. Rubenstein Rare Book and Manuscript Library, Duke University, Durham, N.C.

5. Ad Council, *Public Service Advertising That Changed a Nation* (New York: Ad Council, 2004), 6.

6. Hal K. Rothman, *The Greening of a Nation? Environmentalism in the United States since 1945* (Fort Worth, Tex.: Harcourt Brace, 1998), 10.

7. Ibid., 12.

8. Ibid., 13.

9. Ibid., 16.

10. Ibid.

11. Louis Blumberg and Robert Gottlieb, *War on Waste: Can America Win Its Battle with Garbage?* (Washington, D.C.: Island Press, 1989), 237.

12. Ibid., 238.
13. Ibid.
14. Ibid., 239.
15. Schulman, *The Seventies*, 129.
16. Ibid., 131.
17. Blumberg and Gottlieb, *War on Waste*, 240.
18. Adam Rome, "Give Earth a Chance: The Environmental Movement and the Sixties," *Journal of American History* 90, no. 2 (September 2003): 525–54.
19. John Kenneth Galbraith, *The Affluent Society* (Boston: Houghton Mifflin, 1958), 253.
20. Vance Packard, *The Waste Makers* (New York: David McKay, 1960), 68.
21. Rachel Carson, *Silent Spring* (Boston: Houghton Mifflin, 1962), 17.
22. Ibid., 2.
23. Rome, "Give Earth a Chance," 534.
24. Federal Highway Administration, "How the Highway Beautification Act Became a Law," accessed August 25, 2012, http://www.fhwa.dot.gov/infrastructure/beauty.cfm.
25. Rothman, *Greening of a Nation*, 97.
26. Rome, "Give Earth a Chance," 534.
27. Margaret Mead, *Culture and Commitment: A Study of the Generation Gap* (New York, Doubleday, 1970), 58–59.
28. Rome, "Give Earth a Chance," 545.
29. Ibid., 546.
30. Nelson Institute for Environmental Studies, "Gaylord Nelson and Earth Day: The Making of the Modern Environmental Movement," accessed August 25, 2012, http://www.nelsonearthday.net/earth-day/index.htm.
31. Rome, "Give Earth a Chance," 549.
32. Ibid., 550.
33. Ibid.
34. Ibid., 551–52.
35. Internal Revenue Service, "Exemption Requirements: Section 501(c)(3) Organizations," accessed September 20, 2012, http://www.irs.gov/Charities-&-Non-Profits/Charitable-Organizations/Exemption-Requirements-Section-501%28c%29%283%29-Organizations.
36. Keep America Beautiful, accessed August 18, 2012, http://www.kab.org/site/PageServer?pagename=index.
37. Ibid.
38. Keep America Beautiful, "KAB: A Beautiful History," accessed August 18, 2012, http://www.kab.org/site/PageServer?pagename=kab_history.
39. Heather Rogers, *Gone Tomorrow: The Hidden Life of Garbage* (New York: New Press, 2005), 141.
40. Ibid.
41. Carl Deal, *The Greenpeace Guide to Anti-Environmental Organizations* (Berkeley, Calif.: Odonian Press, 1993), 62.
42. Rogers, *Gone Tomorrow*, 141–42.

43. Ibid.

44. Higgins Productions, *Heritage of Splendor*, 1963, accessed August 26, 2012, http://archive.org/details/Heritage1963.

45. Ad Council, "The Miracle of America," Section 13/2/207: Box 7, Ad Council Archives, University of Illinois, Urbana.

46. Ibid., 12.

47. Orville Schell, "Introduction: Follies of Orthodoxy," in *What Orwell Didn't Know: Propaganda and the New Face of American Politics*, ed. András Szántó (New York: Public Affairs, 2007), xxi.

48. Ad Council, "People's Capitalism: Background—How and Why This Project Was Developed," memo, Section 13/2/305: Box 9, Ad Council Archives, University of Illinois, Urbana.

49. Ad Council, "Copy for People's Capitalism Exhibit," memo, Section 13/2/305: Box 9, Ad Council Archives, University of Illinois, Urbana.

50. Ad Council, "Radio Fact Sheet: Keep America Beautiful," June 1961, Ad Council Collection, Box 28, David M. Rubenstein Rare Book and Manuscript Library, Duke University, Durham, N.C.

51. Ad Council, "Keep America Beautiful Campaign One-Minute Radio Spot #1," 1961, Ad Council Collection, Box 28, David M. Rubenstein Rare Book and Manuscript Library, Duke University, Durham, N.C.

52. Keep America Beautiful, "Check List of Radio and TV Programming Ideas," Ad Council Collection, Box 28, David M. Rubenstein Rare Book and Manuscript Library, Duke University, Durham, N.C.

53. Ad Council, "Keep America Beautiful Campaign One-Minute Radio Spot #2," 1962, Ad Council Collection, Box 28, David M. Rubenstein Rare Book and Manuscript Library, Duke University, Durham, N.C.

54. Reynolds Metal Company, "Dear Broadcaster," 1963, Ad Council Collection, Box 28, David M. Rubenstein Rare Book and Manuscript Library, Duke University, Durham, N.C.

55. Ad Council, "Keep America Beautiful Campaign One-Minute Radio Spot #1," 1963, Ad Council Collection, Box 28, David M. Rubenstein Rare Book and Manuscript Library, Duke University, Durham, N.C.

56. Ad Council, "Keep America Beautiful Campaign One-Minute Radio Spot #1," 1965, Ad Council Collection, Box 28, David M. Rubenstein Rare Book and Manuscript Library, Duke University, Durham, N.C.

57. Best Foods, "Dear Sir," April 1967, Ad Council Collection, Box 28, David M. Rubenstein Rare Book and Manuscript Library, Duke University, Durham, N.C.

58. Best Foods, "Campaign Copy Guide & Fact Sheet," 1967, Ad Council Collection, Box 28, David M. Rubenstein Rare Book and Manuscript Library, Duke University, Durham, N.C.

59. Ad Council, "Transit Advertising Bulletin," August 1970, Ad Council Collection, Box 28, David M. Rubenstein Rare Book and Manuscript Library, Duke University, Durham, N.C.

60. American Can Company, "Dear Broadcaster," September 1971, Ad Council Collection, Box 28, David M. Rubenstein Rare Book and Manuscript Library, Duke University, Durham, N.C.

61. Ad Council, "Help Fight Pollution—1971," Ad Council Collection, Box 28, David M. Rubenstein Rare Book and Manuscript Library, Duke University, Durham, N.C.

62. Ibid.

63. Keep America Beautiful, "71 Things You Can Do to Stop Pollution," Ad Council Collection, Box 28, David M. Rubenstein Rare Book and Manuscript Library, Duke University, Durham, N.C.

64. Keep America Beautiful, "Pollution Control: A Corporate Responsibility," Ad Council Collection, Box 28, David M. Rubenstein Rare Book and Manuscript Library, Duke University, Durham, N.C.

65. Keenen Peck, "Adnauseam," *The Progressive* May 1983, 43–47.

66. John McDonough, "Ad Council at 60—Facing a Crossroads," *Advertising Age* April 29, 2002.

67. Thomas F. Williams, "A Litter Bit Is Not Enough," speech, Keep America Beautiful National Advisory Committee, January 16, 1973.

68. Ibid., 10.

69. Peter Harnick, "The Junking of an Anti-Litter Lobby," *Business and Society Review* (Spring 1977): 47–51.

70. Ibid., 50.

71. Ibid., 51.

72. Ibid.

73. Container Recycling Institute, "Thirty Tears Later Keep America Beautiful Is Still Keeping America Blindfolded," Spring 2000, http://www.bottlebill.org/news/articles/2000/2000-KAB-op.htm.

74. Finis Dunaway, "Gas Masks, Pogo, and the Ecological Indian: Earth Day and the Visual Politics of American Environmentalism," *American Quarterly* 60 (2008): 67–99.

75. Ibid., 70.

Chapter 8. Beyond Integration

1. Robert P. Keim, *A Time in Advertising's Camelot: The Memoirs of a Do-Gooder* (Madison, Conn.: Long View Press, 2002), 26.

2. Marybeth Gasman, *Envisioning Black Colleges: A History of the United Negro College Fund* (Baltimore: Johns Hopkins University Press, 2007), 170.

3. Keim, *Advertising's Camelot*, 26.

4. Library of Congress, "Rosa Parks Was Arrested for Civil Disobedience," accessed September 8, 2012, http://www.americaslibrary.gov/jb/modern/jb_modern_parks_2.html.

5. David Pilgrim, "What Was Jim Crow?" September 2000, http://www.ferris.edu/jimcrow/what.htm.

6. Library of Congress, "15th Amendment to the Constitution," accessed September 8, 2012, http://www.loc.gov/rr/program/bib/ourdocs/15thamendment.html.

7. Kimberley Johnson, *Reforming Jim Crow: Southern Politics and State in the Age before Brown* (New York: Oxford University Press, 2010), 16.

8. Ibid.

9. Ibid., 34.

10. Raymond Gavins, "Gordon Blaine Hancock: A Black Profile from the New South," *Journal of Negro History* 59 (1974): 216–17.

11. Johnson, *Reforming Jim Crow*, 34.

12. James G. Maddox, "The Bankhead-Jones Farm Tenant Act," *Law and Contemporary Problems* 4 (1937): 434.

13. Johnson, *Reforming Jim Crow*, 147.

14. Ibid., 148.

15. Ibid.

16. Ibid., 153.

17. Gasman, *Envisioning Black Colleges*, 3.

18. Ibid., 16–17.

19. Ibid., 18.

20. Ibid.

21. Ibid., 22.

22. Ibid., 23.

23. Ibid., 28.

24. Ibid., 33.

25. Ibid.

26. Ibid.

27. Ibid., 43.

28. Johnson, *Reforming Jim Crow*, 250.

29. Ibid., 2.

30. Gasman, *Envisioning Black Colleges*, 86

31. Derrick Bell, *Silent Covenants: Brown v. Board of Education and the Unfulfilled Hopes of Racial Reform* (New York: Oxford University Press, 2004), 9.

32. Gasman, *Envisioning Black Colleges*, 89.

33. Ibid.

34. Ibid.

35. Ibid.

36. Ibid., 90.

37. John S. Lash, "The Umpteenth Crisis in Negro Higher Education," *Journal of Higher Education* 22 (1951): 432.

38. Ibid., 434.

39. Gasman, *Envisioning Black Colleges*, 119.

40. Raymond D'Angelo, *The American Civil Rights Movement: Readings and Interpretations* (Guilford, Conn.: McGraw Hill/Dushkin, 2001), 279.

41. Gasman, *Envisioning Black Colleges*, 134.

42. Ibid., 171.

43. Ad Council, *Public Service Advertising That Changed a Nation* (New York: Ad Council, 2004), 13.

44. Gasman, *Envisioning Black Colleges*, 169.

45. Ibid., 171.

46. Metropolitan Life, "A Mind Is a Terrible Thing to Waste," 1973, Ad Council Collection, Box 39, David M. Rubenstein Rare Book and Manuscript Library, Duke University, Durham, N.C.

47. Ad Council, "Black Colleges Face a Crisis," 1973, Ad Council Collection, Box 39, David M. Rubenstein Rare Book and Manuscript Library, Duke University, Durham, N.C.

48. Ibid.

49. United Negro College Fund, "For About What It Costs for Riding Lessons, You Can Send a Kid to College," 1973, Ad Council Collection, Box 39, David M. Rubenstein Rare Book and Manuscript Library, Duke University, Durham, N.C.

50. United Negro College Fund, "University President Francis," 1975, Ad Council Collection, Box 39, David M. Rubenstein Rare Book and Manuscript Library, Duke University, Durham, N.C.

51. United Negro College Fund, "Prudence Crandall," 1976, Ad Council Collection, Box 39, David M. Rubenstein Rare Book and Manuscript Library, Duke University, Durham, N.C.

52. Ad Council, "Dear General Manager," 1981, Ad Council Collection, Box 39, David M. Rubenstein Rare Book and Manuscript Library, Duke University, Durham, N.C.

53. United Negro College Fund, "Reachin' for the Dream," 1981, Ad Council Collection, Box 39, David M. Rubenstein Rare Book and Manuscript Library, Duke University, Durham, N.C.

54. United Negro College Fund, "Bus," 1987, Ad Council Collection, Box 39, David M. Rubenstein Rare Book and Manuscript Library, Duke University, Durham, N.C.

55. United Negro College Fund, statement provided to author on the historical impact of the "A Mind Is a Terrible Thing to Waste" campaigns, September 11, 2012.

Chapter 9. Fighting Back

1. Advertising Educational Foundation, "Crime Prevention1979–Present," accessed January 5, 2013, http://www.aef.com/exhibits/social_responsibility/ad_council/2386/:pf_printable.

2. "The Challenge of Crime in a Free Society: Looking Back, Looking Forward." (Washington, D.C.: U.S. Department of Justice, Office of Justice Programs, 1997).

3. Nancy E. Marion, *A History of Federal Crime Control Initiatives, 1960–1993* (Westport, Conn.: Praeger, 1994), 37–67.

4. Ibid., 69–101.

5. "U.S. Department of Justice Federal Bureau of Investigation Uniform Crime Reporting Statistics," last modified March 29, 2010, http://www.ucrdatatool.gov.

6. Marion, *Federal Crime Control Initiatives*, 143–86.

7. Paula Reed Ward, "Kill-for-Thrill Case Drags On after 25 Years," *Pittsburgh Post-Gazette*, August 12, 2006, http://www.post-gazette.com/stories/local/uncategorized/kill-for-thrill-case-drags-on-after-25-years-445874/.

8. Evan Thomas and Bennett H. Beach, "Law: Burger Takes Aim at Crime," *Time*, February 23, 1981.

9. Ed Magnuson, "The Curse of Violent Crime," *Time*, March 23, 1981.

10. "The Plague of Violent Crime," *Newsweek*, March 23, 1981.

11. "The People's War against Crime," *U.S. News & World Report*, July 13, 1981.

12. Robert P. Keim, *A Time in Advertising's Camelot: The Memoirs of a Do-Gooder* (Madison, Conn.: Long View Press, 2002), 110.

13. Ad Council, minutes of meeting of the Board of Directors, February 8, 1979, 13/2/201, Box 13, Ad Council Archives, University of Illinois, Urbana.

14. William M. O'Barr, "Public Service Advertising," *Advertising & Society Review* 7, no. 2 (2006), http://muse.jhu.edu/journals/asr/v007/7.2unit06.html.

15. Keim, *Advertising's Camelot*, 113.

16. R. I. Goodman, "Selecting Public Service Announcements for Television," *Public Relations Review* 7 (1981): 25–33.

17. Needham Porter Novelli, *Survey of Public Service Directors from TV Stations Representing High and Low Play of High Blood Pressure Messages* (Washington, D.C.: National High Blood Pressure Education Program, National Heart Lung and Blood Institute, 1985).

18. Kathleen Reid, "A Rhetorical Approach to Non-Discursive Messages in Information Campaigns," in *Verbo-Visual Literacy: Understanding and Applying New Educational Communication Media Technologies*, selected readings from the 1993 symposium of the International Visual Literacy Association, ed. Nikos Metallinos (Montreal: 3DMT Research and Information Center, 1994), 170–81.

19. Garrett O'Keefe, "Taking a Bite Out of Crime," *Social Science and Modern Society* 22 (March/April 1985): 3, 56–64.

20. Garrett O'Keefe, *Taking a Bite Out of Crime: The Impact of the National Citizens' Crime Prevention Media Campaign* (Thousand Oaks, Calif.: Sage Publications, 1996), 22–28, 76–107.

Chapter 10. Public Service Ads and the Public Interest

1. Walter Gantz et al., *Shouting to Be Heard (2): Public Service Advertising in a Changing Television World* (Menlo Park, Calif.: Kaiser Family Foundation, 2008), 3.

2. Ibid., 6.

3. Clay Calvert, "Imus, Indecency, Violence & Vulgarity: Why the FCC Must Not Expand Its Authority over Content," *Hastings Communications and Entertainment Law Journal* 30 (2007): 1–32.

4. Wendy Melillo, "NBC Nixes Drug Ads," *Adweek*, October 4, 1999, http://www.adweek.com/news/advertising/nbc-nixes-drug-ads-36259.

5. Ibid.

6. Ibid.

7. Victoria Rideout, *Assessing Public Education Programming on HIV/AIDS: A National Survey of African Americans* (Menlo Park, Calif.: Kaiser Family Foundation, 2004): 3, 7.

8. Ibid., 7.

9. Ibid., 12.

10. Advisory Committee on Public Interest Obligations of Digital Television Broadcasters, "The Public Interest Standard in Television Broadcasting," last modified December 18, 1998, http://benton.org/initiatives/obligations/charting_the_digital _broadcasting_future/sec2.

11. Ibid., 2.

12. Ibid.

13. Ibid., 4.

14. Ibid.

15. The Radio Act of 1927, accessed September 22, 2012, http://www.americanradio history.com/Archive-Stevenson-Burgess-Others/Federal%20Radio%20Act%20 1927.pdf.

16. Museum of Broadcast Communications, "Public Interest, Convenience and Necessity," accessed March 1, 2012, http://www.museum.tv/eotvsection.php?entrycode =publicintere.

17. Advisory Committee on Public Interest Obligations, "Public Interest Standard," 2.

18. Ibid., 7.

19. Ibid., 11.

20. Red Lion Broadcasting Co. v. FCC, 395 U.S. 367 (1969),http://caselaw.lp.findlaw .com/scripts/printer_friendly.pl?page=us/395/367.html.

21. Ibid.

22. Thomas Jefferson Center for the Protection of Free Expression, "The FCC Makes Its Indecency Case at the Supreme Court, But Has the Court Already Shown Its Cards?" September 8, 2011, http://www.tjcenter.org/2011/09/08/the-fcc-makes-its -indecency-case-at-the-supreme-court-but-has-the-court-already-shown-its-cards/.

23. Craig L. LaMay, "Public Service Announcements, Broadcasters, and the Public Interest: Regulatory Background and the Digital Future," draft report for Kaiser Family Foundation, April 13, 2001.

24. Ibid., 4.

25. Ibid., 5.

26. "Hundt Blasts PSA Lack," *Television Digest*, March 10, 1997.

27. Richard Katz, "Networks Hit on PSA Loads," *Mediaweek*, April 14, 1997.

28. Ibid.

29. "TV's Foolish PSA Wrangle," *Advertising Age*, May 19, 1997.

30. Ibid.

31. Edward O. Fritts, speech to the National Association of Broadcasters convention, April 7, 1997.

32. LaMay, "Public Service Announcements," 6.

33. Judy Pasternak, "Ad Plan: Your Tax Dollars on Drugs," *Los Angeles Times*, August 20, 1998.

34. Federal Communications Commission, "In the Matter of Public Interest Obligations of TV Broadcast Licensees, MM Docket No. 99-360," *Notice of Inquiry* 14 FCC Rcd 21633 (December 1999).

35. National Association of Broadcasters, *A National Report on Local Broadcasters' Community Service* (Washington, D.C.: National Association of Broadcasters, 2000), 5–7.

36. Paige Albiniak, "NAB Study Says Stations Contributed Billions in Public Service; Not Enough, Say Some," *Broadcasting & Cable*, April 10, 2000, 24.

37. Wisconsin Democracy Campaign, "Network Affiliates Air Just 9 Seconds of Candidates Talking Each Night," April 19, 2000, http://www.wisdc.org/abcmonitorpr.php.

38. Albiniak, "NAB Study," 24.

39. Erik Barnouw, *The Sponsor: Notes on a Modern Potentate* (New York: Oxford University Press, 1978), 40.

40. Advisory Committee on Public Interest Obligations of Digital Television Broadcasters, "Appendix E: History of the Advisory Committee on Public Interest Obligations of Digital Television Broadcasters," accessed March 12, 2012, http://benton.org/initiatives/obligations/charting_the_digital_broadcasting_future/appe.

41. Advisory Committee on Public Interest Obligations of Digital Television Broadcasters, "Executive Summary," accessed March 12, 2012, http://benton.org/initiatives/obligations/charting_the_digital_broadcasting_future/summary.

42. Ad Council, e-mail response to author query, August 16, 2012.

Epilogue

1. Ad Council, e-mail response to author query, September 12, 2012.

Index

A

AARP. *See* American Association of Retired Persons (AARP)
ABC TV show *Webster,* 166
Acheson, Dean (Undersecretary of State), 70, 83, 96
Acheson-Lilienthal report, 83
Ad Council Archives (University of Illinois), 2, 67
ad industry abuses, 20–21
Adamic, Louis, 74
Advertising Age, 104, 123
The Advertising Council (Ad Council). *See also* Conlon, Peggy; propaganda; War Advertising Council
    ad agency reimburses the agency for out-of-pocket expenses for a campaign, 9
    Advisory Committee on Public Issues, 11, 128
    aim to protect the nation's people and resources, 2
    birth of, 25–28
    broadcast networks have right to decide what ads run in the space they donate to public service, 10
    Campaign Review Committee, 6, 29, 44
    campaign-related operating expenses, 17
    campaigns, public service, 2
    campaigns (1942 to 2012), created 423 separate, 2
    campaigns focus on individual actions a person can take to help address a larger societal problem, 3, 10
    campaigns run a minimum of three years, 9, 16
    campaigns use commercial advertising methods, 2
    client receives a series of ads donated by media companies on network television, cable, radio, newspapers, magazines, online, and on outdoor billboards, 9–10
    donated media model, 10, 16, 27
    Executive Committee, 11
    Form 990 tax returns, 17
    goal is to achieve positive social change, 3
    government officials, access to top, 3
    incorporated February 18, 1942, 1, 28
    Kaiser report findings, 171
    "Matters of Choice: Advertising in the Public Interest," 52
    media companies donate more than $1 billion a year in free advertising time and space, 2, 5, 10
    nonprofit organizations and federal government pay $2.4 to $3 million to underwrite a three year campaign, 16
    partnerships with advertising, business, foundation, and media organizations, 17
    politics, religion, advocacy, and direct fund-raising campaigns, shuns, 9
    propaganda campaigns, 56, 88
    Public Advisory Committee, 76, 78, 84
    Public Policy Committee, 101, 154
    public service advertisements (PSAs), 171–73, 175, 179–81, 183–85
    public service role, 3, 162
    radio ads encouraged listeners to write for a pamphlet, 79
    revenue, taxpayer *vs.* private sources, 17
    revenue structure, 16
    total revenue (2001-2010), 17
    War Advertising Council, renamed (May 28, 1943), 1–2
    "wish list," 15
Advertising Council of Rochester, 95
Advertising Federation of America, 21
Advertising & Society Review (Natkins), 158
Advertising the American Dream: Making Way for Modernity, 1920-1940 (Marchand), 20
Advisory Committee on Public Interest Obligations of Digital Television Broadcasters (Gore Commission), 176, 183–85
The Affluent Society (Galbraith), 110
African American
    education, 131, 134, 148
    educational institutions, 129
    Jim Crow order and, 131, 137
    leaders, 133
    teens, 143
AIDS, 170, 174–75
air and water pollution, 112
Albert Lasker (advertising giant), 39
alcohol and drug abuse, 162, 170
Alliance for Better Campaigns, 182
"America at War Needs Women at Work" slogan, 62
American Association of Advertising Agencies, 23

American Association of Retired Persons (AARP), 11
American Bar Association, 153
American Broadcasting Company, 74
American Can Company, 116, 122, 125
American Chamber of Horrors (Young), 20
American Chemistry Council, 104
*The American Civil Rights Movement: Readings and
    Interpretations* (D'Angelo), 140
The American Farmer (ABC), 85
American Heritage Foundation, 100
American Institute of Public Opinion poll (1945), 75
American intelligence officials, 92
American Legacy Foundation's anti-smoking
    campaign, 175
American Monroe: The Making of a Body Politic (Baty),
    59
*American Prometheus: The Triumph and Tragedy of J.
    Robert Oppenheimer* (Bird and Sherwin), 69
American values and ideology, 68
Annenberg Public Policy Center study, 182
anti-black stereotypes, 132
anti-bullying
    campaign, 166
    tricks, 166
anti-childhood obesity, 16–17
anti-communist
    crusade, 89–90, 94
    lectures, 92
    literary journal, 90
    opinions among Western European intelligentsia,
        90
    psychological warfare program, 94
    theme in advertising, 102
anti-communist elements, indigenous, 94
anti-drug abuse, 175
    campaign, 173, 175, 182
    effort, 175
anti-litter
    campaigns, 121, 125, 155 (*See also* Keep America
        Beautiful)
    focus of Keep America Beautiful, 119
    habits, 121
    strategy, 116
    themes, 120
anti-pollution, 122
anti-poverty initiatives, 150
anti-smoking campaign, 175
anti-U.S. propaganda, 91
Arab oil shock, 104
Armstrong, David (National District Attorneys
    Association), 153
Arnold, Thurman (Assistant Attorney General), 23
*The Art of Cause Marketing: How to Use Advertising to
    Change Personal Behavior and Public Policy*
    (Earle), 104
"Assessing Public Education Programming on HIV/
    AIDS" survey, 174–75
At Your Request (ABC), 85
Atlanta University, 135
Atlantic Richfield, 116
atomic energy campaign (1946), 4, 69–72, 76, 78, 80–86

atomic weapons, 69–71, 74–75, 78–79, 82–83

B
baby boom generation, 106, 112
"Back by Popular Neglect" ad, 126
*The Background and Beginning of the Advertising
    Council* (Thomas), 67
Bankhead-Jones Tenant Farm Act (1937), 133
"ban-the-can" and "bottle bill" movements, 108
Barnouw, Erik (author), 169, 183
Barnsdall-Rio Grande Oil Company, 38
Barry Goldwater: Extremist of the Right (Cook), 178
Baruch, Bernard (U.S. representative to UNAEC), 78
Baruch Plan, 78–79, 85
Batt, William L. (Office of Production Management), 24
Batten, Barton, Durstine & Osborn (BBDO), 6–8, 92,
    186
Baty, S. Paige, 59
Beard, David F. (Reynolds Metal Company general
    director of advertising), 120
beer bottle, refillable, 108
Belding, Don (Lord & Thomas), 39–40
Bellah, Robert N., 59
Bellow, Saul (author), 90
Benton Foundation, 182
Berlin Airlift, 87, 93
Berlin blockade, 90
Bernays, Edward ("father of public relations"), 118
Berryman, Cliff *(Washington Star),* 42
Best Crossword Puzzles, 66
Best Foods, 121
Bethe, Hans (physicist), 81, 84
Better Business Bureaus, 21
beverage companies' throwaway plastic bottles, 105
beverage container deposit law, national, 108–9
Big Brothers Big Sisters of America, 170–71
*The Big Burn: Teddy Roosevelt and the Fire That Saved
    America* (Egan), 36
Bird, Kai (author), 69
black citizenship, 133
black colleges. *See also* "Jim Crow"
    America's, 129, 131, 133–34, 137–41, 144–46
    leaders, Southern, 135
    presidents, 135–36
    private, 136
    Southern, 133–36
black higher education, 134
black Southern university leaders, 135
black universities, 133–34
blacks, racist terms for, 132
blacks have same legal protections as whites, 132
Blanding, Sarah (Vassar College president), 76, 101
Blumberg, Louis (author), 108
Bond, Horace Mann (president, Fort Valley State
    College (Georgia)), 133
Booker T. Washington's Tuskegee Institute, 134–35
Borden Company's Elsie the Cow, 42
Borkenau, Franz (Austrian writer), 90
bottle bills, 108–10
bottles and packages, throwaway, 104, 108, 114, 116
Boy Scouts of America, 179

Boyer, Paul, 72, 74
Bradley, Omar (D-Day commander), 89
broadcast networks standards, 10
broadcasting, 1, 176
broadcasting executives, 27
Brown, Allan (Bakelite Corporation), 98
Browning Ferris, 125
Bulletin of the Atomic Scientists, 73, 79, 86, 200n11
Bureau of Forestry, 35
Burger, Warren (Supreme Court Chief Justice), 153
Burnett, Leo (Leo Burnett Company), 27, 96
Burnham, James (American philosopher), 90
"Bus" spot TV ad, 147
Bush, George W. (President), 8
Butcher, Harry (Columbia Broadcasting Company vice
    president), 27
*By the Bomb's Early Light: American Thought and Culture
    at the Dawn of the Atomic Age* (Boyer), 72

C
Calhoun, Jack (president and CEO of the NCPC),
    164–65, 183
California Redwood Association, 40
"Caregiving" effort by AARP, 11
"Careless Matches Aid the Axis—Prevent Forest Fires"
    (slogan), 40–41. *See also* Smokey Bear campaign
"Carelessness Is Treason" slogan, 41
Carnation Contented Hour (NBC), 85–86
Carson, Rachel (biologist), 110–11, 117
Carson National Forest, 46
Carter, Jimmy (President), 152, 160
Cash McCall (Keil), 156
Caudill, Susan, 74
"CBS Cares," 172
Central Intelligence Agency (CIA). *See also* "In the Pay
    of the CIA: An American Dilemma"
    about, 4, 178
    Crusade for Freedom campaign, 87–97, 100, 102
    Psychological Strategy Board, 93
CFFP. *See* U.S. Forest Service's Cooperative Forest Fire
    Prevention (CFFP)
"The Challenge of Crime in a Free Society" (report), 150
Chandler, Raymond, 69, 157
Chase, Stuart, 21
Chicago Roundtable (weekly radio program), 74
child abuse, 163
Churchill, Winston (British prime minister), 72, 83
CIA. *See* Central Intelligence Agency (CIA)
civil disobedience, 131
civil rights
    about, 104, 111, 128, 138
    movement, 129, 131, 140
    struggle, 133, 140
Civil Rights Act (1964), 140
Civilian Conservation Corps, 37–38
Civilleti, Benjamin (Attorney General), 161–62
Clark, William A. (Montana copper baron), 34, 46
Clarke-McNary Act in 1924, 37
Clay, Lucius (General), 89, 93, 97
Clean Air Act (1970), 114
"Clean Community System" campaign, 125

cleanliness ethic, national, 115
Cleveland, Grover (President), 34
Cleveland, Helene (Fire Prevention Program Manager), 43
climate change campaign, 13–14
Clinton, Bill (President), 128
The Closing Circle: Nature, Man, and Technology
    (Commoner), 126
Coca-Cola, 116
Cold War, 88–94, 98, 102
Coldplay (rock band), 8
The Collapse of Cotton Tenancy (Johnson), 133
college access campaign, 15–16. *See also* United Negro
    College Fund
"College Is America's Best Friend" slogan, 129
Columbia Broadcasting Company, 27
Columbus Day speech (1942), 55
commercial radio programs, 81
"The Commissar lies . . . I heard the Truth from Radio
    Free Europe!," 98
Committee to Frame a World Constitution, 75
Common Ground (Adamic), 74
Commoner, Barry (scientist), 126
Communications Act (1934), 176–77
communism, 4, 88–89, 92, 95, 97–98, 101–2, 189. *See
    also* "Crusade for Freedom" campaign
Community Chest system, 136
Conant, James (Harvard University president), 76
"Confidence in a Growing America" campaign, 118
Congress for Cultural Freedom, 90
Conlon, Peggy (Ad Council president and CEO). *See
    also* The Advertising Council
    Ad Council campaigns, anecdotal stories of, 7
    Ad Council is non-partisan, 12
    Ad Council's advertising's gift to America, 2, 19
    climate change, 13
    donated media model, 16
    Huffington Post article, 49, 51
    income from federal government, 17
    industry's charity, 18
    Internet, what it is teaching us, 189
    management of nonprofit organization earning
        $40.5 million (2010), 8
    marriage campaign, value of, 9
    "no drama Conlon," 8
    obesity prevention work, 17
    poster of Rosie the Riveter, 49–50
consumer attitudes, 2
consumer movement, 20–21. *See also* Keep America
    Beautiful
Cook, Blanch Wiesen (historian), 94, 96
Cook, Fred J., 178
Copeland, Royal S. (Senator), 21
Corn Products Sales Company, 121
Council for Democracy (anti-communist group), 93
Council for Financial Aid to Higher Education, 129
Council on Children, Media, and Merchandising, 179
Cousins, Norman (Saturday Review of Literature
    editor), 73–74
Crabtree, Nate (Batten, Barton, Durstine & Osborn
    executive), 92
Crandall, Prudence (young Quaker), 145, 147

Creating Rosie the Riveter: Class, Gender, and Propaganda during World War II (Honey), 53
The Creative Mystique (Keil), 156
crime prevention campaign
  about, 150, 154, 161–62
  alcohol and drug abuse messages, 162
  "Blanket," 165
  "The Gilstraps," 159, 164–65
  Got a Minute? You Could Stop a Crime (booklet), 160
  "Lock your door," 159
  McGruff, copyrights issued for use of, 164
  McGruff booklets, Department of the Army printed 300,000, 163
  McGruff stamp, U.S. Post Office issued, 166
  McGruff the Crime Dog, 150–51, 153–56, 158–67
  McGruff the Crime Dog newspaper ad, 151
  "Mimi Marth," 159–60, 164
  "Real Situations," 165
  Scruff campaign, 165
  "Stop a Crime," 159, 164–65
  Take a Bite Out of Crime campaign, 150, 153, 156, 165
  Taking a Bite Out of Crime: The Impact of the National Citizens' Crime Prevention Media Campaign (O'Keefe), 165
  "Teddy Bear," 165
  TV ads, 158–59, 164, 166
crime rates, 152, 183
"Crusade for Freedom" campaign. *See also* Free Europe Committee; propaganda
  about, 4, 87–89, 92–93, 97–100, 102, 118
  CIA and, 87–97, 100, 102
  communism, 4, 88–89, 92, 95, 97–98, 101–2, 189
  "Day and night Radio Free Europe is exposing communist lies and propaganda," 100
  "Kids on Radio Free Europe Send Hope to Pals behind the Iron Curtain," 100
  "Neither could fly . . . but they soloed to freedom," 101
  newspaper ad encouraged Americans to believe, 99
  two campaigns raised $3.5 million for Radios, 100
  "You Mean I Can Fight Communism?," 101
Crusade for Freedom Organization, 100
"The Crying Indian." *See also* "Keep America Beautiful" campaign, 4, 103–5, 122–27
  was an Italian (Espera Oscar DeCorti), 124
The Cultural Cold War: The CIA and the World of Arts and Letters (Saunders), 90
Czech passenger train, 100

D

Dancer Fitzgerald Sample (DFS) (agency), 119, 155
D'Angelo, Raymond, 140
David Ogilvy (advertising), 140
Davis, Elmer (Ad Council), 60, 78
Davis Jr., Billy (musician), 147
"Day and night Radio Free Europe is exposing communist lies and propaganda," 100
DeCorti, Espera Oscar (Crying Indian), 124. *See also* Keep America Beautiful
delinquency prevention programs, 165

DeMille, Cecil B., 92
Department of Health and Human Services, 179
Department of Justice, 150, 154, 157, 161
deposit laws, 109. *See also* Keep America Beautiful
deposits on beer and soft-drink bottles, 108
Der Monat (The Month), 90
The Dharma Bums (Kerouac), 111
Diegelman, Robert (Justice Department's Office of Justice Assistance, Research and Statistics), 160–62
digital communication, 185
digital technology, 187
DiSesa, Nina (McCann Erickson chairman), 30–31, 43
Dixie Cup Company, 116
Donnellan, Kevin (AARP's executive vice president and chief communications officer), 13
Donovan, William "Wild Bill" (Wall Street lawyer), 90
"Don't be a litterbug" slogan, 120. *See also* Keep America Beautiful
"Don't Waste a Mind" TV ad, 142–43. *See also* United Negro College Fund
Draftfcb (agency), 39, 43, 46
drug industry's lobbying, 12
drunk driving, 2, 163, 170
Du Bois, W. E .B., 135
Dunaway, Finis, 126
Dunne, Pete, 33
Dyke, Ken (War Advertising Council), 60

E

Earle, Richard (Marsteller Inc. executive), 104
Earth Day, 103, 106, 113–14, 121
"East Europe Today" (booklet), 102
Eastern Europe, 88, 91–92, 97, 99, 102
ECAS. See Emergency Committee of Atomic Scientists (ECAS)
"Education is the bridge between opportunity and despair," 145
Egan, Timothy, 36
Einstein, Albert (theoretical physicist), 71–74, 76, 79–81
Eisenhower, Dwight D. (General), 93
Eliot, T. S. (poet), 89
Emanuel, Kate (senior vice president of non-profit and government affairs), 13–15
Emergency Committee of Atomic Scientists (ECAS), 76, 79–81, 84–85
endangered species, 112
"Enterprise America," 94, 96
Entertainment Weekly, 104
environmental crisis, 112
"The Environmental Crisis," 122
environmental groups, 106–7, 114–15, 124–26. *See also* Keep America Beautiful
environmental protection, 107
Environmental Protection Agency (EPA), 106, 114, 124–25
Envisioning Black Colleges: A History of the United Negro College Fund (Gasman), 128
Every Beat Matters site, 187
"Every litter bit hurts" (tag line), 119
Executive Suite (Keil), 156

F

Fairness Doctrine, 178
Falk, Peter (actor), 5
FAS. *See* Federation of American Scientists (FAS)
FCC. *See* Federal Communications Commission (FCC)
FDA. *See* Food and Drug Administration (FDA)
Federal Communications Commission (FCC), 169–70, 172, 177–84
Federal Radio Commission, 176
Federal Trade Commission, 19, 22, 179
Federation of American Scientists (FAS), 70, 73
female empowerment, 4, 59, 68. *See also* Womanpower recruitment campaign
The Feminine Mystique (Friedan), 56
First Lady's Committee for a More Beautiful National Capital, 112
The First One Hundred Days of the Atomic Age (Woodrow Wilson Foundation), 72
Fisher, Chester (Metropolitan Life), 143–44
Flicker, 188
Folgers coffee, 22
Food and Drug Administration (FDA), 12, 21
Foote, Cone & Belding, 39, 42
Ford II, Henry (president of General Motors), 92
forest fire prevention campaign, national, 38–41, 47
Forest Reserve Act of 1891, 34
Fox, Frank (Madison Avenue Goes to War), 87
Francis, Clarence (General Foods Corporation chairman), 76
Francis, Norman (Xavier University president), 145
Franks, Martin (CBS's executive vice president), 170–71
free enterprise, 39, 117
Free Europe Committee, 88, 92, 97, 102. *See also* "Crusade for Freedom" campaign
free speech rights, 176
"free world doctrine," 95
"Freedom Scrolls," 93, 97
Friedan, Betty, 56
Friedman, Stephen (MTV), 174
Fritts, Edward (president of the NAB), 172, 181
"Future of America" campaign, 118

G

G. I. Bill, 56
Galbraith, John Kenneth, 110, 117
Gallagher, Buell (Talladega College in Alabama), 136
Gallup, George (American Institute of Public Opinion director), 76
Gallup poll (1946), 86
garbage disposal, 109
Gasman, Marybeth (author), 128, 135–40, 142–43
Gavins, Raymond, 133
"Get Your Smokey On" campaign, 31, 44–45
Gibson, Henry (actor and songwriter), 121
Giles, Pat (Saatchi & Saatchi creative director), 168
Gillett & Johnston, 93
"The Gilstraps," 159
Gitlin, Todd (Columbia University professor), 3
"Give Earth a Chance: The Environmental Movement and the Sixties" (Rome), 113
"Give jobs. Give money. Give a damn." slogan, 142

glass bottles, throwaway, 108. *See also* Keep America Beautiful
Gluck, Sherna Berger, 53
Gone Tomorrow, The Hidden Life of Garbage (Rogers), 115
Good Housekeeping, 65
Good Housekeeping seal of approval, 165
"Gordon Blaine Hancock: A Black Profile from the New South" (Gavins), 133
Gore Commission. *See* Advisory Committee on Public Interest Obligations of Digital Television Broadcasters (Gore Commission)
Got a Minute? You Could Stop a Crime (booklet), 160
Gottlieb, Robert (author), 108
Government Accountability Office report, 15
Gracie Fields (entertainment program), 67
Graham, Katharine (Washington Post publisher), 112
Gray, Berkeley M. (Mac) (former police officer), 155, 165, 167
Great Depression, 22, 52, 134
The Greater Generation: In Defense of the Baby Boom Legacy (Steinhorn), 56
Greenpeace, 116
Gregg, Allen (Rockefeller Foundation director of medical science), 76
Gromyko, Andrei (Soviet delegate), 83–84
Guardian of the Forest: A History of the Smokey Bear Program, 38–39
gun control legislation, 150. *See also* crime prevention campaign

H

Habits of the Heart: Individualism and Commitment in American Life (Bellah), 59
Hamer, Hilary (Draftfcb's senior vice president), 46
Hammatt, Richard (Forest Service), 40–43
Hancock, Gordon (Virginia Union University professor), 133
handgun purchases, major restrictions on, 152. *See also* crime prevention campaign
Hargis, Billy James (Reverend), 178
Harkins, Ann (NCPC president and CEO), 166–67
Harriman, E. H. (Union Pacific Railroad), 34
Hayes, Denis (Earth Day gathering), 113–14
heart beat of children, 7–8, 186–87. *See also* Save the Children
"The Heartbeat Experiment," 7–8
Heritage of Splendor (Richfield Oil Company), 116
Heyburn, Weldon (Senator), 36–37
Hickey, Margaret A. (chairman of the women's committee), 67
Highway Beautification Bill, 111
Higinbotham, William (Federation of American Scientists chairman), 70, 74, 80
Hiroshima and Nagasaki bombings, 70, 72, 74, 82, 85
HIV/AIDS messages, 173–74
Hoffman, Paul (Economic Cooperation Administration), 76, 96
Holdridge, John (Department of Defense), 155
Holmes, Oliver Wendell (Justice), 176
Honey, Maureen, 53–54
Hoover, J. Edgar (FBI), 178

Hough, Franklin B. (physician and statistician), 33
Houston Chronicle report, 58
"How Industry Can Help the Government's
    Information Program on Womanpower," 61
How to Zig in a Zagging World (Keil), 156
Howe Institute (Memphis), 135
Huffington Post article, 49–50
Huffy bicycles ad, 172
Hughes, John C. (Time-Life executive), 92
human rights, 152
human trafficking and modern-day slavery campaign, 15
100,000,000 Guinea Pigs (Young), 20
Hundt, Reed (FCC chairman), 180
Hungarian revolt (1956), 101
Hutchins, Robert (University of Chicago president),
    74–75

I
In the Name of Sanity (Swing), 74
"In the Pay of the CIA: An American Dilemma"
    (*60 Minutes* report), 87. *See also* Central
    Intelligence Agency (CIA)
Indian occupation of Wounded Knee, 104
The Industrial Discipline and the Governmental Arts
    (Young), 20
industry trade associations, 11
industry's charity, 16–18
International Advertising Association, 21
International Visual Literacy Association, 163
"Invest in America's Greatest Natural Resource" news-
    paper ad, 146
Iron Curtain, 83, 87–88, 92, 94, 97–102
Iron Eyes Cody (actor), 105, 124, 126–27

J
J. Walter Thompson (ad agency)
    about, 4, 19, 24, 51, 60, 62–66, 68, 95, 158
    ad copywriters, 61–64
    campaign's radio spots, 66–67
    newspaper ad (1944), 64
    soldier urges other women to find war jobs, 66
    Womanpower ads, 68
Jackson, Charles Douglas (political warfare specialist),
    88, 91, 93–97, 100–101
Japanese American concentration camps, 47
Japanese submarine attack, 38–39, 47
"Jim Crow" (racial caste system label), 131–35, 137
Johnson, Charles (Fisk University president), 133
Johnson, Edwin C. (senator), 82
Johnson, Kimberley (author), 132
Johnson, Lady Bird, 111, 115
Johnson, Lyndon (President), 111–12, 150
Joint Committee for Sound Democratic Consumer
    Legislation (lobby), 22
Jones, Thomas Elsa (Fisk University), 136
Jordan Jr., Vernon E. (United Negro College Fund),
    128–30, 138, 141, 144
Journal of Broadcasting, 162
Journal of Public Health, 175
Journalism Quarterly, 74

Joyce Jordan, M.D. (soap opera), 67
Julius Rosenwald Foundation, 132, 136

K
Kaiser Family Foundation
    about, 173–75, 184
    Shouting to Be Heard studies, 169–71
Keep America Beautiful (nonprofit group)
    about, 4, 103–6, 112, 114–15
    Ad Council's series of pamphlets and campaigns,
        117
    anti-litter campaigns, 115–17, 119, 121–22,
        124–25, 155
    "Back by Popular Neglect" ad, 126
    bumper stickers with cleanup and beautification
        message, 120
    campaign on radio, 120–21
    charitable organization, 114–15
    Clean Community System, 124
    "Clean Community System" campaign, 125
    core issues are "preventing litter," "reducing
        waste," and "beautifying communities," 115
    Crying Indian, image of the, 105
    "Crying Indian" campaign, 4, 103–5, 122–27
    Crying Indian was an Italian (Espera Oscar
        DeCorti), 124
    "do something beautiful" slogan, 115
    "Don't be a litterbug" slogan, 119–121
    "The Environmental Crisis" fact sheet, 122
    "Every litter bit hurts" (tag line), 119–21
    holistic solutions to the pollution problem, 125
    KAB's founders steered clear of regulating indus-
        try, 116
    lobbying organization, 115
    "The Miracle of America" pamphlet, 117
    "People Start Pollution. People Can Stop It," 105,
        122–23
    "Pollution Control: A Corporate Responsibility"
        (magazine headline), 123
    pro-industry, anti-litter strategy, 116
    recycling campaign, 104, 106, 114, 188
    "71 Things You Can Do to Stop Pollution"
        pamphlet, 123
    "a sophisticated greenwashing operation," 116
    sponsors of, 116, 119, 121, 125
    Susan Spotless (ad character), 121
    website, 115
Keil, Adman Jack (DFS executive vice president and
    creative director), 149–50, 155–59, 167–68
Keim, Robert P. (Ad Council president), 67–68, 87,
    102, 130, 154, 161
Kelley, John (chairman of NBC), 155
Kelly, Clarence (FBI director), 154
Kennan, George F. (chief architect of the Marshall
    Plan), 91
Kennedy, John F. (President), 111, 147, 150
Kennedy, Robert (Senator), 150
Kerouac, Jack (author), 111
"Kids on Radio Free Europe Send Hope to Pals behind
    the Iron Curtain," 100

"kill for thrill" case, 152
Kimble, James J., 49, 56–58, 68
King Jr., Martin Luther, 150
Kirkman, Larry (Benton president), 182
Kiwanis International, 40
Klein, Donna (CEO of Corporate Voices for Working
    Families), 12, 14–16
Know HIV/AIDS, 174
"KnowHow2GO" (college access) campaign, 15–16
Koe, Francesca (Natural Resources Defense Council),
    12–13
Kosek, Jake (University of California at Berkeley
    professor), 29, 46–47
Kremlin, 98, 101
Krivascy, Ray art director), 157
Kroll, Alex (creative director of Y&R), 141–43, 148, 181
Kulzer, Danna (Ad Council's director of non-profit and
    government affairs), 15

L
Larmon, Sigurd (Young & Rubicam), 39
LaRoche, Chester (chairman of Ad Council), 25–27
Larson, Arnold B. (newspaperman), 39
Lash, John S., 139–40
Lasker, Mary (philanthropist), 112
Lasky, Melvin J. (journalist), 89–90
Lavizzo-Mourey, Risa (Robert Wood Johnson
    Foundation president and CEO), 11–12, 14–15
Law, Nick (agency R/GA), 8, 188
Law Enforcement Assistance Administration (LEAA),
    150, 152, 160–61
Lawter Jr., William Clifford, 38
LEAA. See Law Enforcement Assistance Administra-
    tion (LEAA)
League of Women Voters, 125
Lesko, John, 152
Liberty Bell (Philadelphia), 93
'life as it ought to be,' 20
The Light of the World (CBS), 85
Lilienthal, David (Chicago lawyer), 83
"The litterbugs are on the loose," 120
Littleford, William (Billboard magazine president and
    CEO), 155
"Lock your door," 159
Loeb, Carl (chemist, and philanthropist), 154–55, 162
Long, Forest (Y&R copywriter), 141–43, 148
Los Angeles Fruit Growers Exchange, 41
Lowe's Charitable and Educational Foundation, 115
Lucas, Ferris (National Sheriffs' Association), 154
Luce, Henry (Time-Life), 88, 93–95
lumber industry, 116

M
Manhattan Project scientists, 4, 69–70
manifest destiny, 33–34, 88
Mann, Thomas (author), 90
March of Dimes, 135
Marchand, Roland, 20
marriage campaign, value of, 9
Marshall, George Catlett (General), 89

Marshall Plan, 89–91, 96
Martin, Chris (lead vocalist), 8
Martin, Louis E. (President Carter's special assistant), 155
Mary Allen Junior College (Crockett, Texas), 135
mass consumption, 117
mass production and consumption, 118
Massachusetts Department of Youth Services, 164
"Masterpieces of the Twentieth Century" festival in
    Paris, 90
"Matters of Choice: Advertising in the Public Interest"
    (Ad Council), 52
May, William F. (American Can Company chairman of
    the board), 125
May-Johnson bill, 82, 84
Mays, Benjamin (president of Morehouse College), 133
Mazur, Paul (Lehman Brothers banker), 118
McCaffrey, Barry (Office of National Drug Control
    Policy head), 181
McCoo, Marilyn (musician), 147
McDonough, John, 123–24
McGruff the Crime Dog, 150–51, 153–56, 158–67. See
    also crime prevention campaign
McKinley, William (President), 34
McMahon, Brien (chairman of Senate's Special
    Committee on Atomic Energy), 77, 82
McNutt, Paul (War Manpower Commission head), 61
Mendenhall, William V. (Angeles National Forest in
    Southern California), 39
Miastkowski, Anna, 63
microsites, 186
Migraine Research Foundation, 14
Miller, Harold B. (National Committee for a Free
    Europe), 100
Miller, J. Howard (artist), 50, 57, 59, 63, 65, 68. See also
    "Rosie the Riveter" poster
"Mimi Marth," 159–60
"A mind is a hell of a thing to waste." slogan, 142
"A Mind Is a Terrible Thing to Waste" campaign, 5, 128,
    131, 142–43, 145. See also United Negro Col-
    lege Fund
"A mind is" campaigns, 148
"The Miracle of America" pamphlet, 117
missing children, 163
Mobilizing Women for War: German and American
    Propaganda, 1939–1945 (Rupp), 60
Modern Man Is Obsolete (Cousins), 73–74
MomsRising, 11–12
"Monitoring the Future" study, 175
Monroe, Marilyn (actress), 51
Monroe, Rosie Will (Rosie the Riveter), 58. See also
    "Rosie the Riveter" poster
Montgomery bus system boycott, 131, 137
moral superiority of freedom and democracy, 102
"The More You Know" campaign, 172, 180
Morgan, J. P. (Northern Pacific Railroad), 34, 46
Morrill Act of 1890, 133–34
Morris, Edmund (author), 32
Morrison, Ellen Earnhardt, 38–39
Motion Picture Association of America, 14
Mrs. degree, 56

Muir, John (Sierra Club founder), 31–32, 36, 103, 107
multiple offenders, pretrial releases for, 152
Multiple-Use Sustained-Yield Act, 33
murders per 100,000 people, 152
Murray, Scott (Draftfcb), 29–31, 43
myth of feminine empowerment in the wartime work-
     force, 56

N
NAACP. *See* National Association for the Advancement
     of Colored People (NAACP)
NAB. *See* National Association of Broadcasters (NAB)
Nader, Ralph, 112
National Association for the Advancement of Colored
     People (NAACP), 132, 134–35, 137, 139
National Association of Broadcasters (NAB), 172, 180
     Code of Broadcasting, 172
National Association of Manufacturers, 116
National Association of State Foresters, 30
National Audubon Society, 105, 124
National Committee for a Free Europe, 88, 92–93, 95, 100
National Committee of Atomic Information (NCAI),
     79–80
National Council on Crime and Delinquency (NCCD),
     154
National Crime Prevention Council (NCPC), 151,
     154–55, 162, 164–67, 183
National Republic, 66
National Security Act of 1947, 90
National Security Council (NSC), 90–91, 94
National Sheriffs' Association, 154
National Wildlife Federation, 105, 107, 125
Natkins, Priscilla (Ad Council's executive vice president
     and director of client services), 8, 13–14, 158
Natural Resources Defense Council, 12–13
NCAI. *See* National Committee of Atomic Information
     (NCAI)
NCCD. *See* National Council on Crime and Delin-
     quency (NCCD)
NCPC. *See* National Crime Prevention Council (NCPC)
Needham Porter Novelli survey, 162–63
"Neither could fly . . . but they soloed to freedom," 101
Nelson, Donald (Sears, Roebuck and Co. executive), 1,
     25–26, 28
Nemmers, Sherry (Brand Ideas), 156–60, 165
Neri, Dan (creative partner), 44
Nestlé Waters North America, 115
New York Times, 72, 112, 153
New York Times Magazine, 76
New York Urban Coalition, 141
Newsweek, 153
Ney, Ed (Young & Rubicam), 128
Nixon, Richard (President), 105–6, 114, 152–53
Nooyi, Indra K. (PepsiCo chairman and CEO), 103
Northern foundations, 132
NSC. *See* National Security Council (NSC)
nuclear arms control, 152

O
Obama, Barack (President) and Michelle, 147
Obama's Nobel Peace Prize, 147

O'Barr, William (Duke University professor), 158
obesity prevention, 16–17
Office of National Drug Control Policy (ONDCP), 173,
     181
Office of Policy Coordination (OPC), 91
Office of Strategic Services (OSS), 90
Office of War Information (OWI), 59, 93
     Bureau of Campaigns, 60
oil consumption, 107
O'Keefe, Garrett (University of Denver professor),
     162–65, 167
Olson, Lester C., 49, 56–58, 68
ONDCP. *See* Office of National Drug Control Policy
     (ONDCP)
online pharmacy campaign, 12
online universities, 15
"Only Then Shall We Find Courage" (Einstein), 76, 81
"Only You Can Prevent Forest Fires," 44
"Only You Can Prevent Wildfires," 44
OPC. *See* Office of Policy Coordination (OPC)
Operation Backtalk, 89
Oppenheimer, J. Robert (nuclear physicist), 69–71, 83, 89
Orwell, George (author), 90
Osborn, Michael, 58
OSS. *See* Office of Strategic Services (OSS)
O'Sullivan, John L. (author), 33
"Our Carelessness, Their Secret Weapon" slogan, 41
*Our Mothers' War: American Women at Home and at
     the Front during World War II* (Yellin), 58
Owens-Illinois Glass Company, 116
OWI. *See* Office of War Information (OWI)

P
Pacific Coast Advertising Clubs, 39
packaging industry's throwaway containers, 105
Packard, Vance, 110–11, 117
Pardes, Herbert (New York–Presbyterian Hospital pres-
     ident and CEO), 16
Parks, Rosa, 131, 137
*Partners in Plunder, Our Economic Society and Its
     Problems* (Young), 20
Partnership at Drugfree.org, 175
Patterson, Frederick D. (president of the Tuskegee
     Institute), 134–37
Peace Corps, 2
Pearl Harbor bombing by Japanese, 1, 24, 52–53
Peck, Keenen (author), 123
Pelican Island (Florida), 35
Pendray, G. Edward (president of the American Rocket
     Society), 77, 81–82
"People Start Pollution; People Can Stop It" campaign,
     4, 105–6, 122–23
"People's Capitalism" campaign, 118–19
PepsiCo, 115
Perlis, Leo (director, AFL-CIO's Community Services
     Division), 154
Perlov, George (Ad Council's head of research and eval-
     uation), 9
Perry, Katy (singer)7, 7
PET. *See* polyethylene terephthalate (PET)
Philip Morris USA, 115

Pinchot, Gifford (Division of Forestry chief), 32, 34–37, 43, 107
Pittsburgh Courier, 136
"planned obsolescence," 110
"Please Mister, Don't Be Careless. Prevent Forest Fires," 42. *See also* "Smokey Bear" campaign
Poisons, Potions and Profits (Young), 20
"Polaris Project" campaign, 15
polio, 2
political freedom, 95, 118
"Pollution Control: A Corporate Responsibility" (magazine headline), 123
polyethylene terephthalate (PET), 108
"Powers of Persuasion: Poster Art from World War II" (exhibition), 51
Prairie Spring (Dunne), 33
President's Commission on Law Enforcement and the Administration of Justice, 150
President's Council on Physical Fitness and Sports, 179
preventive health care, 162
print ads, 60, 123, 158, 186
Printers' Ink, 21, 23
Pritchard, Marc (Procter & Gamble), 6
Proceedings of the American Philosophical Society, 71
pro-democracy messages, 92
Profiles in Courage (Kennedy), 147
The Progressive, 123
propaganda. *See also* "Crusade for Freedom" campaign; "Rosie the Riveter" poster
    Ad Council was " an important propaganda tool in fighting communism at home and abroad," 95
    to aid the federal government, 88
    anti-U.S., 91
    atomic energy campaign, 80–81
    campaigns, 56
    Council for Democracy (anti-communist group), 93
    Creating Rosie the Riveter: Class, Gender, and Propaganda during World War II (Honey), 53
    "Day and night Radio Free Europe is exposing communist lies and propaganda," 100
    for D-Day, 93
    government-sponsored broadcasts on Radios into the Soviet Union, 88, 97, 100
    Mobilizing Women for War: German and American Propaganda, 1939–1945 (Rupp), 60
    Office of Policy Coordination (OPC), a division of the CIA, 91
    Office of War Information (OWI), 59–60
    overt propaganda programs and covert psychological operations, 91
    posters of 'Rosie the Riveter,' 58
    posters to encourage women to work during the war, 58
    pro-democracy messages aimed at Americans, 92
    psychological warfare, 91, 93, 98, 100
    public, 91
    Radio Free Europe, 4, 87, 90, 92, 97–98, 100–102
    Radio Free Europe/Radio Liberty (RFE/RL), 102
    Radio Liberty, 4, 87, 92
    recruitment campaign, 55

PSAs. *See* public service advertisements (PSAs)
psychological operations, covert, 91
psychological warfare, 91, 93, 98, 100
public health issues, 169
Public Lands Committee, 33
Public Media Center, 178–79
Public Opinion Surveys Inc., 121
Public Relations Review survey, 162
public service advertisements (PSAs). *See also* Kaiser Family Foundation
    about, 118, 170–71
    Ad Council and, 171–73, 175, 179–81, 183–85
    broadcast networks and, 172–75
    Gore Commission and, 183–85
    public interest and, 176–83
"Public Service Advertising That Changed a Nation" booklet, 52, 106, 143
Pure Food and Drugs Act (1906), 21
"Put it there, Sister!" (magazine ad), 65

Q
Quayle, Dan (vice presidential candidate), 143
Quick, Jerry (forest ranger), 37

R
Rabinowitch, Eugene (Manhattan Project chemist), 73
Radio Act of 1912, 176
Radio Act of 1927, 176
Radio Free Europe, 4, 87, 90, 92, 97–98, 100–102
Radio Free Europe/Radio Liberty (RFE/RL), 102
Radio Liberty, 4, 87, 92
Raymond Gram Swing (news program), 67
Reagan, Ronald (President), 152–53
Rector, Milton (National Council on Crime and Delinquency), 154
Red menace, 102
refillable bottle, 108
Reforming Jim Crow: Southern Politics and State in the Age Before Brown (Johnson), 132
Regan, Ronald (President), 116–17
Reid, Kathleen, 163
"the reign of terror in American cities," 153
"Report on the International Control of Atomic Energy," 83
Repplier, Theodore (executive director of the War Advertising Council), 70, 80, 84
Resource Recovery Act (1970), 109
Reynolds Metals Company, 119
RFE/RL. *See* Radio Free Europe/Radio Liberty (RFE/RL)
Richfield Oil Corporation, 116
Rideout, Vicky (Kaiser's vice president and director of programs), 171, 173–75
Ridge, Susan (Save the Children's vice president of marketing), 187
"right war jobs," 61
Robbins, Jim (forest ranger), 37
Rockefeller, Laurance S. (philanthropist), 112
Rockefeller, Nelson, 112
Rockefeller family's General Education Board, 132, 136–37

Rockefeller Jr., John D., 136–37
Rockefeller Sr., John D., 137
Rockwell, Norman (artist), 57
Roger Williams University (Nashville), 135
Rogers, Heather (filmmaker), 115–16
Rome, Adam, 113
Roosevelt, Franklin Delano (President), 1, 28, 37
Roosevelt, Theodore (President), 31–32, 34–37
Roosevelt's Civilian Conservation Corps, 40
"Rosie the Riveter" poster. *See also* Miller, J. Howard;
    Monroe, Rosie Will; propaganda; Woman-
    power recruitment campaign
    about, 4, 49, 51, 58, 67–68
    "We Can Do It!" poster, 4, 49–52, 57–58, 63,
        67–68
*Rosie the Riveter Revisited: Women, the War, and Social
    Change* (Gluck), 53
"Rosify Yourself" (Facebook application), 49
Rothman, Hal K., 106–7, 112
Round, Cynthia (United Way of America's executive
    vice president), 13–14
Rowan & Martin's Laugh-In, 121
Rubenstein, Harry (National Museum of American
    History's Division of Political History), 51
Rubenstein, Paul (Y&R agency), 141
Rupp, Leila J., 60
Russell, Bertrand (British philosopher), 90

S

Safe Streets and Control Act of 1968, 150
safety belt education campaign, 10
San Diego Union-Tribune, 58
San Francisco Chronicle, 58
San Francisco group of scientists, 81
Saturday Evening Post, 57
Saturday Review, 74
Saunders, Frances Stonor (author), 90
Save the Children, 6–8, 186–87. *See also* heart beat of
    children
Schaffner, Joseph (ECAS executive director),
    80–82, 84
Schlesinger Jr., Arthur (American historian), 90, 92
Schlink, F. J., 21
Schulman, Bruce J., 104, 109
Science (magazine), 75
seat belts, 2. *See also* safety belt education campaign
"See Where the Good Goes" campaign, 6
segregated South, 131–34
Seifert, Shona (Ogilvy's executive group director), 173
sentences, mandatory minimum, 152
Servicemen's Readjustment Act of 1944 (G. I. Bill), 56
"71 Things You Can Do to Stop Pollution" pamphlet, 123
*The Seventies: The Great Shift in American Culture,
    Society, and Politics* (Schulman), 104
sewage treatment plants, 114
sexually transmitted diseases, 173
Sherman Antitrust Act, 23
Sherwin, Martin J. (author), 69
Shimaitis, Barbara (Ad Council's senior vice president),
    187, 189
"Should Your Wife Get a War Job?," 62–63

Shouting to Be Heard studies (Kaiser Family Founda-
    tion), 169–70
Sierra Club, 31, 103, 105, 107, 124
Silent Spring (Carson), 110
Simpson, Christopher, 92
Sipuel, Ada (University of Oklahoma law school
    student), 138–39
60 Minutes report, 87
Smith, Robert (Assistant Attorney General for Public
    Affairs), 161
Smith–Dungy public service ad, 171
Smithsonian's National Museum of American History, 51
Smokey Bear 20252: A Biography (Lawter Jr.), 38
Smokey Bear Act of 1952, 44
"Smokey Bear" campaign
    about, 2–4, 29, 38, 43–46, 156, 161, 164, 187–88
    "Careless Matches Aid the Axis—Prevent Forest
        Fires" (slogan), 40–41
    "Carelessness Is Treason" slogan, 41
    "Get Your Smokey On" campaign, 31, 44–45
    "Only You Can Prevent Forest Fires," 44
    "Only You Can Prevent Wildfires," 44
    "Please Mister, Don't Be Careless. Prevent Forest
        Fires," 42
    public service advertising campaign, longest-
        running, 29
Smokey public service ad (PSA), 43
Smokey's Twitter feed, 188
social media, 187
Social Science and Modern Society, 163
Social Security Board Building, 1
"Socially Conscious Capitalism" (speech), 95
soft-drink bottles, plastic, 108
solid-waste disposal, 112
Southern California Committee for Open Media, 179
Soviet Union, 71–72, 77, 83–84, 88, 90, 92, 96
Spellman, Francis Joseph (Cardinal), 97
The Sponsor: Notes on a Modern Potentate (Barnouw),
    169, 183
Staehle, Albert (artist), 42–43
Standard Oil, 113
Steinhorn, Leonard, 56
Stephens, Harvard (print ad story), 144–45
Stole, Inger (University of Illinois advertising professor), 20
"Stop a Crime," 159
Straub, Eleanor, 54
Stroock, Mark (Y&R's senior vice president of corporate
    accounts), 129
Sullivan, John, 166
Sunkist (California Fruit Growers Exchange), 39
Super Bowl game, 170–72
Supreme Court
    Brown v. Board of Education, 129, 137–41
    Plessy v. Ferguson, 134, 137
    *Red Lion Broadcasting Co. v. the Federal Commun-
        ications Commission,* 178
    Sipuel v. Board of Regents, 138
    Sweatt v. Painter, 138
    University of Oklahoma's "Negro law school," 138
Sweatt, Heman (University of Texas law school student),
    138–39

Swing, Raymond Gram (American Broadcasting Company newscaster), 74, 86
Szilard, Leo (Hungarian-born physicist), 73, 81

T
Taft, William Howard (President), 35, 97
"Take a Bite Out of Crime" campaign, 150, 153, 156, 165
Taking a Bite Out of Crime: The Impact of the National Citizens' Crime Prevention Media Campaign (O'Keefe), 165
Taylor, Joseph (college fund's campaign manager), 130, 142
Tedder, Ryan (singer), 187
Telecommunications Act (1966), 183
Television Commercial Monitoring Report, 180
Tennessee Valley Authority, 83
"That's Not Cool" campaign, 188
"The American Century" (Luce), 88
The Bomb's Early Light (Boyer), 74
The Greening of a Nation? Environmentalism in the United States since 1945 (Rothman), 106–7
Theodore Rex (Morris), 32
Thomas, Harold B. (Centaur Company), 25, 67
throwaway bottles and packages, 104, 108, 114, 116
"throwaway spirit," 110
A Time in Advertising's Camelot: The Memoirs of a Do Gooder (Keim), 154
Time magazine, 153
Torrance School of Race Relations (Virginia Union), 133
Transfer Act of 1905, 35
Travaglia, Michael, 152
Truman, Harry (President), 149
    anti-communist crusade, 89–90, 94
    atomic energy campaign, 69–73, 75, 82–84
Truman administration, 89
Truman Doctrine, 84, 89
"Truth Dollars," 93
Tugwell, Rexford G. (assistant secretary of agriculture), 21
Tugwell bill, 21–22
Tuskegee Project testing syphilis on African Americans, 47
TV Guide, 104
TV spots, thirty-second broadcast, 186

U
"The Umpteenth Crisis in Negro Higher Education" (Lash), 139
UNAEC. *See* United Nations Atomic Energy Commission (UNAEC)
Uncle Sam, 63, 117–18
Uncle Sam's Forest Rangers (radio program), 37
Understories: The Political Life of Forests in Northern New Mexico (Kosek), 46
Union of Concerned Scientists, 13–14
Union Oil well leak (California), 112
United Airlines, 22
United Church of Christ, 179
United Nations, 74–75
United Nations Atomic Energy Commission (UNAEC), 77, 82–83, 85

United Nations Day, 97
United Nations Security Council, 75
United Negro College Fund (UNCF)
    about, 15–16, 128, 130–31, 136–38, 141, 143–48
    birth of, 134–37
    "KnowHow2GO," 15
    "A Mind Is a Terrible Thing to Waste" campaign, 5, 128, 131, 142–43, 145
United Way, 179
University of Denver's National Opinion Research Center, 55
University of Oklahoma's "Negro law school," 138
Unsafe at Any Speed (Nader), 112
Upson, Stuart (chairman, Saatchi & Saatchi), 156
Urban League, 125
Urey, Harold (University of Chicago Nobel Prize-winning chemist), 75, 81
U.S.
    ad industry, 19
    annual consumption of raw materials, 114
    atomic energy policy, 82
    capitalism, 95
    commitment to help noncommunist countries, 84
    delegation to UNAEC, 77–78
    drug manufacturers, 12, 22
    foreign policy in Germany and Europe, 90
    foreign policy injected fear of the atomic bomb into American children, 86
    government countered anti-U.S.propaganda, 91
    government gave land to robber barons, 46
    international business interests reflected "Enterprise America," 94
    nationalism, 46
    pace of consumption, 118
    population increase, 20
U.S. Administration on Children, Youth and Families, 164
U.S. Constitution, 132
U.S. Department of Agriculture, 16, 33, 44
U.S. Department of Commerce and Labor, 176
U.S. Department of Health and Human Services, 16, 179
    Administration for Children and Families, 8–9
U.S. Department of Justice, 150, 154, 157, 161
U.S. Department of Transportation
    national safety belt education campaign, 10
U.S. Employment Service
    survey of attitudes about women in the labor force, 54
U.S. Environmental Protection Agency, 106, 114, 124–25
U.S. Forest Service, 33, 35–47
    Cooperative Forest Fire Prevention (CFFP), 3–4, 29–30, 35
U.S. Geological Survey, 34
U.S. Justice Department, 23
    crime survey, 150
U.S. National Archives, 51
U.S. News and World Report, 153
U.S. Office of Education report (1943), 135
U.S. Office of Production Management, 25
U.S. Patent Office, 12
U.S. scientific knowledge/plans to build more atomic weapons, 82

U.S. State Department, 68
U.S. Supreme Court decision in *Roe v. Wade,* 104

V

Vermont bill banning sale of throwaway bottles, 116
Vermont's Green Mountain National Forest, 43
Vietnam War environmental devastation, 112–13
Vinod, Paul (BBDO's creative director), 7
"Visual Rhetoric Representing Rosie the Riveter" (Kimble and Olson), 49
Vittorini, Carlo (president and CEO of *Parade* magazine), 155
Voting Rights Act (1965), 140

W

Walker, Darren (Ford Foundation vice president of education, creativity, and free expression), 15
Wallace, Mike (CBS), 87
Wallace, Robert (Keep America Beautiful spokesperson), 106, 116, 124
Walt Disney's *Bambi,* 42
War Advertising Council, 27–28, 38, 60–61, 68, 70, 76–77. *See also* The Advertising Council
War against Crime, 152–53
War against Poverty, 152
War Manpower Commission (1942), 4, 51, 55, 59–62, 66–67
"war on poverty," 111
War on Waste: Can America Win Its Battle with Garbage? (Blumberg and Gottlieb), 108
War Production Board, 1, 27, 54, 57
War Production Board's Labor Division report, 54
War Production Coordinating Committee, 57
"Wartime Forest Fire Prevention" campaign, 41
Washburn, Abbott (executive from General Mills), 92
The Waste Makers (Packard), 110–11
Waste Management, 115
Waste Management Inc., 125
Watergate conspiracies, 104
Watson, John B. (behaviorist), 65
"We Can Do It!" poster, 4, 49–52, 57–58, 63, 67–68. *See also* "Rosie the Riveter" poster
Weeks Act, 37
Weinman, Rosalyn (NBC's executive vice president), 173
Wendelin, Rudy (artist), 31
West, Paul B. (secretary of Ad Council), 23, 26–27
Western European intelligentsia, 90
Westinghouse Electric and Manufacturing Company, 57

Westinghouse Magazine, 57
Wharton, Dennis (National Association of Broadcasters), 172
Wheeler–Lea Act (1938), 19, 22
"When There Is a Need, We Are There" (pamphlet), 17–18
White House's anti–drug abuse campaign, 175
"Why General Motors, Ford, and Chrysler Put Thousands Every Year toward the Development of New Ideas." (headline), 147
Wickard, Claude (Secretary of Agriculture), 40–41
wilderness protection, 112
Wilderness Society, 107
"Wildfire Awareness" widget, 188
Williams, Thomas (EPA's Solid Waste Division), 124
"Winds of Freedom," 100
wiretappings, 152
Wisner, Frank (OPC), 91–92
woman would be considered equal to a man, 62
Womanpower recruitment campaign. *See also* propaganda; "Rosie the Riveter" poster
    about, 2, 4, 51–52, 54, 59–62, 65, 67–68
    "We Can Do It!" poster, 4, 49–52, 57–58, 63, 67–68
    Womanpower ads, 68, 189
"Women War Workers," 62
Wooden, Ruth (Ad Council's president), 10, 180
Woodrow Wilson Foundation, 72
World Freedom Bell (Berlin), 92–93, 97
World Trade Foundation, 94
World War II. *See also* propaganda; "Rosie the Riveter" poster
    about, 1, 4, 38, 49, 51
    Womanpower campaign: "We Can Do It!" poster, 4, 49–52, 57–58, 63, 67–68
Wright, Steven J. (president of Fisk University and Bluefield State College in West Virginia), 140–41

Y

Yankee ingenuity, 1
Yellin, Emily, 58
Yellowstone Forest Reserve, 34
"You Mean I Can Fight Communism?," 101
Young, James Webb (J. Walter Thompson agency), 19–20, 24, 158
Young, John Orr (Young & Rubicam), 25
Your Money's Worth (Chase and Schlink), 21
YouTube, 188

Printed in the United States
by Baker & Taylor Publisher Services